Bridge Ahead

Also by Keith Dahlberg:
Edwin T. Dahlberg: Pastor, Peacemaker, Prophet
Flame Tree, A Novel of Modern Burma

Bridge Ahead

A Medical Memoir

Keith Dahlberg

iUniverse, Inc.
New York   Bloomington

Bridge Ahead
A Medical Memoir

Copyright © 2008 by Keith Dahlberg

iUniverse books may be ordered through booksellers or by contacting:

iUniverse
1663 Liberty Drive
Bloomington, IN 47403
www.iuniverse.com
1-800-Authors (1-800-288-4677)

ISBN: 978-0-595-49258-9 (pbk)
ISBN: 978-0-595-61030-3 (ebk)

Printed in the United States of America

To my parents, Edwin and Emilie Dahlberg,
who taught me the basics.

Cure Thy people's warring madness,
Bend our pride to Thy control;
Shame our wanton, selfish gladness,
Rich in things and poor in soul.
Grant us wisdom, grant us courage,
Lest we miss Thy kingdom's goal.

Harry Emerson Fosdick

Contents

Preface

This memoir traces four ideas in my life: the basic integrity of science and medicine; the reality of faith; the clash between war and the commonly stated values of the human race; and finally, the goals I tried to reach, building upon these foundations.

Not all will agree with some things I have to say. A few readers will call some of my actions and beliefs unpatriotic, self-serving, or misguided.

No one can match the special bravery and sacrifice of soldiers who must spend months or even years in combat. Nevertheless, my fifteen years of work as a doctor in Southeast Asia, picking up the wreckage that wars leave behind—the Shan rebellion in Burma in the 1960s, the Cambodian genocide in 1979, and the excesses of the Myanmar military along the Thai-Burma border in the 1990s—may lend some authority to my views on war and peace.

Along the way, I also consider some ways in which American medicine falls short. Contrary to what we are often told, America's medical system is not always near the top of the list.

I do not intend this to be an inspirational book or a political statement. Instead, I write to describe some of the events that have shaped my life, and to encourage readers who find obstacles blocking the road to their own goals. I have discovered that bridges often appear at unexpected places, making goals attainable.

Keith Dahlberg, April, 2008

Acknowledgments

My wife, Lois, has been of immeasurable help and inspiration during the years I have spent putting this story together: proof-reading, occasionally correcting my memory, and providing companionship in what otherwise would have been a lonely job.

Although I find many of the events still clear in my memory, they are enhanced or corrected by many family letters, often copied for family distribution by my sister, Margaret Torgersen, during my overseas years.

I am grateful to all those who have critiqued my writing—Melanie Rigney, Barbara Smith, and their students at the 2007 Green Lake Writers' Conference; Dr. Karen Lentz Clark of the University of Arkansas Quality Writing Center; Dennis Held, former faculty member at Lewis & Clark State College; members of the local writing club *Pen and Quill* in Kellogg; Doris Fleming and her writer colleagues in Kellogg; and members of Juliene Munts's reading group in Coeur d'Alene.

I thank my computer guru Jack Hendryx for his skill in blending the graphics. George Goetzman of Goetzman Portraits, Coeur d'Alene, did the back cover picture. I thank the crew at iUniverse for formatting the book.

For reasons of confidentiality and right to privacy, few of my patients and professional colleagues will find their names in this book, unless their story has at some time been featured in news media. It is not my purpose to embarrass or criticize anyone. General policies of medicine, organizations, or governments, on the other hand, sometimes need public re-examination.

My thanks go to the daughter of Harry Emerson Fosdick, Elinor Fosdick Downs, for permission to use some lines of his hymn as an epigraph. The quotation on the wall of Memorial Chapel, Stanford University, in chapter 54; the quotation from *The Autobiography of Benjamin Franklin* cited in chapter 54; and Felix Adler's hymn *Hail the Glorious Golden City,* quoted in chapter 17, all predate the twentieth century and are in the public domain.

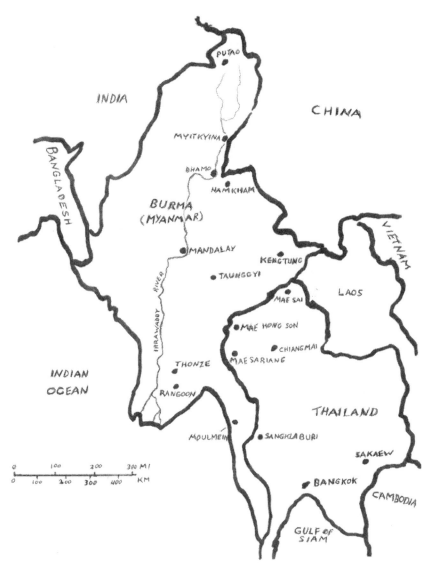

Map of Burma (Myanmar) and Thailand

1

Far Away Places

I was born in 1929 in Buffalo, New York, but when I was two years old my family moved to St. Paul, Minnesota, and that's where my memories begin.

A lot of kids in those days wanted to grow up to be a fireman or policeman. I thought that might be okay, but from my earliest memories I wanted to be a traveler. The lure of a new town always beckoned, from the first sight of its water tower on the horizon ahead. So did the exotic stamps my older brother Bruce collected—a brightly colored triangular postage stamp with a giraffe gazing out of it fascinated me. What was Nyasaland like? Or Tanu Tuva, or Hong Kong?

Much as I felt loved by my family, and loved them, I had a private personality as a little kid. I'd rather read a book or go hiking by myself than spend precious time playing organized sports. At picnics, I favored exploring the river bank over joining group games.

This sense of independence played a large part in my ambitions and actions. When I first learned to read, I spent one noon hour showing my new ability to a schoolmate, while we sat on a curb on the way home from school. When I finally showed up for lunch, my mother was frantic: "*Where* have you been?" But that didn't stop my exploration of the unknown. At age five I set out one hot summer day to see what lay beyond my St. Clair Avenue neighborhood in St. Paul. About a half mile from home, I found winding streets, stone archways and beautiful big houses. Just beyond them a stone stairway led me down to a street we often traveled from downtown, so I had no trouble finding my way home. I kept my adventure to myself at first, but then couldn't resist telling my teen-age sister, Margaret. Mother overheard, and said to Dad, "So that's why his face looked so flushed before supper!" But she didn't give me the scolding I half expected.

Although Dad's work as a minister included many evenings of committee meetings or calling on church members, he saved Saturday nights for family. Mother and Dad were reliably home that night, to play games with us or read to us. I remember them reading to me from *The Wizard of Oz* a dozen times, with only mild complaints at my insistence that we start at the beginning each time.

The high point of every year was family vacation. Most of the Dahlberg clan lived in Colorado. About every second year during Dad's vacation, we would drive westward to Denver, two days journey from St. Paul. Even the trip itself was fun, reading the Burma Shave ads and watching for the next town, across the endless corn fields of Iowa and Nebraska.

The old black Dodge sedan had a flat vertical windshield, and the engine's temperature gauge sat above the radiator cap on the front of the hood. The car's trunk was strapped to a carrier rack above the back bumper. Either Mother or my sister sat in the back seat between my brother and me to see that we behaved.

We sped along the two-lane highway at the 50 mile per hour limit, slowing to 25 in towns to see the sights. The gas station man pushed a pump handle back and forth, lifting the colored gasoline up into the big glass measuring chamber on top of the pump. Then he turned a valve to let it drain through the hose and into the car's gas tank. Twenty cents a gallon. He would check our oil, water, battery level, and tire pressure too, and clean the spattered bugs from the windshield. Even road maps were free.

Lunch time at a roadside diner was a 15-cent hamburger with fried onions, ketchup and a slice of dill pickle, and maybe a piece of pie and a bottle of root beer or Lime Rickey. We boys saved the bottle caps for our collection. And in the middle of a hot afternoon, Dad might find a drugstore in some town where we could stop for an ice cream soda or a milkshake.

Sunset found us somewhere around Grand Island, Nebraska. No relatives anywhere; we stayed overnight at a row of tourist-cabins lined up behind an office whose light attracted a swarm of moths and bugs. One or two dollars a night for the family, back in those depression years of the 1930s. The night sounds were quiet and reassuring—

crickets chirping, a screen door slamming, a train whistle far away. Bruce and I lay there in the dark, guessing what time tomorrow the Rocky Mountains would come into view, and whether there would be pancakes for breakfast, until we drifted off into a sound sleep.

Gray-green sage brush lined the highway next day on the flat plains of eastern Colorado. Soon a purple line of mountains would appear far away in the west and we could make out snow on the peaks, even in July.

Denver wasn't the chief attraction, even though we had grandparents and three sets of uncles and aunts there. We and our cousins could catch crawdads at Washington Park or visit the Natural History Museum at City Park, but the main thrill was a week in Uncle Henry's cabin up in the mountains near the small village of Ward. Ward wasn't an easy place to get to; a sixty-mile trip. We'd go through the city of Boulder then up Left Hand Canyon along Jim Creek (where car-sickness often got the best of me), and finally reached the forest-covered mountainsides surrounding Ward's one store and gas station.

The cabin in Ward could hold twenty, if the kids climbed the ladder to sleep in the loft and the grown-ups set up cots in the main room. A hand pump supplied the sink in the kitchen, and a two-hole latrine was just down the slope.

We built dams in the little creek and searched piles of waste rock at abandoned gold mines for "fool's gold," pyrite with a gleaming yellow sheen. It impressed friends back home who had never seen it, just like bringing home seashells from the ocean shore.

The older folks would cook, fish for trout, and take us to look for wild animals, Indian paintbrush flowers, or whatever else the hillsides might yield. At night, bright stars pierced the cold black sky while we roasted marshmallows around the campfire or learned the endless number of songs our older cousins knew.

After a few days to get used to the thin air at elevation 10,000 feet we would set out for the high mountains beyond Long Lake. Navajo Peak, Paiute Horn and Mount Audubon, at 14,000 feet, were part of the Great Divide separating the rivers bound for the Atlantic or Pacific Oceans. The country above timberline still held patches of snow in August, with lichen-covered boulder fields and soaring golden eagles. The conies, marmots and other animals had little contact with humans and were unafraid of us. All of it was a whole different world.

To me, the Rocky Mountains became a spiritual home. Later, in my teen-age years my day-dreams featured sharing a wilderness home with some as-yet-unknown girl, up in the isolated rocky reaches of Lake Isabel in Colorado.

World War II came along with its gas rationing, and trips to Colorado became rare. By that time I had learned to ride a bicycle and had new worlds to explore nearer home. But always, I dreamed about places far away.

2

Learning to Grow Up

Mrs. Wembly sat in an extra seat in the sunlit row by the window, testing us second-graders on the week's spelling words. She paused, seeing my upraised hand. "Yes, Keith?"

"What was that last word?"

"Omit."

I frowned, puzzled. Mrs. Wembly's voice took on a slight edge. "Didn't you study this spelling lesson, Keith?"

"No, Ma'am," I admitted, ashamed.

"Come over here."

I went to her chair by the window, uncomfortable under the collective gaze of my classmates. I looked out the window at bright sunshine and spring greenery, wishing I were out there.

She spoke quietly as I stood in front of her. "Why didn't you study your spelling lesson?"

"I never do. I already know the words. But I never heard this one before."

"I see," she said. She was silent a moment. Then, "All right, go to your seat."

There must have been a parent-teacher conference. Later that week they moved me up a half-grade, from 2-A to 2-B.

That gave me a couple of problems. I didn't comprehend the first right away, but its effect lasted for years afterward. I was now the youngest in the class—always the little kid. The second was more immediate: I hadn't any idea what the new teacher was talking about in arithmetic.

Long division: "Divide, multiply, subtract, bring down." I had no clue what all that meant, and was ashamed to ask. Instead, I looked over the shoulder of the kid in front of me and copied. My parents had taught me never to cheat, and I never had before. Eventually I learned how to do long division with help from my brother and sister. But I always remembered that I had cheated, and didn't like that feeling.

Mostly school was no problem. I got acceptable grades. A fight or two on the playground bloodied my nose, but usually my classmates and I got along well. Once, in fourth grade, a bunch of us were called in from recess for throwing snowballs at the school building, something the principal had banned that very morning. Two teachers cross-examined us, sentencing each pupil to stay after school, as each claim of innocence was disproved. My turn in the line-up came. The teacher asked me where I had been during the time in question. What the heck, I thought to myself, we were all throwing snowballs and the marks are still there on the brick wall; why try to lie about it?

"I was throwing snowballs at the school," I said. The teacher praised me for admitting it, and (as an example to the others, I suppose) gave me no penalty.

I was the classic weakling pictured in magazine ads for Charles Atlas body-building courses, the skinny kid who gets sand kicked in his face by bigger guys on the beach. I wasn't much good at fighting, though I sometimes did. My opponents were usually stronger.

Once in fourth grade I asked one of my classmates, who often hassled me, if we could be friends for a while. Sure, that was fine with him. Later that same day, he slugged my arm again while we were on the playground at recess. I said, "Hey, Sid, I thought we were going to be friends for a while."

"That's right and we were, for a while," he pointed out. I learned to define words at an earlier age than most kids.

That's not to say I had no friends. When I was eight or nine, the two Grayson brothers, E.C., Dick and I roamed the neighborhood, went hiking, flew balsa-wood glider planes, or laid four-inch nails on the railroad track to be pressed into miniature swords by the next passing train. We traded misinformation on a variety of topics with all the earnestness of kids who are always sure they are right. In short, we were average pre-teenagers.

One afternoon, we met a gang of toughs a year or so older and bigger than we were, who outnumbered us. E.C. and Dick and I were hiking a little farther than usual from home, and found our way blocked while crossing a culvert. I don't know what was on the gang's minds, maybe just asserting their turf or maybe glee in tormenting somebody. They surrounded us—you don't really consider escape by jumping into a ravine twenty feet below. I was held, my arms pinned behind me by one gang member, while another "gave me the old one-two" punch to my face and stomach several times. I don't remember the physical pain, but the humiliation is still vivid. Yeah, I was scared too, but there wasn't much to do except just stand there and take it. They finally tired of us and let us go. It didn't stop us from exploring new territory, but we were more careful after that.

I had alternating warfare and partnership with Donna, the tomboy over on the next block. Sometimes the two of us tried terrorizing someone else. I am not proud of the day when Donna confronted "Skinny Joyce" on the way home from school, and I sneaked up behind Joyce to make her scream when she turned around to flee. Nor am I proud of the time in sixth grade when someone—I don't remember who—tried to extort quarters from me. I figured *I* could do that, if I gave more attention to organization than he had. But my crime syndicate folded even before it started when the biggest classmate I could find said he didn't want to be my enforcer.

Nowadays, I suppose the verdict on my childhood might be "low self-esteem." I don't know—I was as cocky as any other kid most of the time. But physically I wasn't as strong, and certainly I had low self-esteem when sides were being chosen for baseball or even for playing red-rover. I hadn't the coordination to hit a baseball, except by chance, and I hadn't the arm strength to get more than three feet off the ground in rope climbing in junior high school.

We moved to Syracuse, New York, when I was ten. I joined the Boy Scouts at age twelve (the minimum age in those days.) Memorizing the Scout Oath and Scout Law was no problem, and I worked my way through knot-tying, Morse code, first aid, canoeing, and all the rest.

Hikes and camping in the woods were kind of fun, even though the older boys sometimes hazed us Tenderfeet.

In the summer of 1942, America's first year of World War II, Victory Gardens and the national food supply were big topics. Scout Troop 18 held Farm Camp for two weeks that year, setting up tents in a patch of woods on nearby Pitcher Hill. We worked in farmers' fields, transplanting cabbages, weeding tomatoes, picking beans, throwing dirt clods at each other, and then had campfire in the woods at night. None of us liked the work in the hot sun very much. It felt good to get the weekend off to go home and collect clean laundry, etc. I told Mother I didn't plan to go back for the second week. "Oh yes you will," she said, and added a succinct lecture on finishing work begun.

Scouting was okay. Moving up the ranks from Tenderfoot gave me no real problems. I even became a patrol leader, lead man in a group of eight. But I never made Life or Eagle ranks because of the required merit badge in athletics (later called personal fitness.) For the life of me, I could never manage to climb a rope or do more than two chin-ups.

But learning to ride a bicycle was my turning point. I had not learned to ride until age thirteen. My brother put me on his bike one afternoon and patiently kept me in balance, trotting along beside me with a hand on the bike's back fender. Time after time we moved down the alley behind our house until that glorious moment when I took off in triumph on my own. I spent the rest of the afternoon going around and around the block, relishing my new ability to go faster than walking—faster even than running. I had the worst case of leg cramps in my life that night but didn't care—I could do it! Riding a bicycle opened up a new world.

My first paying job came from this new skill. I answered a want-ad for boys with bicycles, at a low-rent hotel on the edge of downtown Syracuse. Along with a handful of other boys, I reported each morning to a lady in charge of a row of telephone girls. The Veterans of Foreign Wars Auxiliary (maybe the real one, maybe a sales fraud borrowing the name) solicited phone orders for furniture polish, lemon extract, and a dozen other household products. We boys delivered the orders and collected the money, for which we received ten cents per delivery. Each of us was assigned a region of the city. With a carton of bottles in my bike basket, I would go make my deliveries and report back in the afternoon.

It was an ideal job, getting paid for riding my bike, and the only drawback was the moment at the customer's front door when she realized she was paying double the local grocery store price. When I mentioned this to the boss lady, she said the money went into their "patriotic fund" in a tone that did not invite further questions. The operation closed down after a few weeks.

Not many months later, Scout Troop 18 took a bike hike to Camp Woodland, about 30 miles northeast of Syracuse. The campfires, cooking, hikes and songs have faded from memory, but the trip home still stands out clearly. We were strung out haphazardly along the highway on our bicycles in a drizzling rain. I somehow got ahead of the group. Once ahead, I found it possible to stay ahead, even ahead of the scout leader. For the first time in my life, I not only kept up but excelled in something physical.

For the next three or four years I lived on my bicycle. I rode it to school, fall, winter and spring. I took it apart, repaired it, maintained it. One of my first Boy Scout merit badges was cycling. It required a fifty-mile-in-one-day bike hike. I trained on the hills around Syracuse and passed the test easily. When I was fourteen, my friend Amby Smith and I took a 300-mile trip in four days. The following year we did 700 miles, through northern New York State.

Bicycling helped me discover that different people can excel in different things. You don't always have to struggle to keep up with the crowd; it's sometimes okay to be different. Learning that does wonders for a boy's confidence.

3

Science, Stone, and Silver

The earliest I can remember an interest in science was a library book, *The Story of the Earth and Sky*. Its pictures of the solar system and planets, mountain formation, and prehistoric animals—giant amphibians, dinosaurs and mammoths—riveted my imagination and filled my daydreams.

Then and now, I never have seen any real conflict between science and religion. I'll leave it to the theologians to argue about God's word written in scripture versus his word written in rock strata and DNA. In my simplified opinion, the Bible talks about who created the world; science talks about how.

My fascination with science blossomed after my brother Bruce and I set up a five-dollar Gilbert chemistry set on a bench in the basement. In those days, the set came in a blue wooden cabinet with racks for small vials of chemicals like copper sulfate, sodium bicarbonate, potassium nitrate and so on. There was a tiny measuring spoon, an alcohol lamp, test tubes and a set of instructions for experiments that usually made something fizz or change color. Later, when Bruce was in high school, I devoured his chemistry textbook's description of atoms, elements and compounds. I memorized the list of all the chemical elements, the ninety-two natural substances from which all matter is formed, and I knew some of the minerals they came from.

After moving to Syracuse at age ten, I learned that I could buy some chemicals in drug stores. For about fifty cents, my friend Dave Lee and I could buy powdered charcoal, sulfur and saltpeter to make fireworks; we packed the mixture into soda straws for flares, and added strontium to color the flame scarlet, or barium to make it green or iron filings for sparkly stars.

I was soon experimenting on materials a ten or twelve-year-old should not have messed with. One quiet afternoon I packed an explosive compound (best left unnamed—"don't try this at home, kids") into a device I made from two steel bolts screwed into opposite ends of a steel nut. I experimentally dropped it from the top of the basement stairs to the cement floor below. The satisfying BOOM, followed a second later by the musical clink of one of the bolts bouncing against the far wall, brought the thump of my mother's feet hitting the floor upstairs and her scream, "Keith!" When she opened the basement door my nonchalant "What?" failed to soothe her.

A later experiment, making nitroglycerin, fortunately did not succeed. Kids that age rarely have any sense of real danger in what they try to do.

In sixth grade, a young and pretty teacher visited our class for an hour each Friday to teach geology. I already knew about a few minerals like pyrite from the Colorado Mountains; now I learned about the rocks all around us. We students brought her samples of granite, sandstone and limestone. She was very patient with her eleven and twelve-year-old admirers and encouraged our collections, at least until we began including pieces of brick or cement when we ran out of new rocks to bring her.

After getting a bicycle, I gradually increased my exploring range. Clark Reservation State Park, a few miles away, has limestone cliffs formed by a giant waterfall, comparable in size to Niagara and formed during the time when the ice-age glaciers melted. And a small hill in a farmer's field near Dewitt had a vein of peridotite, the same kind of rock that bears diamonds in South Africa and Arkansas (but not in New York.) I found a railroad cut that exposed sheets of selenite gypsum, transparent as glass. I got an "A+ Excellent" for my high school paper,

11

"Interesting Rocks of Syracuse," complete with diagrams of strata and an Indian legend of the ancient waterfall.

I had passing interest in amateur radio, model airplanes, electromagnets and the like, but the chemistry of minerals always remained my main hobby. My friend Dave Lee and I lived two blocks from the Syracuse University campus. Bowne Hall was the chemistry building. If we were quiet, no one would throw us out when we came to gaze at the shelves in the hall where many of the pure chemical elements were on permanent display. We learned what bromine, mercury, silicon and tellurium look like in pure form. We found a sympathetic clerk in the basement stockroom who would give us (I suspect he paid out of his own pocket) small quantities of some chemicals the neighborhood drugstore did not carry.

Dave and I upgraded our basement laboratory with a Bunsen burner, set on an old orange crate, and began analyzing our mineral specimens with its hot blue flame. Borax heated on a platinum wire loop would melt into a clear glass bead, which turned color when a small amount of powdered mineral was added—yellow for iron, blue for cobalt, green for chromium and so on. The gas flame itself could change color: red for strontium, green for barium, brilliant yellow for sodium, etc. And a mineral's degree of hardness, color, luster and crystal form all gave clues to its identity.

During World War II, at age fourteen, I went with my Dad to Colorado by train to visit my brother in the army. I recall two things about that summer. One was the discovery of someone's abandoned mineral specimens by the hoist room at an old deserted mine. One piece from this find, a fist-sized chunk of pure, gold-colored chalcopyrite, became the first item in my permanent mineral collection. The other memory was the Denver Museum of Natural History in City Park, where I spent most of the next two weeks writing down the name, chemical formula and place of origin of every mineral they had on display. To my surprise, quite a few came from my home state, New York.

I already had a small handbook with pictures of common minerals, but this new knowledge sent me to the library back in Syracuse, to check out *Dana's System of Mineralogy*. The four-inch-thick volume not only described every mineral known to the world at the time it was published, but listed the most prominent locations where each had been found. Over the next couple of years, that book was in my house more often than on the library shelf.

I wanted to take a three-day bicycle hike into the St. Lawrence country of northern New York, to look for the minerals I had read about. My parents said no, not unless I could find a friend to go along. None of my classmates could go. So I asked Ambrose Smith— the other nerd in Boy Scout Troop 18. He was into mechanics and I into chemistry; we shared interest in bicycles, hiking and camping. It was the start of a life-long friendship. We left the week before school opened in the fall, and on the first day we made 120 miles, a record we never exceeded. We quickly learned that a mineral site listed merely as "St. Lawrence County" covers an awful lot of territory. We scouted several sites between Watertown and Ogdensburg and found only a few specimens, but we learned a lot about tracing old records and maps.

The next year, 1944, Amby and I wrote down all the mineral sites we could find listed in Dana's Mineralogy for the Adirondack area of northern New York. We earned money mowing lawns and picking farm crops and set out on a 700-mile, three-week bike tour circling the edges of the Adirondack Mountains. We went from Syracuse to Albany, northward to Ticonderoga and Plattsburgh and back through Potsdam and Watertown, with many side trips to small towns, mines or farmers' fields. Township clerks and local residents were very helpful in directing us. We found quite a few good specimens, some by chance, some from our references: feldspar, sheet mica, talc, hexagonite, tourmaline, hematite, fluorite and others, to add to what by now were becoming respectable mineral collections. At the end of my high school junior year, in 1945, two of my classmates and I got summer jobs at the newly opened Northern Baptist Assembly conference grounds at Green Lake, Wisconsin—more about that later. My roommate, Chuck Perrine, a gregarious type, introduced me to hitch-hiking. Thumbing a ride was safer then than it is now, and during war time most people gave any young man a lift.

I was soon traveling to some new place every week on my day off. I first heard the news of the atomic bomb while getting a haircut in Wisconsin Dells—"a piece of this new stuff the size of a stove could blow up a whole city," the barber told me. A week later, coming back from Wausau with samples of moonstone, I heard church bells ringing in all the towns signaling V-J Day, the end of the war.

But my biggest trip that year was at the end of summer when I set out alone, age 16, to the Keweenaw copper-mining country on Michigan's northern peninsula. I hitch-hiked as far as Green Bay, Wisconsin, and then took an overnight Greyhound bus to Houghton. The copper there comes as pure metal in the rock, uncombined with other elements. The mining school in Houghton had a 1,000-lb mass of pure natural copper on the campus lawn. I had no trouble finding specimens of several copper minerals, and one lady I rode with even gave me two so-called "half-breed" nuggets with swirls of natural silver mixed in with the copper. I stayed in the area a couple of days, took the bus back to Green bay, and hitch-hiked again sixty miles south to Fond du Lac where I used the rest of my round-trip train ticket to get home.

For several more years, I continued traveling and prospecting, whenever I had a few days free and the weather was good. Amby and I even went commercial in 1949, augmenting our next-year college expenses.

People at church occasionally told me I should become a preacher, like my father. I liked my father, but there was almost no job that interested me less than preaching. In high school I drifted toward mineralogy or mining engineering, until events turned my attention in another direction.

4

The Church of My Childhood

First Baptist of St. Paul, Minnesota, was not your everyday small-town church. My father accepted a call to be its minister and heal the rift between conservative and liberal factions left by the former pastor, who had taken two hundred church members with him when he left. We moved to St. Paul from Buffalo, New York, in 1931.

First Baptist was a study of contrasts, standing downtown on the corner of 9th and Wacouta Streets, lifting its tall spire to the sky in the midst of a neighborhood already going downhill, although the Great Depression had barely begun. Street bums and low-income residents of the neighborhood mixed with business people and office workers, farmers and families from all parts of the city. Dad had a relaxed preaching style that filled the personal needs of those who worshiped there, as well as addressing the root causes of such needs in twentieth century America. In seminary in Rochester, Dad had been a student of, and personal secretary to Walter Rauschenbusch, a leading teacher of the so-called "Social Gospel." Rauschenbusch taught that unless you address the needs, both for personal salvation and for fixing society's wrongs, you don't have the whole Gospel of Jesus Christ.

Such matters were way beyond me back then, of course. I knew the church as a place for Sunday school, and later for "Junior Church" where the children in the congregation marched off to a separate room before the sermon began. The last Sunday of each month was "Temperance

15

Sunday" when our teacher, a registered nurse during the week, showed us the physical effects of alcohol or compared the weekend expenses of two fathers. One spent his weekend in the bar room, while the other took his family to the park. The money spent was the same amount, but when the weekend was over the first man's child had a black eye from his drunken father, while the second man's child had some candy left over from his picnic.

Church was the place where we had Vacation Bible School for two weeks in the summer, shouting out the school cheer, learning Bible verses, and building things. Church was the scene of the Watch-night Service on New Year's Eve, where we had stories, drama and games from 8 to 10, then food till 11, and finally a worship service to see the New Year in. Everyone kneeled in prayer for the last five minutes of that hour while the organist chimed out the number of minutes remaining in the old year.

Church was where my brother and I sat with Mother on Sunday nights and sang old hymns, her alto voice blending with the people in the pews behind us. (My sister was old enough to be in the teen-age Baptist Young People's Union [BYPU] so there were only we three.) Mother always had a pencil and some cards in her purse for me to draw with if I got restless during Dad's evening sermon.

Church meant being invited to Sunday dinner at the Ballians, or the Speisers, or the Mears's farm, where Elwood Mears and I could play in the hayloft. Church included Sunday-school picnics in the park, where each kid got a ticket redeemable for an ice cream cone, or some years even a ride on a Mississippi river boat. One of my most pleasant memories pictures coming back up the river on the stern-wheel steamboat *Capitol* at sunset, while the steam calliope on the upper deck boomed out *Stormy Weather,* and cars on the nearby highway slowed to keep pace and listen.

There was no mixing of church and public school, but the school did allow an hour off on Wednesday afternoons for those who went to a nearby church for religious instruction. This was sort of a group church effort, several churches worked together. Miss Jenny Doige had us memorize the books of the Bible in the right order, so we wouldn't have to fumble around when looking things up. Several years afterward, she happened to be working on some committee with Dad, and he called me into the room and asked her if she could still recognize me. "Oh yes," she said, "I'd know Keith's non-committal look anywhere."

Dad's call to pastor the First Baptist Church of Syracuse, New York, was quite a shock to me. I was ten by then, and had firmly idealized Colorado and the West, where we went on summer vacations, as the place I wanted to live. It never occurred to me that we would move to the *east*, which I imagined as endless cities. In fairness to Dad, he had accomplished what he had set out to do in St. Paul eight years before, and now felt it was time to move on to new challenges.

Syracuse was a city of about 200,000 when my family moved there in 1939. First Baptist owned a parsonage (a house for the pastor and his family) at 862 Ostrom Avenue, about two miles from the downtown church, near Syracuse University. It would be our home for the next eleven years. The Syracuse church was bigger than the one in St. Paul, and had been served by several prominent preachers in the Northern Baptist Convention (now renamed American Baptist Churches/USA.)

It was unique in owning a hotel within the church building. The Mizpah Hotel was probably Syracuse's third largest, after the Hotel Syracuse and the Onondaga. The hotel lobby had a separate entrance, connected by elevator to rooms on the fifth and sixth floors, with a restaurant in part of the building's basement. The fourth floor held Sunday school rooms and the third floor held church offices; most of the second and third floors were displaced by the church auditorium which, including the balcony on three sides, seated close to 1,800 people. There was a penthouse on the roof, occupied by the ministers of music, Mr. and Mrs. John T. Clough, and a walkway across the flat roof to access the bell tower.

Our family immediately felt welcome; there was none of the guarded wariness that had begun Dad's pastorate in St. Paul. If there was any dispute in this church, it was about finance—whether to keep a large savings account as shelter against further years of depression, or use the money to improve church facilities and serve more people. The latter option won and First Baptist was well-positioned to minister to the hordes of service men and women who passed through the city as America geared up for World War II. Families with a member in the military displayed a small flag with a star. The church's own service flag eventually held two hundred stars, representing members who had gone to war. By 1945, ten of the stars were gold—those who had died for their country.

I was ten when we came to Syracuse, my brother Bruce almost fifteen. My twenty-year-old sister Margaret stayed in Minnesota to finish college and became a school-teacher in the small town of Wells, near to St. Paul and close to her fiance, Gordon Torgersen.

I have uninteresting memories of Sunday school during my first years in Syracuse, but the church music was good. George Oplinger, research chemist during the week and dean of the Syracuse Society of Organists, played the huge pipe organ in the choir loft above the pulpit. The *a capella* choir entered in procession as the worship service began, singing as they marched, with Mr. Clough pacing sedately behind them. He and his wife managed all six choirs in the church: two adult, one youth (high school and college age) and three children's choirs, besides giving professional voice lessons during the week.

Preachers' kids in a one-car family had to wait half an hour after church, while Dad visited with people at the door. I soon made friends with gray-haired Miss Carlotta Matthews, who counted the church offering upstairs in the office. "Can I help count?" I asked one Sunday.

"Ayuh, if you're careful." She taught me how to count coins rapidly, using two fingers to sweep pairs of coins into my other hand, counting the correct number for each paper roll for the bank. She made sure I did it right, until she knew she could trust my count. This occupied me every week thereafter while Dad finished talking with people at the church door. On rare occasions when an Indian-head penny turned up in the offering, she allowed me to trade a penny of my own for it.

Sunday afternoons were spent quietly reading, playing, or listening to the radio. Movies on Sunday weren't actually forbidden, but were something we kids went to on Saturday instead.

My attitude toward Sunday school changed when I entered high school and the Baptist Youth Fellowship (BYF). Partly, it was because of a couple of adult leaders who involved us in discussions, taught us to speak in public, and sponsored occasional bowling parties or square dances during the week. And partly it was because some of my weekday classmates in high school were also in BYF.

Onondaga County had about ten Northern Baptist churches, and their BYF groups would meet together two or three times a year. There was also a New York State BYF annual convention, attended by maybe a dozen young people from our church. The counselor for the state BYF, Lew Johnson and his wife, lived in Syracuse and encouraged us in state-wide activities. He took a team of a half-dozen of us on weekend trips to other churches in the state to hold "Discipleship Clinics" in the five-point BYF program (Personal Christian Living, Evangelism, Missions, Citizenship and Leadership). We would lead workshops for the teen-agers of the church on Saturday afternoon, have a party Saturday night (and if we included square dancing, we were careful to call it "folk games" because some churches objected to dancing.) Often we would take part in leading the Sunday morning worship service before heading home.

It was educational for city kids to see other churches. The Northern Baptists had about five hundred churches in Upstate New York, some of them tiny and isolated. We visited a group of three churches around Northville, in the Adirondacks, during their "Mud Week" when the schools closed because the spring time rains made most of the roads impassable.

Mr. Clough's youth choir played a larger part in my life than I realized at the time. It numbered thirty or forty high school and college students and young working people, and rehearsed from 4 to 5 pm each Sunday. Mr. Clough was a professional yet friendly man in his forties, low-key in his conduction style, who led us with small hand motions, not arm waving. We paid attention because we knew our music sounded good. A few of the best voices were promoted to the top-ranking *a capella* choir, but even the rest of us enjoyed learning to sing in four- or eight-part harmony. I can't read music, except to tell whether a note is higher or lower than the last one, but I found I had a sense of harmony. Mr. Clough coached us until the music became fixed in my brain, easily recalled decades later.

In my junior year in high school, the Cloughs were invited to take charge of the next summer's music program at the newly founded Northern Baptist Assembly Grounds in Wisconsin. I suspect Mr. Clough wanted at least a small nucleus of singers already accustomed to his style of leading. In any event, he publicized the Green Lake summer staff's impressive opportunities, and managed to recruit three of us from his Syracuse youth choir.

Church influenced my life in several ways, including that summer at Green Lake, where the direction in my life began to change.

5

Nottingham High

High school is a time of many changes for any teenager. Still more so, if the teenager is a dissident. And I was a pacifist, in the middle of World War II.

I felt strongly about this. I took my cues from my Dad, whose sermons from the pulpit were pro-people, but against all war. To him, peace did not mean merely absence of war. He believed war went against the word of God and solved very few issues. It did not mean that a Christian should be a weakling or a doormat. On the contrary, Christians are expected to be strong in order to help the oppressed, enslaved, or lost to find a personal relationship with God, and so far as possible help them find a way out of suffering and injustice.

As a young man at the time of the first World War, Dad at first had refused even to register for the draft. He finally registered as a conscientious objector, although the draft board would have allowed him a clergy exemption. He continued to preach against war during World War II, even while he ministered to the needs of two hundred service men and women among his congregation in Syracuse. The FBI had him on their list for a while; they listened to him preach, and questioned the church members, but never found anything to even suggest that he was seditious or unpatriotic. (Years later, I read their conclusion in the FBI's dossier on Dad, released under the Freedom of Information Act.) His congregation, in fact, highly respected him, even though many members had questions about his message.

During World War II, a pacifist teenager was hard for most of my classmates and teachers to figure out. Following Pearl Harbor, the whole nation had mobilized to the war effort. Buy war bonds. If you can't afford a bond, buy war stamps each week until you have enough for a bond. Turn in your aluminum cooking pots to build airplanes. Plant victory gardens. Save gas. Knit sweaters. Write the boys overseas. The time I spent at Boy Scout farm camp, in 1942, weeding cabbage fields and picking beans, was to help the national effort to raise more food, and I had no problem with that.

But I had a decision to make on my own in wood-shop class in junior high school. The whole class was assigned the project of making scale-model wooden airplanes, about five inches long, used for training aircraft spotters and gunners in instant recognition. To me, that was supporting war and I told the shop teacher, Mr. Pepper, that I couldn't do it. "I understand," was his gruff reply, but I don't think he ever really did.

It got worse in high school, during home-room period each day. Students were expected to buy at least one war savings stamp (twenty-five cents) each Friday. If even one student in the whole school did not do so, the school could not display the 100% banner on the flag pole that week. Nottingham High never got to fly the banner when I was a student. Some of my classmates resented this, although most adopted a neutral attitude. Things improved after about a year when the school held a Red Cross fund drive one day. I figured up what I had not invested in war stamps over the past months, and gave it to the Red Cross, possibly more than the rest of my home room combined. A hostile classmate accosted me one morning, "How come you can give to the Red Cross but not to the war effort?"

I told him the Red Cross healed people. I added that I wouldn't get any savings investment returned after the war, like he would from his war bonds. He didn't like that at all; I thought he might hit me, but I stood my ground. The class president and his girlfriend were standing nearby; both took my side and told the guy to back off. After their endorsement, things got better.

During 1945, the Baptist Youth Fellowship at church became active in drama. I had a bit-part in *Elmer and the Love-Bug,* found that I liked acting, and when a drama club at school presented *Why I Am a Bachelor,* I got the lead role, playing a misanthropic lecturer. It was a corny play, but the student body liked it. In looking back, perhaps part of its popularity was their opinion that the role fit me exactly.

In my senior year, I happened to have Miss Frederica Smith as my English teacher. "Sister Smith" was a middle-aged, self-possessed soul in horn-rimmed glasses who believed in getting the whole class involved. After we had studied poetry and verse-making for two weeks, Miss Smith announced that, tomorrow being Valentine's Day, each student would choose some character from literature and write an appropriate valentine to him or her. After making sure that the Bible was considered literature, I submitted my valentine, from Samson to Delilah, with a straight face:

> *All the while I've been making your people feel blue,*
> *Though I'm fighting with thousands, yet think I of you.*
> *I've torn city gates from their place in the wall,*
> *But your icy cold heart I cannot move at all.*
> *In times of distress I've relied on my brawn,*
> *But that's no help at all when to you I am drawn.*
> *Of all the Philistines I think you're most fair—*
> *But Baby, I can't keep you out of my hair.*

The class, Miss Smith included, burst into laughter. To my surprise, I was later elected senior-class poet based on this offering, and was invited to join the staff of the school newspaper, but I never wrote any more poems worth remembering.

The year went by quickly after that, and on June 24, 1946 graduation night came for 256 of us. Our principal, Harold Coon, was graduating too, moving up to a post in the school district headquarters downtown. There was the usual procession to *Pomp and Circumstance,* speeches, awards etc. My mind was chiefly on summer vacation; I would go directly from school to the railroad station and catch the night train west for my second summer of work at Green Lake, Wisconsin, along with one of my classmates.

I was startled out of my reverie by hearing my name called at the tail end of the athletic and citizenship award presentations. Mr. Coon announced that the class had voted me the one they would most like to represent them in life. I hadn't known there was such an award, but it's the one I would most like to have.

6

Green Lake

The same year that I entered Nottingham High School, 1943, the Northern Baptists were offered an opportunity to buy 1,100 acres of property on Green Lake in Wisconsin. This had originally been the show-case farm of a rich Chicago newspaper publisher named Lawson. In the Depression a holding company took it over and built a five-story hotel and gambling casino on the lake front, with a world-class golf course, each of the eighteen holes patterned after some famous hole elsewhere in the world. But the resort went bankrupt in the Depression, and the whole of Lawsonia was on the market for $250,000.

Luther Wesley Smith, an executive at the Baptists' national headquarters, immediately saw it as a possible national conference grounds of unparalleled beauty. He took Baptist layman J. L. Kraft (of Kraft Cheese) and several others to see it.

Both men were salesmen, one spiritual and one financial, and the Northern Baptist Assembly grounds soon became a reality. The slot machines were consigned to the deepest bottom of the lake, where I guess they still remain, and the hotel was renamed Roger Williams Inn, after the first pioneer Baptist in America, who founded the state of Rhode Island.

Don Folkes, a member of the older BYF group in Syracuse, attended the first Youth Conference at Green Lake in 1944, and came home with a glowing report. But interest in Green Lake really took hold when John

Clough accepted the summer appointment as music director there for the 1945 season, and began recruiting a nucleus for the staff choir. He announced to our Youth Choir in Syracuse that Green Lake sought student staff members. The pay was nominal—$25 a month plus tips—but it came with free room and board, free attendance at any and all conferences, and free use of the extensive recreation facilities. Not to mention seeing a new part of the country and meeting people from all over the world. Minimum age for applicants was sixteen in 1945, because almost everyone eighteen and over was still in the military or had a wartime job.

Three of us applied, Chuck Perrine as a dining room waiter, and Ed Boyd and I as pot and pan washers. The three of us took the train west as soon as school was out.

Green Lake Conference Center, as it is known today, has about two miles of shoreline on a lake eight miles long by three miles wide. There were about seventy on the student staff—bell hops, waiters, waitresses, life guards, and kitchen help. Adult volunteers also worked for a nominal stipend, like the Cloughs on the music staff, and Claude Bush, another Syracusan, who managed the golf course. Some others were missionaries on home furlough. The only salaried people were a few department heads and people from surrounding towns working in year-round maintenance and housekeeping jobs.

We students stayed out by the gate, two miles from the Inn where most of us worked, the boys at "The Farmhouse" and the girls at "Shepherds' Lodge", a quarter mile apart. Buses provided transport to the Inn; those who preferred to walk could do so. Many couples did, in the moonlight after work.

When we worked, we worked hard. Scrubbing grease and baked-on crusts from enough pans to feed six hundred people three meals a day is a hot, sweaty job. Ed and I each had an eight-hour shift, and it was hands-on work, not mechanized like the dish-washer crew.

But the time-off was great. The scenery, sports, hiking, swimming and boating were hard to match anywhere else. A new crowd of guests came in every week. I made friends from across the country.

Norman Gano, a staff member from Opportunity, Washington, and I discovered a mutual liking for hillbilly music, and we formed a singing act for the occasional talent night, with such memorable numbers as *The Crash on the Highway,* and *Glory-Bound Train.* We got mixed reviews from some of the conference leaders, including two evangelists who got up and walked out because of the jug I used as a stage prop.

One of the first and largest groups of guests that summer was the BYF Conference, bringing kids our age and a little older from all parts of the country. We mixed freely with conferees, and attended sessions that caught our interest.

Some of the conference speakers met with the student staff in the evening after working hours, shared experiences and answered our questions. Clarence Jordan had pioneered inter-racial cooperative farming in Georgia, at a time when treating blacks as equals meant social ostracism at best, and gunfire at worst.

Jessie Burrall Eubank talked quietly about what we could accomplish when we put our lives in God's hands, and how she had survived near-fatal illness by doing so. Chuck Boddie taught us the rhythms of Black Gospel songs. Victor Sword told of his mission to the Naga headhunters in the far north of Burma. Nels Ferre, a theologian from Sweden, talked about the nature of faith. Salman, the artist, recreated his famous painting *Head of Christ* before our eyes.

There were week-long conferences for Christian educators, for evangelists, for missions, Bible study, music, and recreation leadership. Lexie Ferrell, the leader of the rec lab recruited student staffers to fill in as participants in the games and parties she and her team demonstrated each evening.

It wasn't all contemplative. Some high-spirited students once tied up our house father, Dick Beers, and threw him in a tub of cold water when they disagreed with his latest edict. And a plan to put a cow on the small island just offshore from the Inn at midnight had to be abandoned when the cow refused to enter the rowboat, and had to be quietly returned to pasture.

I returned to the Green Lake staff in 1946, 47, 50, 51 and 53. By the end of my second summer, I had graduated to cook's helper, no longer having to scrub an endless stack of encrusted pans, but helping instead to prepare mashed potatoes for five- or six-hundred people, or help dish out salads and desserts. One of my first lessons, learned the hard way was, if you fill a potato kettle from the cold water tap instead of the hot, you must then explain to twenty waitresses why the potatoes will be half an hour late.

One guest owned a coffee company and taught me the fine points of brewing good coffee, thirty-gallons at a time. All I remember now is that he advised using 170 degree hot water, not boiling, on the drip-grind coffee, to avoid extracting bitter oils. My coffee skill became a sought-after commodity that year.

But overall, that first summer in 1945 prepared me for taking Christianity more seriously when it came time to choose a career the following year, my senior year in high school. The experience wasn't just about being away from home. I had already been to Scout camp, and had taken two extended bicycle trips, one of them more than three weeks long, in previous summers. Green Lake gave me contact with a Christian peer group, irreverent enough to question hypocrisy. And I met many adults who had chosen to follow Jesus in their life work and yet were still in daily contact with the world.

Christianity appeared to be something more than just going to church, but I wasn't really sure what, yet.

7

Changing Direction

Whatever war's roots, I agreed with Dad that war was wrong. As I grew older, I sympathized with several young men of like mind who chose to work as non-combatant medics in the armed services, or as civilians in the camp for conscientious objectors (CO's) at Elmira, NY.

Larry, one of my co-workers at my first summer at Green Lake, was a CO. The county sheriff came and took him to jail one day, and several of us went to visit him in his cell. He was unconcerned with the future and not angry with the sheriff or the government. It was just something he had to do, and he did it.

I realized that no one was going to stop World War II, and that the CO's function in the midst of war could be little more than a reminder that there are choices involved in war that someone, in some future decade, might discover in time to use effectively. Meanwhile my prayers included the daily request, "May there soon be peace all over the world forever."

The introduction of the atomic bomb raised the question, might "peace all over the world forever" describe a desolate radioactive wasteland? I gradually modified my wish to something more like "Peace in the hearts of humankind."

By 1946, the war was over and my pacifist stand was no longer irritating anyone. I had gained some experience in public speaking and leadership in the BYF and drama group. I began to see myself as more than just an athletic team's last choice. Someone who, even if unable to bring about world peace single-handed, might at least make a difference.

My attention began to turn away from a career in chemistry or minerals and focus more on people. My senior year in high school taught me that most people are likable. And although mineral specimens and chemistry represented permanence, stability and reliability, peace would come about through some change in people, not through study of unchanging rock.

I wouldn't have put it this way at the time, but that first summer working at Green Lake had opened the world like the pages of a book. I met other teenagers who shared some of my ideals, and older people whom I could see as role models.

During my senior year in high school I felt restless inside. I heard no voice, saw no vision, but had an urge to commit my life to serving God through serving other human beings. I resisted this for weeks. My life was going to be in some chemistry or mineralogy lab, somewhere working with the pristine geometric shapes of crystals, purity hidden in the rocks.

Church? I liked my Dad and Mother, enjoyed the church youth group, and I respected those who, down through history, had stood up for what they believed. But sermons? Endless church services? Old people repeating their "testimony" every week at prayer meeting? C'mon, God, that's not my style.

The restlessness persisted, and I sensed that God wanted something from me, but what? I had already been baptized at age 11, when the church deacons asked us kids whether we would like to be. Dad had encouraged me to consider it, and I had not seen any reason why not. But this was different, in my last year of high school, like someone waiting patiently for me to decide something important.

In reading a Bible chapter each night, I had come across Isaiah, who wrote, "*In the year that King Uzziah died, I saw the Lord, sitting upon a throne, high and lifted up ... Also I heard the voice of the Lord, saying, "Whom shall I send, and who will go for us?" Then said I, "Here am I! Send me."*

The prophet Isaiah's words resonated somehow with the restlessness I was feeling. But I still felt no interest in church work. Being a preacher didn't seem to be my thing.

Finally, one evening in May, alone in my room with the window open to the warm spring air, I decided that whatever God wanted me to do, I would do. And with that act the restlessness disappeared, to be replaced by a peaceful sense of having made a right choice.

That second summer at Green Lake, I began examining the chances for being a foreign missionary while staying in my field of mineral chemistry. Had anyone ever done that, besides maybe teachers? All I discovered was one Catholic priest who had been an authority on glaciers. But I gradually realized that medical missions combined science and service to people, and there seemed to be quite a need for that. The American Baptists had hospitals in many countries, and the hospitals needed doctors.

I enrolled in pre-med at Syracuse University, two blocks from home. I signed up for freshman courses—English, chemistry, advanced algebra, sociology, a foreign language, and managed to pass them. I still had no athletic talents; the only way I got a B in physical education was to volunteer as a sacrificial lamb in an intramural wrestling meet. (I got pinned to the mat in the first fifteen seconds.) I admit being pleased when, on a cold January night, the athletic building caught fire, and burned to an empty brick shell. No, I had nothing to do with causing it, but it was a spectacular fire to watch, and without an athletic building the University waived all mandatory physical ed. classes for everyone, for the rest of my four years.

Pre-med required credits in four courses: basic chemistry, organic chemistry, zoology, and physics. I managed to stay about in the middle of the class in most subjects, but did less well in economics and sociology. In declaring a major, at the end of my sophomore year, it probably surprised no one that I chose chemistry. But I also enjoyed electives like psychology, comparative anatomy, and astronomy. I found it easy to memorize anything set to music—even country music and advertising jingles. An elective course in folksong was a pleasure.

But the odds of getting into medical school were one in sixty, in those years when the war veterans came home. I tried to better my chances by applying to multiple schools. That process was traumatic in itself.

"Well at least you don't look like your picture, thank God!" The Dean of Albany Medical School looked at me critically, glancing down again at my application for the next year's entering class. "Your college grades aren't all that good. What makes you think you can be a doctor?"

I had already learned not to repeat the mistake made at my first interview, at Syracuse. "I want to help people" was what admissions committees heard from every student applicant who couldn't think of anything else to say. And in 1949, three hundred thousand of us were competing for the five thousand seats in next year's class of America's medical schools.

I mumbled some reply to the dean. It was clear that he had already decided, as had the dean at Rochester School of Medicine a few days earlier, that I was not the right material. I drove the 130 miles home wondering if being a doctor was a realistic goal.

Universities overflowed with students in the late 1940s. Returning veterans, holding "GI Bill of Rights" scholarships, were intent on making up for lost years. More mature than we new high school grads, they were tough competition, deadly serious in their studies. No nonsense about joining fraternities, or wearing orange freshman "beanie" caps. They wanted education and a diploma.

So did I. In the end, I applied to ten medical schools, and was accepted at Syracuse and at Temple in Philadelphia. I chose Syracuse because of the possibility of a state scholarship. Long odds, but as it turned out, I got one. The State of New York at that time gave one hundred in-state scholarships annually for the study of medicine or dentistry. The $750 per year provided all the tuition but $50, and I am sure the help was a relief to my parents.

8

Hunting the Rare Rocks

I took the longest of my hitch-hiking trips after my first year in college in 1947, at the end of my summer job. Heading from Green Lake northwestward to St. Paul, I stayed overnight with my boyhood friend, Dick Grayson, then went on north to Hibbing, Minnesota, to see the huge open-pit mines of the Mesabi iron range.

At a coffee shop in Hibbing, there were only a few customers, and the Greek proprietor struck up a conversation. Learning I was a pre-med student, he declared he had studied psychology for a long time. "I can tell people by their faces," he said in his broken English. "You going to be a good doctor."

Maybe so, I thought. The memory of his encouragement gave me a little extra boost in times of doubt later on.

Leaving Hibbing the next morning, I went on through Duluth and along the north shore of Lake Superior. The Immigration officer at Pigeon River, on the Canadian border, almost refused me entry but I persuaded him that my thirty-nine dollars was enough to get me through Canada to New York State.

I had researched mineral sites along my route; the Bureau of Mines in Ottawa had referred me to an engineer near Thunder Bay, Ontario. He in turn gave me the address of a Dr. Peter Wenger, who collected minerals. Dr. Wenger cordially invited me to stop by when I came through. I did, and he and his wife and five-year old daughter packed

31

a picnic lunch and took me out to a remote site to dig amethyst. In almost no time I had half a dozen good-sized specimens of the large purple crystals. The doctor dropped me off at my hotel on his way to a concert where he and a neighbor were to play in the orchestra that evening.

I had not anticipated the road conditions beyond Thunder Bay. The Trans-Canada Highway was not yet finished, and the only road connecting western and eastern Ontario was a gravel two-lane route through Nipigon, Geraldton, and Hearst to North Bay. I had plenty of company—half a dozen other hitch-hikers were having a hard time getting across this stretch of Ontario too. I got as far as Geraldton, a logging and mining town celebrating its tenth year of existence that week, and found that no cars were going farther east except local traffic. A sign "No gas for the next 75 miles" said it all.

I finally went into town to the only hotel. Ten dollars a night. I asked if there was a less expensive place in town, and the clerk disdainfully gave me an address on the edge of town that charged two dollars.

The family there spoke mostly French, the room was a dump, the shadeless window looked out on a brick wall, the toilet down the hall didn't flush and the washbowl didn't work. The bed had a ragged blanket and a single worn sheet. But it was the only place I could afford. A girl carried my bag to my room, and as soon as she set it down and left, I locked the door.

Next morning, as I came out the front door at 6 o'clock, the window panes were frosted and the eastern sky a rich deep rose color. Standing on the silent street, I was chilled to the marrow. An old car finally came slowly out from town, and I hitched a ride. The elderly miner took me two miles out to the crossroads at Highway 11. He asked where I had stayed, and when I told him, he said that was the local whorehouse. That would account for all the noise in the hall most of the night.

The sky now shone fiery orange and gold. A mile away, a refinery's smoke stack was pouring a column of black smoke that floated off in a narrow path on the still air over the endless trees until it reached the eastern horizon. A smaller trail from an auxiliary chimney went along beside it. The eastern sky changed to pale orange and blue as I stamped my feet in the cold and tried to warm my numb fingers in my pockets. A signpost at the crossroads bore the initials of many hitch-hikers, some of them probably those I had stood with the day before. I added mine, next to the word Toronto, for luck.

At seven o'clock I could stand the cold and wind no longer. I caught a local bus back into town. I would have to take a train; at least the station would be warm. The station door opened at 7:40, though no tickets were on sale until 8:00. The fare to North Bay was $17.00, most of the money I had left.

Thank God for that twenty minutes of warmth before ticket sales began, because about eight o'clock I found courage to make another try at hitch-hiking. Two rides took me back to the crossroads and after another hour, a car took me to Longlac, a tiny lumber town at the head of a lake stretching south, the jumping-off place for the long uninhabited stretch of road to Hearst, 130 miles to the east.

Amby Smith was hitch-hiking up from Syracuse, and we had agreed to meet next day in the town of Cobalt, still 500 miles away. By noon I was still in Longlac. Two of the hitch-hikers I had met yesterday joined me for a while; they had spent the night under a bridge. After entering the Longlac railroad station to see what it cost to reach Hearst, they came back in disgust. It was more money than they had, and it would take forever to get there, after changing trains at some place called Oba. As they moved on up the road, they said they would try to hop a freight. Waiting for a ride, I watched idly as logging trucks dumped their loads into the lake, where two tug-boats marshaled the logs into rafts.

By now, I knew that my hope rested on several cars parked outside Longlac's small railroad station, especially one with a Quebec license. When the Quebec people came out, I asked them if they were going to Hearst. They looked at me suspiciously and said no, then drove off eastward. That made me angry, but I couldn't blame them. Who could trust anyone on this lonely road? I went to the lunch counter in the station and bought a glass of milk and a small bag of peanuts for fifteen cents. I thought of asking about taxi rates, but a policeman was talking with the two taxi drivers, and I didn't want to attract his attention.

Finally about noon, I acknowledged I was beaten. And then, strangely, everything felt good; no more worry. I would take the train next morning to North Bay. I'd wire Amby tonight and tell him to meet me there at noon, day after tomorrow. There was plenty of driftwood on the lake shore, plus kindling from dry bark cast off the lumber trucks. I had matches somewhere in my bag. If God sent me no help by 3 p.m. I would start gathering firewood and spend the night under the bridge.

The weather had warmed in the afternoon sun, and I shoved my bag and my sweater under the bridge. At ten minutes to two, I was leaning against the concrete wall of the bridge watching another car come up the road. I raised my thumb with little hope, then lowered it again when I saw the sign on its bumper, "TAXI." It sped by, then suddenly stopped at the other end of the bridge. I stood in amazement a moment, then broke into a trot. "Would you be going to Hearst, sir?"

"Yup."

"Wait just a minute, I have a bag back there under the bridge," and I dashed back, grabbed my things and ran back to the car.

"Let's go, buddy, I'm in a hurry!"

"So am I, sir!" I said. He grinned and told me to throw my bag into the back seat. Asked me where I was going. "Cobalt." I saw him half-smile again. "You aren't going there, are you?"

"Darn near."

And everything was all right again. He had to be in Kirkland Lake that night, only about seventy miles from Cobalt. We passed the two hitch-hikers I had talked with that morning, and I suggested they needed a ride too. He looked annoyed and said one hiker was enough; he would never pick up two together. I drew one other look of annoyance from him by saying that I had about given up hope of a ride and had planned to spend the night under the bridge.

"S'matter, no money?"

"Sure, but I would have needed it to take the train." He looked a little relieved and said some hikers expected him to buy their meals and even give them cigarettes. I said I didn't smoke, and he finally seemed assured I wasn't a drifter.

We sped along the dusty dirt road. Ten miles farther I saw three other guys I had met two days before, back near Nipigon. They forlornly lifted their thumbs in the air beside an old road-grading machine. I mentioned my surprise that they had passed me two days ago. The driver ground to a stop, swearing. "I can't leave them in the middle of nowhere. You say you know them?" (fearful of robbery again.)

"Well, I've seen them along the road a couple of times. One's bound for Ottawa, the other two for Toronto, I think."

"Damn! Now we can't make good time, with the back end loaded that way."

The three reached the car, out of breath, and I gave them a hello. The driver didn't pretend they were welcome, but they didn't refuse the ride, after waiting two days. They dozed in the back seat after their long roadside vigil; once in a while the boy who didn't speak much English would reach over the front seat-back to offer us a cigarette.

Even with the car loaded, the driver averaged sixty miles per hour (this was before Canada converted to kilometers.) But two hours later, at the gas station in Hearst, he opened the back door. "I picked you fellas up because you were foolish enough to get stuck way out in the woods. Now you're in a town again, you'll have to get out. I'm in a hurry, and want to travel light." He turned to me, "You can stay." The three looked disappointed, but at least they were over the worst.

I was fortunate, the first to be picked up and now had the favor of the man with the car. I felt sorry for the others, but not sorry enough to join them.

The driver chuckled as he rolled out of town over the unpaved gravel, ruts and pot-holes of Highway 11. "Did you see the looks on those three when I made 'em get out? That stocky one was the only one had the presence of mind to thank me. They'll get rides now, though. Dam' fools to get stranded way out in the bush."

We made good time on the poor road. Often we hit a pot hole with a hard jolt, raising a cloud of dust that penetrated everything. Sometime past five o'clock we stopped at a garage in Mattice. The driver wanted a front tire fixed; rim cuts from the jolts were making it leak air. We looked for a place to eat, found a small store with several stall-like wooden booths. The waitress spoke little English.

The driver waved my money away, after he had ordered us two sandwiches, and said he'd take care of this. Sandwiches eaten and the tire fixed, we sped onward. I told him about being a student at Syracuse U, he told me what it was like to be a long-distance taxi driver, with sometimes a little bootlegging on the side. He, Peter Doran, grew up in Kirkland but now lived in Rossport, over near Nipigon; had a repair shop and ran his taxi between there and Kirkland for those willing to pay the price—faster than train, cheaper than plane. His wife was in

Kirkland now, but was leaving on the 11 p. m. train; he wanted to get there in time to see her off.

We reached Kapuskasing at dusk where we had to slow to 45 or 50 when the road bumps made the headlights flicker. One really bad hole made them go off entirely, and by the time the car could stop, we were aimed diagonally toward the ditch. Even so, we reached Cochrane by 8 o'clock, but found no garages open to get the lights fixed. We stopped for gas, hamburgers and thick yellow coffee, which I paid for this time. At one point near the Timmins cut-off, a car was stalled on a railroad crossing and we pushed them a short way. The man and his family asked where the nearest garage was, but being a garage man himself, Mr. Doran raised the hood and fixed the problem, refusing payment. Nearing Kirkland, we reached paved highway again, passed through Swastika, a village the Canadians re-named Churchill during the war. We got to Kirkland near midnight; I never found out if he met his wife. He left me at a small hotel and said to drop him a line someday. I did, ten years later, but never got a reply. But thanks, Peter Doran, for the lift and more. My original journal of the trip, written nine months afterward said, "That day remains one of the chief reasons for my faith in prayer." I still believe it, more than fifty years later, as I ponder God's sense of humor in answering my prayer with a taxi.

Ironically, a hotel room and shower that night cost the same two dollars as I had paid for the hole-in-the-wall in Geraldton the night before.

Starting out the next morning, I took temporary shelter from the rain under a movie marquee, along with a sullen-faced boy of about thirteen who was playing hooky from school. He didn't like school, didn't like the teacher. He thought a long-distance hitch-hiker obviously had the better life, and he asked where I was going, where from, and all about the road generally. I told him I was still in school, which would re-start in a couple weeks, and that school was where he should be now, but I don't think he was listening.

I covered the last eighty miles to Cobalt easily and met Amby Smith on schedule that noon. We collected specimens around the mines, adding only a few to our collections, but laying the groundwork for later trips. The going was much easier as we hitch-hiked our way down through Toronto and Niagara Falls and reached home in Syracuse two days later.

Although I was already in pre-med studies at school, Amby and I spent the next two summers, 1948 and 49, searching for the rare rocks: crystals and ores of exotic metals that no one but a mineralogist or metallurgist had ever heard of.

I had already traveled through northern Ontario in the fall of 1946, at the end of my second summer at Green Lake, hitch-hiking home by way of Sault St. Marie, Sudbury, and Ottawa, with a side trip to Cobalt. By 1948, the year after my long trek across northern Ontario, Amby and I both had driver's licenses, and I persuaded my Dad to loan us the family car when he and Mother would be out of town anyway. That was the summer between my sophomore and junior years at Syracuse University. I was nineteen, and had a summer job at Solvay Process Co., while Amby worked at Crouse Hinds at their traffic light plant. After our jobs ended in late August, we drove out to a youth conference at Grand Rapids, Michigan, and afterward continued northward to Sault Ste. Marie, on further north to Cobalt, and southward to a new area for us in the hills around Bancroft, Ontario.

We had much better information, more up to date on what minerals were there, and were more savvy in networking with local miners and teachers. In varying quantities, we collected ores of bismuth, uranium, cobalt, nickel, niobium, yttrium, and a few rocks containing sheets of pure metallic silver. In addition, we picked up decorative rocks like rose quartz, blue sodalite, beryl, and fluorescent hackmanite.

We cut our expenses by splitting cost of gas with the passengers we drove to the conference at Grand Rapids and again from there to North Bay, Ontario. We also sold some duplicate specimens for about thirty dollars to a mineral shop in Berkeley, California, that we had contacted through *Rocks and Minerals Magazine*.

In 1949 we went commercial. We had the use of the car again (Dad and Mother were in Europe, at a World Council of Churches meeting.) We planned trips through New Hampshire, Maine, Ontario and Quebec. The owner of the shop in Berkeley, California, wanted more material and we made contact with a shop in Colorado and a few other possible customers.

We brought back a wide variety of minerals. I have no narrative record of the 1949 trips, but kept a list of the specimen lots: 220 lb. garnet, 8 lb. tourmaline, 23 lb. sapphire (not gem grade), 443 lb.

fluorescent minerals, 160 lb. nickel ore (niccolite and annabergite), 80 lb. cobalt ore (cobaltite and smaltite), 104 lb. uranium ore (autunite), 110 lb. rare-earth metal ores (cyrtolite, columbite and fergusonite.) Also many more ordinary minerals, totaling close to 2,000 lb. in four trips.

We were naive in pricing, charging only fifteen to seventy-five cents a pound for our specimens. I am sure we could have commanded several dollars a pound for some of it, but even so, we made over four hundred dollars (in today's dollars around four thousand) to help with our college expenses for the coming year. Amby made sturdy wooden crates, and we shipped our merchandise to California and Colorado by truck. 1949 was the last of our mineral travels, though I still collect specimens when I get a chance. My life had already changed direction after my high school senior year, but one event stands out in memory:

Coming back from one Ontario trip, we wanted to get home, and planned to drive all night. We arrived at the U. S. border about midnight. The lone customs officer asked what we had acquired in Canada. We showed him our list of mineral specimens, and he rummaged through the boxes in the trunk and back seat. He ignored the corundum, and nickel and cobalt ores, and stopped at "108 lb. nephelite".

"That's jade, isn't it, boys?"

"No, Sir. Jade is nephrite. This is nephelite, kind of like feldspar. We got it near Bancroft."

This was out of the officer's field. He looked at his list again. "This is all highly irregular, boys. I can't let you through until the assessor comes on duty tomorrow morning. You can sleep in the jail cell, if you like."

Amby and I shared the damp-floored cell with a resident bullfrog. At nine the next morning, the assessor looked over our freight, passed us with no import duty, but charged five dollars for the inspection. And that's been my only time in jail so far.

Since that time, I have picked up occasional mineral specimens over the years—barite, ruby, ores of silver, tin, zinc, antimony but mineralogy is now only an enjoyable hobby. I have found that people, and their infinite differences and variations from normal, are far more intriguing.

9

Coming Of Age

My parents provided a warmth in our home that I never appreciated until I had a wider view of what happens in some other families. Seeing them hug was just part of the scene, not producing so much as an "Oh, *ick*!" from us children. We learned that mature adults express love for each other. We learned manners, learned honesty, and learned about right and wrong.

I received two books of instruction from my parents. One was my own copy of the Bible at about age eight, with encouragement to read a chapter each night. The other, around the age of twelve, was called "In Training", and was about puberty. I was glad to get it; sex was an interesting topic that I didn't yet know much about, and this short booklet was a combination of facts and advice. The volumes of Encyclopedia Britannica in Dad's study had been no help, with their anatomic description of seminal vesicles and Cowper's glands. And even my own limited knowledge told me that the whispered tales at Scout camp, at night after lights-out, were wildly inaccurate.

Even at age ten or eleven, I was aware that some girls were pretty. I enjoyed the sight of Beverly, a quiet brunette in my sixth grade class, but I was too shy to do anything about it. A couple of years later, when I was selling Tasty-Jel (for the Scout troop) door-to-door in a nearby neighborhood, it was she who answered one door. Her casually friendly greeting sent me into incoherent mumbling confusion.

The first girl of interest with whom I could converse was a petite blonde whom I knew from school. I would sometimes ride my bike along the route she took to walk home from school, just on the chance of seeing her and saying hello. My calf-like admiration lasted a few months. Then another girl from church happened to share a Greyhound Bus seat with me, while a group of us were coming back from some event near Binghamton. She fell asleep with her head on my shoulder, and I didn't move a muscle for fifty miles, so entrancing was the closeness. I was brave enough to go out on several group-dates with her, square-dancing and the like, and maybe her head on my shoulder had not been entirely a random event.

But I was still lacking in worldly wisdom. At someone's birthday party when I was 13 or 14, the group decided to play a version of "Post Office" in the dark. We were paired off, boy and girl, with the lights out, and I felt too embarrassed to do more than sit motionless. The girl next to me finally muttered something like, "I might as well be sitting by myself." I stood up, went out to the lighted kitchen where the mother of the house was chaperoning-at-a-distance, excused myself and went home. Even my own Mother thought that was a little strange.

There were occasional dates with other girls, more friendly than romantic. Once I was appointed chairman of some committee, I don't remember what, at BYF. I needed committee members, and thought they might as well be pretty girls, so I chose Laura, Katie, and Nancy. This brought no immediate improvement in my social life (nor in the committee's function.)

During most of my teen years, school and the church youth group were the biggest maturing influences in my social growth, partly through amateur drama, youth choir, and Boy Scouts. And I had enough interest in additional loner-type activities like bicycling and mineral prospecting to not really care whether I had a date to the sock-hop or the junior prom, or sports events. But I always dreamed of meeting the right girl someday, and I kept my eyes open.

Things gradually changed as I gained more social confidence in high school. By the time I was a senior I could muster enough courage to go out with a college freshman I knew, and we "went steady" for a while. I have always felt grateful that, brushing aside my objections, she taught me to dance—well, the fox-trot at least. I never really managed the waltz or jitter-bugging, but watching those from the side-lines was socially acceptable. When big-band leader Tommy Dorsey came to town we went, and really enjoyed it.

We shared an interest in music, and both of us sang in the church's Youth Choir. She also played the church carillon in the bell tower, and taught me how. We pulled ropes to ring the bells, and played several hymns each Sunday evening, sending the clear notes out over downtown Syracuse. You had to know the tune first, and write the sequence of rope tugs on a card, after working it out on the piano.

But looking back on the relationship, I was awfully immature and self-centered. Escorting her home on the bus one winter night, we passed a roaring building-fire surrounded by fire trucks. I assumed fire fighting would be as interesting to her as it was to me, and persuaded her to get off the bus with me several stops before her house. Five or ten minutes later, she mentioned that it really wasn't very comfortable walking around in the snow and ice in thin shoes, something I hadn't thought about at all.

She was a sociable sorority girl; I was an introverted pre-med student, and our goals began to drift apart. I wasn't ready for a serious commitment, acutely aware that if I wanted to be a doctor, I wouldn't be in a position to marry for another six or eight years. To my shame, I considered only my own feelings, oblivious to hers.

For a while, I had interest in a girl from the midwest. We had met on the Green Lake, Wisconsin, student staff when I was 17 and she 19, and we sort of went together that summer. She didn't plan to return to the staff, so the next year I planned a route home from Wisconsin by way of her home town, and then on to Saskatchewan and home through Canada. But at the beginning of the summer, I had to repurchase a lost train ticket to get out to Wisconsin, and so had less money to finance that very long homeward trip. I had to settle for a shorter route home through Duluth and Ontario.

She and I met again a couple years later, when we both attended the National Youth Conference. A long-distance romance re-blossomed, and when she came east to graduate school, I hitch-hiked three hundred miles to visit her over the Christmas holidays, staying nearby at a college dorm. She was a beautiful, talented girl. We could talk together as we walked, or listen to Grieg's *Song of Norway* while sitting on the floor copying magazine portraits on a winter afternoon, or play records softly while she baby-sat for a faculty couple. She returned the visit, coming to Syracuse for Easter weekend and staying with my family. Mother and Dad welcomed her hospitably but a little guardedly, not seeing her in quite the same light that I did.

I graduated from Syracuse University in 1950 and returned to Green Lake to work as a bus driver before starting medical school. She sent me a letter saying that she didn't think she should see me anymore, giving no real reason, but sounding depressed. Alarmed, I asked my boss at Green Lake for several days off, and spent most of my funds for a train ticket back east. I didn't want to lose this girl. Arriving at her city in the afternoon, I went out to her campus. She was surprised and disconcerted to see me. The letter she had sent had not exactly been a "Dear John" message, but that's what it amounted to. She had become engaged to another young man and would marry him in a few days. She was touched by my effort, but that's the way it was. I was stunned, but what was there to say? We parted friends—she and her husband still exchange Christmas cards with my wife and me—but we never again met. The return trip to Wisconsin was glum, made worse on arrival there by the comment of another staff member who attended the same school she did. "I could have saved you the trip if I'd known you were going," he said when I got back, and he showed me the engagement announcement from his home town paper.

Even so, I was glad I had gone. I knew that I had cared enough to pursue her. It hurt, but things like that happen, and you discover that it was not God's plan.

That was the summer of 1950, just before entering medical school. Sometimes God says "No," because the star performer is still waiting, just offstage in the wings.

10

Learning to Work

By 1948, after three summers work in the hotel kitchen in Wisconsin, I wanted some experience besides a vacation resort. I was a college chemistry major by then, and got a job at Solvay Process, a bus-ride across town in Syracuse. This huge chemical plant on the lakeshore used Onondaga County's natural resources of salt wells and limestone to make soda ash, a basic industrial chemical.

The operation converted sodium chloride (salt) and calcium carbonate (limestone) to sodium carbonate (soda ash) and calcium chloride, using ammonia as a catalyst. The conversion towers had a problem with calcium buildup blocking the cooling pipes. The job of the four of us in the pilot project was to carefully regulate the alkalinity in the pipes of the two-dozen towers by blending lye from a big tank, out in the factory yard, with the cooling-pipe water. We would test pH in hourly samples drawn off from each pipe. We had no physical contact with the corrosive lye, but sometimes the ammonia overflowed, flooding the building with choking fumes, and each of us carried a gas mask for emergencies. The first such overflow taught me not to put the mask on over my glasses; the mask distortion allowed ammonia vapor to enter; I had to hold my breath and flee to fresh air outside.

The pay was good, fifty to sixty dollars a week. Since the job would only last two months, the union waved mandatory membership dues. Solvay Process was my first job punching a time clock, and taught me

43

what was expected of a wage earner: stay awake, do the job, and don't punch out even one minute early. But we had to change shifts, advancing eight hours every week, making it hard to adjust my sleep schedule. I satisfied the minimum duties of the assigned tasks, but didn't yet get the idea of improving my performance. If a flow meter was stuck, I noted it on my clipboard, but had no idea how to get it working again. The boss found me asleep on the job one night, and soon after that the company dismissed me, a few days earlier than the job would otherwise end. That shook me, and taught me that minimum job performance was not enough.

During my third and fourth years of pre-med at Syracuse U, I found a part-time job at Good Shepherd Hospital, a few blocks across campus from home. I started in the kitchen, but soon got promoted to orderly. That was sort of a male nurse-aide, passing out trays, giving back-rubs, and wheeling big oxygen tanks and suction units from storeroom to bedside. One evening the head nurse sent me to mop an especially bloody operating room, needed for more surgery. I did the job thoroughly, and soon after that she started assigning me to clean the emergency room. I was working there one afternoon when a man arrived who had fallen into a circular saw. It had severed his left arm and plowed onward into his chest. His treatment and progress fascinated me and I visited his hospital ward each of the next several days.

Later, I applied to be ambulance attendant, and was soon staying overnight in the ambulance call room. Some trips were only to pick up an ill patient or take someone home. I learned to walk backwards, carrying the foot of the stretcher in and out of houses, and up and down stairs. Three staccato rings on the phone signaled emergencies, ranging from major highway accidents to false alarms like, "See, Bobby, I told you I'd call the doctor if you didn't eat your cereal!" The ambulance crew was just the driver and me, with sometimes an intern. We "scooped and ran," rather than treating at the scene, and the only training I had was how to tell if the patient was already dead.

But we learned a lot about human nature, drunks, hysteria, and crowds at accident scenes. Dr. Ellen Cook, an intern at the time, recalled a trip with the daytime driver, Joe Buschle, a massive man with many years experience. The police were restraining a wildly agitated young man who had run amok downtown on the main street. Joe stopped the ambulance in the middle of Salina Street, walked over to the police and ordered, "Let go of him!" and then to the young man, "Come with me, son." Such was his presence and calm authority that the young man meekly accepted transport to the hospital.

On another trip, we found squad of firemen supporting a gasping 500-lb. woman sitting on the floor in heart failure. We lifted her onto the stretcher and into the ambulance, thankful for the whole fire crew's help. Her sagging flesh overflowed the stretcher by about a foot on each side, and there was no way to secure the stretcher to the wall brackets. So I sat on the ambulance floor, my back braced against her and my feet against the opposite wall the whole trip to the hospital, to keep the stretcher from rolling around. In the hospital she required two beds wired together.

The next year, 1949, was the summer Amby Smith and I went into business for ourselves, prospecting for minerals and selling them to retail rock shops.

I continued my ambulance job in 1949, and was promoted to relief driver. The main lesson I learned was caution. On one of my first emergency runs with red lights and siren, the intern beside me growled, "Stop at each cross street, siren or not, buddy," he said. "I don't need to be an accident victim myself."

One intern unwittingly taught me that not all who have a doctor's degree know what they are doing. "Adrenaline," he said, searching the ambulance bag, "Where's the adrenaline?" The patient had a history of heart disease and was having trouble breathing.

"Naw," said Wally, the driver, "we don't carry that." We did, actually, but he sensed the intern's uncertainty, and knew most interns didn't use adrenaline in that situation. "We got digoxin, if you want that. Let's just get him to the hospital."

I continued ambulance work through the first couple weeks of my first year in medical school, then realized I didn't have time for both that and studying. Two years later I returned to Good Shepherd as a medical student on rounds.

When I graduated from Syracuse University in 1950, I hitch-hiked out to Green Lake again. The job was on the "Young Adult Staff," a step upward from the Student Staff I had served on earlier. About eight of us worked in Transportation, at $50 a month plus room and board, probably the most enjoyable work I have ever had. We picked up guests and baggage at the train stations in Fond du Lac and Portage, made travel reservations, drove tours around the grounds. We brought the student staff back and forth from their dormitories to the Inn, moved furniture and equipment, kept the Coke machines filled, and tended the gas station. We had a fleet of about five buses and a half-dozen cars and pickup trucks, and large sheets of paper on which to plan each day's interlocking trip schedules.

In the summer of 1952, I again wanted experience in the "real world." I wanted to drive an 18-wheeler truck, even though common sense told me I didn't have the smarts to handle such a vehicle. After a week of walking the pavement in Syracuse, I finally settled for driving with City Taxi. Drivers got 45% of the fare, plus tips (rarely exceeding a quarter.) I got maybe twenty fares in a good day. The main thing the job gave me was better knowledge of human nature and of the seedier sections of Syracuse at night.

11

Almost-a-Doctor

I walked through the autumn leaves in the fall of 1950, toward my first day as a real medical student with a feeling of exultant expectation. Up till then, I had found that being a "pre-med" didn't make as much impression as I would have liked. With coeds, especially, the attitude seemed to be "Forget this one; he'll be buried in the books for four more years." But now my embryo medical career was finally on track. I had at least made it in through the door.

Classes for first year medical students were all held in one building, across campus from my home. I joined seventy would-be doctors in the lecture auditorium that first day, all of us waiting with apprehension for the professor of anatomy to appear, who would rule our lives for the next five months. First semester in medical school covered only two subjects: Human Anatomy and Histology, which is anatomy viewed through a microscope.

Dr. Phillip Armstrong was a deceptively bland man in his fifties, who made no effort to put us at ease. His aphorisms were memorable:

"We will address you here as 'Doctor'. For some of you, this will be the only time you will ever hear it applied to you."

"Up until now, you have worked to achieve a well-rounded education. Here, we intend to flatten you out."

We spent that first day getting organized into working groups of four, and learning detailed instruction for the care and study of our

47

cadavers. We took notes on everything; one nervous student even jotted down the professor's "Good morning." We entered the dissecting room that afternoon, wondering what our reaction would be to studying the dead. We four, Onas Morgan, Tony Rivera, Tony Slivinski, and I grouped ourselves around our dissecting table, and surveyed the motionless shape swathed in pungent, formaldehyde-soaked layers of sheeting beneath the yellow oil-cloth.

Following the instructor's directions, working one pair on each side, we laid bare the groin area and made a first incision along the inguinal ligament, surprised at the toughness of human skin, careful to go slowly and meticulously, exposing and identifying each nerve branch and blood vessel. We would spend most of the first week on the abdominal wall, laying open each muscle layer under the critical eyes of the instructors and Dr. Armstrong himself.

Dissecting a dead person brought a feeling of awe, different from working with dead animals in my pre-med courses. All of us had a healthy fear of making a mistake in the work and earning Dr. Armstrong's displeasure. Perhaps he kept us off-balance on purpose during these first uneasy encounters with death.

"The name of the muscle is not pronounced 'ili-op-soas' as it is spelled," he said. "Say 'ilio-soas.' The 'p' is silent. As in swimming."

Three students dropped out that first week. One fainted dead away. Another threw down his scalpel, cursing, and stalked out. We never saw him again. Rumor had it that the third decided to take his girl-friend's advice to study pharmacy instead.

We compensated for our insecurity with a certain amount of dark humor. Medical students learn a large number of limericks and memory devices, ranging from the fate of nymphomaniacal Alice or the efficient young man from Bel-Air, to the names of the eight bones in the wrist or the sequence of the twelve cranial nerves.

We four lab partners learned that our cadaver's name had been Peter B_____, who had died in a state hospital of "old age." Weeks later, deep in the abdomen, we found that undiagnosed urinary obstruction had destroyed his kidneys.

A month after entering medical school, I had acute appendicitis. The operation went well, but spinal headaches from the anesthetic kept me on my back for a week. I still recall trying to study, holding the six-pound Gray's Anatomy textbook on my sore abdomen. I also remember, when I was exhausted by the four-hour work sessions in the anatomy lab the following week, that even Dr. Armstrong had a compassionate streak. He stopped at my table to ask quietly how was I, and to tell me it was all right to take a rest break occasionally.

We four, and most of the rest, survived that five months and the examination at the end. One of my tense friends panicked when the examiner thrust a skull at him, jabbed a finger at the large opening at the base and barked, "What goes through there!"

"Food!" the student blurted, then winced as he realized the answer should have been spinal cord. Our universal wish, we all agreed, was that we could repeat the whole course, now that we knew what we were supposed to be learning.

We celebrated the end of anatomy the last weekend in January, a double milestone for me. That night I first met the girl I would marry.

12

Lois

Shortly after I started medical school, my parents moved to St. Louis, Missouri, where my father had accepted the pastorate of the Delmar Street Baptist Church. So I rented a room a few blocks south of the medical school, where my lab partner, Onas Morgan already lived. Onas, a Jamaican, had earned part of his way to medical school loading banana boats. In his forties, he was the oldest in our class.

The occupant of a third room, Jack, a factory worker, was rarely home. We only saw him on weekends, usually when we asked him to turn down his radio so we could study. Onas and I studied together most evenings, quizzed each other to prepare for tests, and shared a kitchenette where we ate breakfast and drank hot tea in the evening, to keep us awake during 4-hour sessions at the books. Our landlords, Mr. and Mrs. Henderson lived downstairs, and occasionally came up to visit, but realized that medical students live to study.

Well, almost. We went our separate ways most Saturday nights. Onas had several girls interested in a relationship with a doctor-to-be, and I had friends around town. One evening the phone rang. "This is Nancy Mercer, Keith. How are you?" I knew Nancy from several years acquaintance at BYF, but hadn't heard much from her lately. I vaguely remembered that she was now a student nurse at Syracuse General Hospital. Quite a pretty girl, vivacious, brown hair, a couple years younger than I.

I made some friendly reply indicating I was glad she called, and waited.

"Our nurses' dance is Saturday night the 31st. Would you like to go?"

With Nancy? Yeah, I would.

"Yes, I would!" I said.

"Okay. The girl you'll take is Lois Coleman. She's a classmate of mine. She's nice; you'll like her."

"Oh." Wait a minute, I thought, what just happened here? But it was too late to back-pedal.

"You two can go with Lin and me, if you like. We can double-date." Lin was the brother of my high-school classmate Chuck Perrine. I had not been aware of this pro-active side of Nancy before, but it looked like she already had the blind-date set in concrete.

"Okay, Nancy. Give me the details."

The night of the dance, I had on my best (and only) suit. Having had bad experience with florists delivering brown-edged gardenia corsages, I hand-carried a single orchid for this girl I had not yet met.

I remember my first vision of her, as she came down the stairs at the nurses' dorm. She was a slim brunette, wearing a strapless, red, ankle-length dress and sparkling earrings and necklace. She was as shy as I was, but she smiled at me. I gave her the orchid.

The dance was at a country club near Fayetteville. The January night outside was well below zero Fahrenheit, and we sat close together in the back seat of Lin Perrine's car. I don't remember much about the dance except that Lois was easy to talk to, and seemed to like my tentative hands on her waist as we watched a jitter-bug dance that neither of us felt up to trying.

She chides me now that it was more than three weeks before I asked her out again. I point out that, for medical students beginning the struggle with biochemistry and physiology, that's average social life. I phoned her and invited her out for cocoa. It was another freezing night, and we walked two blocks from the nurses' dorm to Ivan's Diner. We sat and talked for a long while.

She lived in Bridgeport, fifteen miles out of town, was nineteen years old, a second-year nursing student in Syracuse General's three-year course. She had worked as a nurses aide on the medical floor at

Good Shepherd Hospital while I was an orderly there on orthopedics, but we had never met.

It wasn't love at first sight, but we liked each other. We were both on a low budget, and our dates were things like the cheapest chow-mein at the Chinese restaurant downtown, or taking long walks.

That spring, I came down with a severe case of chickenpox, and spent a week in the student infirmary with the personal attention of two visiting student nurses, Nancy and Lois.

The first kiss, while walking in the park in May, took Lois and me beyond just friendship, but it wasn't until fall, after my return from my summer job in Wisconsin that things moved ahead. We double-dated with my friend Amby and his girl Helen, at a Saturday night dance at Drumlins, a local dining and dancing spot. When we saw each other, she gave me that smile again and held her arms out, and I was captivated.

She took me out to meet her folks. Her Dad was a part-time farmer and full-time night-shift station agent in Syracuse for the New York Central Railroad. Lois was second oldest among four girls and a kid brother. From the first, I felt at home there, totally accepted as were all of their large number of relatives and friends. My brother and sister had long since moved away, and my parents now lived in St. Louis. It was as though I had re-discovered family. One evening early in my second year in med school, Lois's siblings and several others were gathered in the living room. Her fourteen-year-old brother Burt said loudly, to torment his sister, "Well, Keith, looks like you'll be my next brother-in-law!"

I heard Lois gasp and whisper in fury, *"Burt!"* But I didn't mind. It sounded like a good idea to me.

In Lois's last year of nursing school, she took her three-month rotation in pediatric nursing at Buffalo Children's Hospital. I stopped in Buffalo to see her when I hitch-hiked out to St. Louis for Christmas break. The student nurses' dorm did not allow men even in the downstairs lounge, and Buffalo was living up to its reputation of coldest, windiest, most wintry city in the East. The city even puts up ropes to hang onto on some corners. We shivered along the downtown streets after dinner, taking refuge in store doorways to warm up, between passersby, but after an hour or two we gave it up and I took her back to the dorm.

We promised each other we would find a warmer place when we both returned to Syracuse.

A year after we first met, I proposed to her while we were walking in Oakwood Cemetery. This choice of location has always amused our children, but Oakwood was like a huge park, with a side entrance halfway between her dorm and my house, and there were fewer muggings at night in those days. My parents were to visit Syracuse a few weeks later, and I wanted our engagement, even though secret at first, to happen before they met her—establishing the decision as my own, I suppose.

When Mother and Dad arrived in town, the four of us went out to dinner. Afterward, outside the restaurant, Dad pulled me aside while the two ladies were conversing. "Keith, that's the girl I want for a daughter-in-law!" I've never regretted my choice.

I gave her a diamond—I only had enough money for a very small one—the night she graduated from nursing school that June. I spent the night in the Bridgeport guest room again. Halfway through breakfast, Lois said to me, "Well, they haven't even noticed it, so I'll have to stick it under their noses. Look what I got!" she held her left hand in front of her mother's face.

"Oh, I never even saw! Let me look!"

I turned to Mr. Coleman and asked, "Is it all right if I marry your daughter?"

He looked up from his breakfast. "Why sure," he said, and that was that.

Lois still had to complete her three-month psychiatry nursing rotation at Marcy, New York, that summer, and was gone during the time I drove taxi. In the fall, her alma mater hired her, on night shift in the newborn nursery, and after six months promoted her to charge-nurse on the newly opened gynecology ward. She and her sister Edna shared an apartment on South Crouse Avenue, not far from the med school, and Edna and her boyfriend Conrad made themselves conveniently scarce on Friday evenings.

Lois and I had at first decided on a wedding in June, but as our Friday night visits grew more prolonged, we changed the date to February. My parents were returning from a meeting in India then, and came through Syracuse. Some of Lois's and my classmates attended the Friday night ceremony. Edna was bridesmaid, Onas was best man. My brother Bruce and Lois's brother-in-law Ebin were ushers, and my Dad and Lois's pastor, Baden Mudge, officiated together at the ceremony in Bridgeport Methodist Church.

My job was to pick up Lois's sister Jeannette, almost at term with her third pregnancy, and give her a ride to the church because her husband was already there. It was getting late; I stopped by for her, tooted the horn and got out. She shouted at me from the porch, "Don't you blow the horn at me, Keith Dahlberg, I'm in labor!" I was already nervous enough; several people at the hospital cafeteria that evening had remarked on my failure to turn my water glass right-side up before trying to fill it. What to do now? In the end, I took Jeannette to the church, figuring some one else could drive her the fifteen miles to the hospital if her labor continued. It didn't; my nephew Steve didn't arrive until two weeks later.

My best man and I arranged ourselves before Rev. Mudge and my Dad. The previous month had been filled with uncertainty about assuming all the responsibilities of a husband, but when the organ began the wedding march I looked up the aisle. She was beautiful, and smiled that smile of hers at me. As her hand slipped into mine and we turned to face the ministers, I knew she was the right one.

Edna loaned us her car for the weekend honeymoon in Ottawa, and vacated her part of the Crouse Avenue apartment afterward. Lois and I extended our weekend through Monday, causing some ribald comments by my classmates when I returned to class on Tuesday.

She worked nights, I was gone twelve hours in the day. Like the Star Spangled Banner, we saw each other by the dawn's early light, those first weeks. Her $170 per month (182 when she became a head nurse), plus my scholarship and occasional nights driving taxi, supported us till the end of med school sixteen months later.

We had a second honeymoon during summer break, on the Young Adult Staff at Green Lake—she as camp nurse, I as a bus driver again. I had not done well in third year internal medicine the previous fall and, along with several other students, would have to repeat the work for six weeks during summer vacation.

We got a free ride out to Wisconsin, driving a new station wagon on loan to the Assembly grounds from a Syracuse car dealer. In mid-July, I had to leave my Methodist bride to fend for herself amid all the Baptists of various viewpoints. She found some of them strange, she said later, but she had discovered that the mother-in-law of one of the executives was also a Methodist. "Lois," the old lady told her, "don't let these Baptists think they can *vote* you into the Kingdom of God." Though Lois eventually chose to join the Baptists, I heard that phrase many times in later years.

I did much better on my second passage through Medicine clerkship, spent a weekend or two helping my father-in-law with his corn crop, then returned to Green Lake to take up our second honeymoon where we had left off.

For the last year of medical school, we moved into a basement apartment, bought a sixteen-year-old Plymouth for $100 and painted it blue.

Early on in our marriage, we had some tension about sharing decision-making. I was mostly clueless about this, deciding matters as I had when I was single. And often Lois would say nothing, rather than make an issue of it. But one night during my senior year on internal medicine service, my instructor had told me he was going to give a cardiac patient quinidine for his heart rhythm problem. He said that quinidine was rarely used any more, and it might be instructive to stay and observe its effect. I thought (a) this might be my only chance to see this procedure and (b) it's not wise to be uninterested in instructors' suggestions. I phoned Lois to tell her I was staying at the hospital that night and explained why. Next day she made clear her thoughts on being told, rather than consulted, about extra nights alone at home. It took me many years to learn that my ideas of logic do not necessarily trump someone else's feelings.

Medical school seniors are reasonably sure of graduation, and much of the final few months' curriculum is non-stressful orientation courses like Ear-nose-throat, Ophthalmology (eyes), and Public Health. We spent a day at the State School at Rome, NY, on a guided tour among the mentally deficient. Some had tragic deformities: crippling cerebral palsy, or hydrocephalus with a head the size of a state-fair pumpkin. We saw an idiot savant, mentally retarded in all fields except one: given any date in the past several hundred years, he could accurately tell the day of the week on which it fell. We watched a whole ward full of children unable to help themselves in any way; an attendant pushed a mop along the floor, and when he reached the far end of the room, he would have to come back to begin again, hour after hour. "The population's lower two percent," our guide said, as we left.

In Psychiatry class, toward the end of one session, the attending psychiatrist demonstrated some aptitude tests and gave a bit of advice I have never forgotten. He showed us a number of jagged fragments of jigsaw puzzle and asked us students to put them together. We all sat there looking at it blankly, until I noticed the big piece had five barely detectable flat areas, and I quickly assembled the pieces into a hand with five fingers. "Very superior," the doctor said, and my colleagues looked impressed.

"Do we get a chance to get tested to see what our IQ really is?" I asked him.

He thought a moment, then asked me, "Well, put it this way. Are you happy?"

"Yeah ... I guess so."

He leaned forward with raised eyebrows and a shrug of his shoulders, palms up. "Well, then, the hell with it." And we left it at that. I'm thankful for the brain God gave me to use, but rarely worry about whether my IQ is "high enough." It got me through medical school in the middle third of my class. I always figure that even if I ever place in the top one per cent of the population, that would still mean that any town of a couple thousand contains some people smarter than I am.

At graduation in June 1954, we all marched across the stage one by one in our rented caps and red-and-black academic robes as our names were announced. One of the older war veterans had his wife and four children in attendance. And the whole audience cheered as the only girl in the class received her diploma.

The next week, Lois and I loaded up our ancient bright-blue Plymouth and set out for the West. In the hospital-intern matching program, I had submitted all my applications to Denver hospitals. Denver's Presbyterian Hospital, a good place for the type of training I wanted, accepted me and one other of my classmates, Carl Janovsky.

We and the Janovskys took separate routes, meeting in St. Louis where Carl and I and our wives had the use of my parents' apartment while Dad and Mother were away somewhere. We continued on, two cars together, across Missouri and Kansas while I extolled the beauty of

Colorado scenery to Lois, who had never been beyond the Mississippi River before.

We will never forget our crossing the state line into Colorado on US 40, where we stopped for a photograph. Colorado had had a dust-bowl year, out on its flat eastern plains, and fine dust lay in drifts like gray snow, half-covering the barbed-wire fence beside a decaying wooden barn. We stood by our car, contemplating the flat landscape stretching ahead of us, radiating shimmering heat waves. No mountains in sight.

Lois turned to me. "Are you sure we're in the right state?"

13

Denver

Denver was a good-looking city in those days, before the smog. We chugged over the last rise of the prairie and stopped to let our car's boiling radiator subside, as the Janovskys pulled off behind us. We looked at the city spread below the down-slope and at the snow-topped Rocky Mountains rising into the clear air just beyond. "Yup, it's the right state," I told my wife. It had been eleven years since I had been there; the view was reassuring.

We moved into the row of interns' apartments behind Presbyterian Hospital; small living room and kitchenette downstairs, with a sleeping balcony overlooking it. The Janovskys lived next door. The hospital's back door, across a parking lot from the courtyard, was about a hundred yards away. This was our home for the next two and a half years.

Lois's family had made me welcome two years before; now it was her turn. My immediate family had fragmented to Missouri, Massachusetts and New Jersey, and our contacts with them had been pleasant but brief. Now we were cooped up in the same city with dozens of Dahlbergs spread out across town. Lois encountered her first Swedish hospitality at a July picnic in the mountains. "They brought hot coffee to a picnic in July," was her bemused comment afterward. She probably had drunk three cups in her entire life; now it appeared at every family gathering.

Lois was half-way through her first pregnancy when we arrived in Denver. She worked as a general-duty nurse on the obstetrics floor. I started with two months on OB, at a salary of $75 a month plus my meals. The hospital took back $77.50 per month in house rent. House staff families could eat free each Sunday noon. Lois's wages covered everything else, but only barely.

Presbyterian had a reputation as good as the big hospitals, and the doctors and house staff meant to keep it that way. Jerry Young and I were the only two house staff on obstetrics. Dr. Waddell was chief of service, a jovial politician-type. He and two other obstetricians were always worth making rounds with, another one wasn't, and the half-dozen others fell in between. The delivery nurses were superbly competent, and kept Jerry and me on our toes despite our schedule of thirty-six hours on duty and twelve off. He and I worked together each day and alternated nights, watching labor, assisting in an average of six deliveries a day, and keeping track of postpartums and newborns. My twelve hours off every two days was mostly spent unconscious on the couch or bed at home.

The trick was knowing when to call the attending doctor to come deliver: not too late, but not so soon that he had to wait at the hospital several hours. "I buy my children's *shoes* with these deliveries, Doctor, and I expect to be called in time," Dr. Longwell reminded us every time we cut the timing too close.

I learned to time duration and frequency of labor contractions at the bedside with my fingertips on the mother's abdomen, and learned to gauge, to the centimeter, the dilation of the cervix and descent of the head. I gradually acquired an instinctive knowledge of how to encourage the woman to push and to recognize when the baby was really coming and when it was not, all invaluable in years to come when I would be the only doctor within miles. More immediately, Jerry and I learned from the nurses to load the patient on the gurney and get her on the elevator for the delivery rooms (next floor up) just as the attending doctor arrived.

We were heartened to overhear Dr. Tucker telling Dr. Harvey one morning, "The new interns are pretty good."

Lois's obstetrician was one of the best; friendly, expert, and careful to see that his patient's pain was controlled but without oversedation. I was on my four-month internal medicine rotation, the November night she began labor. I walked her across the lot to the hospital, rode the elevator with her to 4th floor and saw her settled in a labor bed, and then I had to respond to a call on the medical floor. A man with chest and back pain had become worse and his doctor was on the way. Instead of being with Lois all through her first labor, I had to spend part of the night kneeling on a bed in another ward, giving CPR to a dying man with all his family gathered around watching him. It was a long night, back and forth from medical ward to labor room. Finally, the next afternoon, she went to the delivery room. Dr. Roessing gave her a saddle-block anesthetic, smoothly applied outlet forceps, and introduced us to our daughter, Susan Jean.

New mothers customarily remained in hospital a week in those days. Visitors were limited to husband and parents, but several of my aunts and cousins convinced the hospital's desk clerk that they were Lois's mother.

On the day Susie came home to our small apartment, all was ready—crib, diapers, baby clothes—all except us parents. Susie was used to the 24-hour lighting of the hospital nursery and cried the whole night. Both Lois and I were exhausted. Lois began crying, too, around midnight, and by five a.m. I felt like joining in.

Six weeks after Susie was born, Lois returned to night duty, working every other night while I baby-sat on my nights off. (The schedule on internal medicine service was not as demanding as it had been on OB.) A week later, my father-in-law phoned us from Syracuse. Did I think turning yellow was anything serious? I told him it surely could be, and to go see a doctor; it wasn't something to be diagnosed over the phone. He was soon in a Syracuse hospital, under the care of the professor of surgery. His painless jaundice proved to be caused by impacted gallstones. He went on to develop pancreatitis and diabetes; the warning signs were somehow missed, and after surgery he died a slow and painful death over the next two months. Lois and the baby flew back to Syracuse toward the end. I learned that a doctor is not always free to come and be present during family crises.

The year 1955 brought other changes. I was nearing the end of internship and the Baptist Mission Board wanted to confirm my military draft status by officially appointing Lois and me to the foreign mission field. When Lois and Susie returned from Syracuse, we parked Susie with Jerry and Lee Young and took the train to Kansas City, where the Board was holding its semi-annual meeting and examining new candidates. The job was not a foregone conclusion; each of the ten candidate couples was questioned at length on various attributes that Board members wanted in their appointees. As we sat in an anteroom waiting our turns, one of the first couples seemed to be taking a very long time in the Board room. As far as the rest of us could tell, the husband, Donald Deer, was giving a dissertation on each question, covering far more than the Board expected to hear. Our turn came next, and the questioning was brief, until elderly Mr. Swenson spoke up.

"Mrs. Dahlberg. Do I understand that you have never been immersed?" (a method of baptism favored by Baptists.)

"That's right," said Lois, "I was baptized as a baby into the Methodist church, then confirmed in my teens, and later transferred my letter of membership to First Baptist Church in Syracuse."

"Are you willing to be re-baptized by immersion?"

"That would deny the validity of my faith when I was confirmed," Lois said.

Well, that tore it, for the most conservative members of the Board. There was a good deal of discussion among them whether they could be represented by a missionary who had never been immersed. Some said she should be sent as an "associate missionary" whatever that might mean. Others said that her Baptist home church had accepted her statement of faith, and that should be enough. I was proud of her for standing up for what she believed. The temporary solution was that, since I had two more years of medical training to complete, she "would have time to pray about it."

"I've *already* prayed about it," she told me after we had left the room.

"It'll work out," I said. "Give it time."

Another intern and I competed for the first-year surgical resident's spot at the end of internship. The hospital wanted to keep us both, but there was only one position. They offered me an alternative. Obstetrics & Gynecology was opening a residency program for the first time. Would I like a year of OB/GYN, mixed with some surgery, and then move into the surgical resident spot the following year?

I hadn't been assigned a mission field country yet but knew that wherever it was, I would probably be one of the few doctors in the area, perhaps the only one. I could use all the training I could get in both surgery and OB. I accepted.

Residents got raised to $150 per month. Money was still tight, and had always been that way in Lois's home. Growing up, she had learned a hundred ways to prepare hamburger (3 lb. for 99 cents.) She remembers the women at a Denver church inviting her to attend a missionary dinner, but when she learned later she was expected to buy a ticket for $1.65, she had to call back and say she couldn't come. A month often ended with two gallons of gas in the tank and half-a-jar of peanut butter on the shelf, but most of the young doctors were in the same position. We held low-rent parties at each others' apartments Sunday nights. A surgeon once took one of the residents hunting, and we all shared barbecued antelope that Sunday.

The hospital ran a prenatal clinic in the Hispanic part of Denver, providing me with up to thirty deliveries of my own each month. The staff surgeons supervised my hysterectomies and Caesarian sections, and let me take out an occasional appendix. There was no preventive vaccine for Rh babies in those days, and there were enough of them for me to create a small research project in diagnosis before birth. I learned to manage pregnancy with leukemia, pregnancy with advanced cancer, pregnancy with toxemia, severe allergy, heart disease and many other complications. Abortion was still strictly illegal, and there were many victims of whatever home method the neighbors gossiped about over backyard fences. That year, women with severe hemorrhage were common. During pelvic exam of such patients I would often find a round ulcer on the uterine cervix, briskly bleeding from a damaged artery. "You used the purple pill (potassium permanganate) didn't you," I'd say.

"How did you know!" she'd say.

"Don't ever use it again. It's dangerous. There are other ways to prevent getting pregnant, if you don't want another baby."

But for all I learned in the OB/GYN residency, some of the best lessons came from outside the hospital's program. Lois and I took a few days vacation time at Thanksgiving that year to explore westward. We put one-year-old Susie and her crib in the back seat of our old Plymouth, and set out over Loveland Pass on Highway 6 with Salt Lake City as our goal. Neither of us had ever been as far as Utah. We stayed overnight at Grand Junction, toured the misty crags and spires of the Colorado National Monument next morning, and drove across the sagebrush-covered Utah desert. We stopped to buy gas at Price, before heading over the pass at Soldier's Summit.

The sky darkened, a wet snow began falling. The road was soon three-inches deep, and slippery. The windshield wiper on the old car worked poorly at best, and now I had to stick my head out the window to see where I was going. A truck ahead of us was dropping cinders on the road, and I tried to steer in his tracks. We were still headed uphill, with no idea how far to the top.

The engine sputtered, died, then caught again. This happened several times, allowing the cinder truck to pull far ahead of us in the blinding snow. The car began to skid; other cars and trucks honked as they pulled around us. Susie was warm enough in her snowsuit, but she was hungry and there was no way to warm a bottle. She didn't like the cold milk, and began to cry. Lois held her on her lap, singing a lullaby. Our progress became slower and slower, snow blurred my glasses when my head was out the window. Maximum stress. "Can't we have a little quiet in here till we get to the top!" I finally snarled.

The engine gave one last cough, and died for good. I coasted to the shoulder of the road, tried the starter several times. It didn't catch. I got out, raised the hood, stared at the engine as snowflakes hissed on its hot rusty metal. Lois looked frightened; I felt the same way. Without the engine, the car's heater grew cold. It was dark now, and we were miles from anywhere.

About fifteen minutes later, a large car pulled over, a Buick maybe, or a Lincoln. The driver offered us a lift; we thankfully got the diaper bag and one suitcase; locked our car and climbed into the warmth of our rescuer's back seat. I don't know what he thought of two young kids and a baby out in the snow, but he took us over the pass, down to the tiny town of Thistle, and let us off at the only motel. I found a tow-truck number, phoned, and rode back with the truck to our car. The mechanic said it was probably the timing, and towed it to his garage till morning.

Next day, with a new timer and a towing bill receipt for half of our cash, we were on our way again. Soon the engine sputtered and died. We talked about just heading home, but the towns lay ahead of us, and a hundred miles of desert behind. I pulled into a garage in Provo. "It keeps sputtering and dying," I said.

He raised the hood. "When did you last get new spark plugs?"

"I dunno. Not in the two years we've had it."

"That's probably it, then." He put in new plugs, charged us six dollars, and we headed toward Salt Lake. Our money supply was almost gone. The engine kept on skipping; we nursed it along until Salt Lake City, and headed into another garage.

"This is the third garage today," I told the gray-haired mechanic. "If you can't fix it, we'll give you the car for enough bus fare to get us back to Denver."

"Well, tell me just how it behaves," he said. I described in detail what had been going on since we had refueled at Price the day before. He listened, asked several questions, then told me, "You don't need to sell your car." He handed me a can. "Pour this in your gas tank. It'll take the water and ice out of your fuel line." He charged us fifty cents. We had no further trouble the whole five hundred miles back to Denver.

He taught me how to question a patient, a lesson I've carried through my whole professional life: Don't assume a diagnosis. Listen to the patient's story first. Med school taught me the right questions to ask. The garage man taught me to listen to the answers.

14

Jumping-off Point

The war ended in 1945, but the draft continued under the name "universal military training(UMT). There was no problem about my pacifism during my eight college years. America needed doctors, and pre-med and medical students were exempt from the draft. But near graduation from medical school, I got my "Greetings" letter from the draft board. Report for registration. I had no objection to registering, but I did it as a conscientious objector (CO).

Everyone has this right, though the people at the draft board would have you believe that you are the first one they have ever met or even imagined. They put me through all the usual questions. Did I object to *all* war or just the Korean conflict? All war is wrong, I said. Was I a Quaker? No, a Baptist. Well, there are lots of Baptists in the army, what makes you so special?

I did my best to explain about Baptist belief that each individual must interpret the Bible according to his conscience, with the guidance of the Holy Spirit. I had my papers and letters of reference in order. I listened to a fatherly lecture from the draft board; I endured a few half-contemptuous remarks from the other draftees, and took the very brief physical exam which almost all of us passed. ("If you can see lightning and hear thunder, you're in.") Finally, grudgingly, they classified me 1A-O.

My commission as a medical missionary in the [then] Northern Baptist Foreign Mission Society during hospital internship later that year got me a draft re-classification similar to clergy. 2-A was the designation, I think.

And though I remained a CO, I would get first-hand experience with war in the next five years.

In late June of 1956, the Foreign Mission Society met near Seattle to orient its new missionary candidates. I still had no assignment to a country, but the Mission Board thought the next need for a doctor would probably be in Congo. There would be plenty of time to decide; I was just completing the year of obstetrics and about to begin my year of surgery. All future missionaries also were expected to take at least a year of theology. The Board suggested I look at Berkeley Baptist Seminary in California.

A new obstetrics resident arrived at Denver Presbyterian on July 1, 1956. I moved over to surgery, where I had already been doing some work. There was no problem of surgical residents getting in each other's way in this second year; each worked six months as resident surgeon at a hospital in Pueblo and six months in Denver. My colleague, Bob Linnemeyer, would do the first half-year in Pueblo and we would change places in January. After that, I was due for the year's study at Berkeley, beginning July, 1957, before going overseas.

Our second child, Patricia Leanne, arrived a month later during morning surgical rounds. Missing 6 a.m. daily rounds was unthinkable, according to the surgeons, but when the paging system called, "Dr. Dahlberg to the Delivery Room stat!" I left in a hurry. Lois hadn't expected to deliver for several hours yet, and visions of complications filled my head as I raced to the fifth floor. I arrived to see the baby already there, with Dr. Roessing finishing up the delivery of the afterbirth. Lois and I have often discussed a surgical resident's priorities since then.

Lois's non-immersed state of baptism had never been a problem for her or me (or for God, either, as far as we could tell) but the mission executives, whenever one passed through Denver, continued to ask her whether she was still praying about getting re-baptized. After two years of listening to this, she laid the impasse before our pastor, Harleigh Rosenberger, at Denver's Calvary Baptist Church. He agreed with her that her statement of Christian faith was as valid now as it had been when she was confirmed. But we could also see that some of the more conservative Mission Board members were uneasy about letting any upstart Methodist dare to challenge their life-long belief that immersion was the only way to go.

Harleigh offered to include her in the next group of those being baptized, and to preface her own part in the ceremony by saying that she was re-affirming the faith that she had expressed years before. She agreed, and that seemed to reassure the Mission Board that they were sending out fully qualified workers to the field.

As things turned out, we would travel farther than Pueblo or Berkeley in 1957. One of the mission appointees, Dr. John Bissett, had been assigned to re-open the hospital in Kengtung, Burma. But Burma, newly free from British rule, refused him a visa because he had been a medical officer in the British army. The Mission Board had thought Lois and I might go to Congo, but now they wanted us in Burma, and the Bissetts in Thailand.

This was the situation in July, 1956 as I began surgery and as Lois took leave from her nursing job to deliver our second baby. The mission board applied to the Burmese Embassy for our visas. Burma was a sticky government to deal with, often taking a year or two to accept anyone. To everyone's surprise, our visas came through that autumn, good for entry within the next six months. We were told to wind up our affairs in Denver by December 31 and prepare for embarkation. Our year at Berkeley was canceled.

The hospital had no objection to my leaving six months early; I would have been working at Pueblo in any case. I drove to Greeley one December afternoon to accept a donation of a set of instruments from a surgeon's widow. Lois's obstetrician, Dr. Roessing, wanted to take me into partnership in his practice; I thanked him but said I would have to decline. (It had never been a real option to me. I had been committed to overseas work since starting college ten years before.) We attended farewell parties at church and hospital.

My eldest aunt died just before we were to leave. On an early January Saturday afternoon, we attended her funeral and then set out eastward on highway 40, a U-haul trailer in tow, ahead of a gathering blizzard. Susie was two years old, Patsy five months. We stopped for the night at a motel in Limon, Colorado, 85 miles out on the wind-swept high plains. Our children wept themselves to sleep that night. "I want my own bed!" Susie wailed. I thought to myself, how do I tell a two-year-old it will be five years before she comes home?

We arrived at my parents' home in St. Louis two days later. Our new used car ran well on the winter roads, (the old one had succumbed to a broken axle, some months earlier) and there was no repetition of our Utah experience. The children were quite happy to stay with Grandma and Grandpa, while Lois and I took a week's orientation course in the management of leprosy at Carville, Louisiana. The Public Health hospital there was one of only two places in the US treating leprosy, and had pioneered the use of a new medicine called Dapsone, the first to offer real hope in an up-until-then hopeless disease.

Rejoining our family in St. Louis, we drove on eastward to Bridgeport, NY to stay with Lois's mother until departure time, still an undefined date. There was planning, studying, and purchasing to do for the life ahead, but even with all that I still had more time on my hands than I had had since beginning medical school. I watched more hours of television's *Captain Kangaroo* with Susie than I cared to count. Studying the ancient history of Burma was not much more riveting. The Mission Board had advised us to wait to study Burmese language until we had linguistic help.

Burma was a developing country, newly independent, impoverished by World War II. Supplies taken for granted in America could not be counted on. Ignoring the outdated mission lists of what to take with us (*corset covers? ... what are they?*) we made our own plans. Among them, five years' supply of sanitary pads, minus nine months for one more pregnancy ... how many glass mason jars should we pack to allow us to preserve food between crop seasons ... how to minimize breakage in transit ...

I was merging solutions to all this one afternoon when a group of missionary-minded church women came to visit. Lois usually entertained such groups, but this bevy had wandered into the dining room where I sat on the floor beside a 2 x 2 x 3-foot wooden packing crate. Assuming that Lois was behind them, I nodded a greeting and continued removing dozens of sanitary pads from their boxes and stuffing them in and around four dozen glass mason jars in their clean cardboard cartons.

"Oh, and here is the doctor himself, getting ready for overseas adventure!" gushed one woman. "What is that you're doing, Doctor?"

"I'm canning Kotex," I said.

That seemed to end the conversation, allowing Lois to guide them back into the next room.

The Mission's New York office finally sent the word: we would sail from New York for England on the Queen Elizabeth on March 3, and transfer there to the Derbyshire, bound for Rangoon. (Air transport was still too expensive to be routine.) We already knew our journey would take us around the southern tip of Africa, because the war between Israel and Egypt had closed the Suez Canal with sunken ships.

Our crates of bedding and supplies were nailed shut, steel-banded, and shipped. We took the train to New York City with our two kids and eleven pieces of luggage. At the hotel, I phoned the shipping line to ask about disposable diapers on the Queen.

"We've been trying to reach you," said the voice on the phone. "There's a tugboat strike in New York, and the Queen Elizabeth is too large to dock by herself. You'll be on a smaller ship, and will board the Queen up in Halifax, Canada. And no, we don't supply disposable diapers."

15

At Sea

On the first of March, we met Mother, Dad, and my brother Bruce for breakfast, and went to NewYork's Pier 90, where my sister Margaret and her family were waiting. We boarded the *Scythia* for the two-day journey to Halifax, Nova Scotia, and found our small cabin. "This is the troop ship that took me to war in 1944," Bruce remarked. We had an hour to explore it before the "All ashore" announcement, and photos show all of us bundled up against the weather, standing at the ship's stern. We said our good-byes, realizing our parents might no longer be living when we returned.

Snow was falling, two days later, as we moved through the harbor at Halifax. The *Queen Elizabeth II*, largest liner in the world at the time, loomed impressively over its pier, waiting for all of us from New York. It departed that afternoon, its deep booming whistle echoing off the silent snowy hills surrounding the harbor. We shivered on the deck, and looked forward to the tropics.

The Cunard Shipping Line's on-board travel agent was most helpful to us and our small children, but he had a problem. The delay in the Queen's sailing meant that we would arrive late at Southampton, England, and would have only a very short time to reach our next ship in Liverpool, 250 miles farther north. Our crated freight would have to go on the next ship to Rangoon, a month later. But if he put us first in the debarkation line, we might just make the 3:20 train to London.

On Friday, March 8, we approached Southampton, with England's shoreline at its greenest on this early spring-like day. We passed the liner *United States* departing for New York as we neared the harbor. The two vessels, British and American, sounded a deep-toned salute to each other in passing, crowds lining the rails of each, waving at the other. We stood next to a group of American school teachers on tour. One of them had tears streaming down her cheeks at this last view of the American flag she would see for six whole weeks. She kept saying, "I don't think I'm going to like it over here!" Lois and I smiled at each other. We knew how she felt, but for us "over here" would be five years.

At 2:30, the travel agent took us to the First Class gangplank and put us at the head of the line with our accompanied baggage. We sat there for an hour, waiting for the ship to dock. By 3 p.m., we knew we would miss the train, and wondered what we were going to do with two babies, age eight months and two years, in a London hotel for a whole month until the next ship. But when the gangplank finally touched the dock, a Cunard official rushed us through customs and put us in a taxi for London, a trip through the green countryside down the "wrong side of the road," at speeds of up to eighty miles an hour. We entered London in the evening rush hour and pulled up to the train station with four minutes till train departure time. Two travel agents and some porters hurried us through the station and down the platform, while I was counting, "Wife, two children, suitcases, diaper bag, baby stroller—yup, four people and eleven pieces of baggage—as they put us on the train. We could breathe again. We even had several relaxing conversations with British people during dinner in the dining car.

Then the tension built once more as the train pulled into Liverpool. A travel agent met us, hurried us into another taxi, drove through the rain along dark backstreets to an office rear-door where an official stamped our passports, and then onward to the docks. A drawbridge was up; we looked at our watches nervously. The *MV Derbyshire* was still waiting for us (or for the American dollars our tickets represented) an hour past its sailing time, but now the tide was ebbing. Two British ship's stewardesses met us at the top of the gangplank, gently took our sleeping children from our arms and showed us to our room, as a crew of chanting East Indians cast off the lines and the ship slowly moved into mid river.

The Motor Vessel Derbyshire was a rather small ship, carrying perhaps eighty passengers and 500 tons of cargo. We would be aboard her for the next six weeks, with brief stops at Dakar, Capetown, Mauritius, and Colombo. Lois and I had informed ourselves about the "culture shock" we would experience in the Orient, but we hadn't expected to find it as the only Americans among the British. We had had no idea that language and customs could be so different on opposite sides of the Atlantic.

Children ate separately; one of us was expected to come feed our children, but nannies would watch them while we ate. British and Oriental fathers alike were nettled when their wives told them that the American took *his* turn feeding the children, so why shouldn't they?

At adult meals, we shared a table with the ship's third officer, plus a Sinhalese couple, and the principal of Rangoon's prestigious Methodist High School. The latter, Doreen Logie, was returning from the north of England with her sixteen-year-old daughter Gillian. I made what I thought was an innocent request, on one of our first evenings, asking, "Mrs. Logie, may I have a roll, please?"

She drew herself up and her eyes flashed. "*That* is a request usually made in the sanctity of one's cabin!" Her eyes softened to an amused twinkle and she passed the plate. "Here, Keith, you may have a *biscuit*."

There were many other misunderstandings. The British kept referring to American money as "greenbacks," and had such unintelligible items on the menu as "bubble and squeak," "flan," or simply "shape." Seeing pancakes listed at one meal, I told the Indian steward I would have three. His eyes widened, and he withdrew to a lengthy consult with the head steward. The latter came over to me, listened to my request, and suggested I might have two. They proved to be crepes Suzette.

We found the Burmese passengers more accepting. Most were young men, students or soldier-technicians, returning home after several years training abroad. Not only did they agree that the British were a little odd, but our request to teach us a few phrases of Burmese delighted them. They adopted our babies, tried to share their beer with them at the swimming pool, and told us about Burma.

The voyage was a leisurely blur of hot sun, changing diapers, reading murder mysteries, taking the children to the playroom or to meals, getting to know our travel companions, competing at deck quoits and table tennis competitions, and sedate evening entertainment of a British sort. We checked the map by the purser's office each noon, to see our position advance by about 350 miles each day. Exotic seaports punctuated this ennui about every ten days—African Arabs at Dakar, Senegal; fall weather south of the equator at Capetown, South Africa; rows of small Indian and Chinese shops in Mauritius.

Colombo, Ceylon (now Sri Lanka) was our first major stop. A holiday and a dock strike kept us in port there six days, watching the ship's cranes unload automobiles and pallets of canned milk, counting the number of chili peppers the dock workers sliced into their cooking pots, and shopping for footwear less confining than our leather shoes. Our table partners, Henry and Patsy Pereira, home now after years of surgical and pediatric training in Britain, showed us their house and the huge hospital where they would work. We took a tour to Kandi in the center of the island to see a rather dusty temple, renowned as a repository for one of Buddha's teeth. Our children made us the center of a crowd wherever we went, an opening for conversation. Sinhalese children crowded about us to stare; mothers smiled at us and asked jokingly if they could adopt Patsy.

Only four days voyage now to Rangoon. Our young Burmese passengers lined the rail the last day at sea, pointing out the muddy water from the mouth of the Irrawaddy River, the flashing lighthouse far away at night, the small villages next morning, each with its white pagoda, among the dense greenery lining the river. Their first sights of home. I wondered if we would like this strange land.

I turned age twenty-eight on the Indian Ocean.

16

Welcome to Burma

Rangoon, the capital of Burma, had few dock facilities; immigration and health officials came on board where we anchored in the river. After two hours of paperwork, we transferred in rickety boats to a large open Customs shed on shore. Outside its fence a crowd waited for the returning Burmese students. Methodist High School had turned out in force to welcome Doreen and Jill, and some of our colleagues from the Burma Baptist Mission soon found us. It was April 21, Easter Sunday morning, 1957.

Peggy Smith, a missionary nurse, rescued Lois and the children from the crowd and the heat and drove them to the Mission Guest House. I stayed behind with another missionary to clear our baggage, and rejoined them about 2 o'clock.

The mission guest house at 143 St. Johns Road became our temporary home. Thra Tun Shein, the Burma Baptist executive, and Erville Sowards, American mission field secretary, both welcomed us warmly. Most missionaries lived up-country but Ray and June Beaver, whom we knew from Green Lake staff days, came to visit that afternoon. Susie became immediate friends with their four young daughters.

"The Burmese will welcome you this evening at church, you know," someone said. "You'll only have to say a few words. Oh, and this is Naw Gertrude," introducing a middle-aged Karen woman. "She'll baby-sit your children tonight while you're at the reception." Lois and I felt caught up in a swift river, speeding downstream out of control. But this seemed to be the way of things here. We went off to our church welcome and the reception that followed.

We gradually adapted to large cockroaches in the bathroom at night. What we could not accept, a few nights later, were Patsy's screams from her crib. We turned on the light, lifted her mosquito net, and found her covered with ants. She had had a piece of hard candy in her fist at bed time. We cleaned her off, took her into our own bed, and next day learned how to place the crib legs in cups of water as an ant barrier.

Most of the mission, other than Tun Shein and Erville Sowards, didn't seem to know what to do with us, or why we were in Burma. We learned we would start language study when the monsoon rains arrived next month. We would study in the town of Thonze, but the well there had dried up. Meanwhile, I should go visit the mission hospital at Moulmein, an hour's flight down the coast. Lois was left to tend the kids for several days while I was out of town. Mission orientation was only for husbands, and became a recurring sore point over the years, even when our children grew older.

I dutifully went to see how they did things at Moulmein Hospital. A week later, Erville Sowards and I flew to Kengtung, where I would eventually re-open the hospital that had lain dormant since the war.

One of my first discoveries on that trip was that Erville, the mission executive, spoke no Burmese, only Karen language. When our Burma Airways DC-3 plane blew a tire landing at a halfway stop, we watched from the edge of the airstrip as a group of men tugged and pushed the weary old plane off the runway. Nothing further happened for the next three hours. Then word came that a plane would arrive next day.

There was nothing to do about this delay, except catch a ride to Taunggyi, the nearest town with a mission station, and stay over night with the missionary there, Ruth Christopherson. Life in Burma so far seemed to be about waiting.

Next day's plane took us to Kengtung, landing smoothly on an airstrip where armed soldiers kept vigilant watch on the surrounding bushland. We met Paul and Elaine Lewis, only a little older than I but already ten-year veterans of mission work with the Lahu tribe. They would be our only American neighbors within a hundred miles.

Kengtung at that time was a partially walled city of 20,000 in the middle of a flat rice-growing valley, the latter perhaps eight by fifteen miles in size. Mountains rose several thousand feet above its 2,500 foot elevation. Erville and I stowed our bags in the back of Paul's pickup, and rode into town for a brief meeting with local Christian leaders. Paul then drove us to his home at Pangwai, seventeen miles up in the hills, its beautifully cool weather and blossoming cherry trees a pleasant contrast to the unending heat of Rangoon. The Lahu meeting where we had been expected the day before was just ending, but a few people remained. One man had hobbled for nine days' journey when he had learned a doctor was coming. He had dislocated his hip a year before. I could do nothing that late without anesthesia, but we took him to the civil surgeon at the government hospital when we returned to Kengtung. We spent the rest of our time in Kengtung checking over our hospital's buildings and the remnants of US Navy hospital equipment stored there. American planes had strafed the building during the war, when the Japanese had used it as a command post. It needed repairs to the roof and windows, but had sturdy brick walls.

The Shans appointed a language committee to supervise our studies after we finished Burmese down-country. We were the first missionaries in many years to work in the Shan language. We would study in Kengtung. The demands of medical work would probably interfere, but no other region used the same dialect. We met the leprosy committee, who managed sixteen villages stretching from Thailand to the Chinese border, many of them in rebel-controlled territory. We slept in my future home, and I made a map of it and the mission compound for Lois. The children would love the big yard and trees we shared with two other houses, across the road from the hospital.

And I knew Lois would enjoy the town bazaar, almost like a county fair in the center of town. As Paul and I approached it, a medicine show on the back of a truck blared music from a PA system. Just beyond it, a crowd of rubes from the hills gaped at a wooden wheel spinning cotton candy, apparently the latest thing from the big city. Open stalls sold everything from pottery to vegetables to Colgate toothpaste and whiskey. Akha women in silver-and-feather headgear, Lisus in turbans and brightly colored leggings, and all sorts of other strangely costumed people roamed the aisles. I suppose that to them, we were the strangest of all.

Several groups in town hosted dinners for us, and as far as I could tell, it was always the same group under a different name, looking for an excuse to get together and eat again. They heaped my plate high with rice, then passed eight or ten bowls full of meat, fish, vegetables or eggs, each flavored with strange spices. The first serving was twice as much as I could eat, and if I was not on my guard, someone would shovel another spadeful of rice onto my plate. My reputation became established as soon as people heard I was a doctor. They expected any American to know all about medicine, so a real doctor is besieged for a shot to cure Granny's hunchback or baby's hare-lip, everywhere he goes.

This largest of the Shan States, also named Kengtung, had a population of 300,000 spread over a radius of sixty to one hundred miles of mountains, roughly the size of West Virginia. The one existing hospital had two physicians, with another "licensed medical practitioner" in charge of a small military hospital. Most of the population went to unlicensed and largely untrained village midwives and native practitioners. Those partially filled a need, but had no knowledge of surgical or medical crises. The mission office in Rangoon may have been uncertain what to do with the new mission doctor, but I knew there would be all the work I could handle when Lois and I moved to Kengtung.

Meanwhile, there was the Burmese language to learn before we shifted to Shan.

17

Culture Shock

We had been in Burma almost a month. We seemed to be marking time, going on walks with our kids, visiting with other Americans, or reading books. I was getting impatient. When would we start language study and get to work?

U Ba Hmyin, a Yale graduate, and his wife, Daw Hnit, supervised our study of Burmese. We liked them, and they started daily lessons soon after I came back from Kengtung, but they explained the problem: new missionaries tended to learn the language poorly in Rangoon, with so many English speakers around. We would begin study in earnest by moving to Thonze, seventy miles north. A new British missionary, Muriel Soper, would also live there and study with us. But the mission house at Thonze had no source of water until a week after the monsoon rains began. Plan on early June, be there for six months. Very few spoke English there.

Lloyd and Eileen James were leaving for stateside furlough in a few days. Their children's nanny, Naw Carrie, and the Claspers' cook, Naw Ohn Shwe, had agreed to work for us during the year the Jameses and Claspers were gone.

We had expected hot climate, new foods, and occasional illness. We dutifully took our chloroquine every week to prevent malaria, and we boiled our drinking water. But what blind-sided us was "culture shock," a form of depression that hits many foreigners adrift in a strange country after about a month. Most adults adapt and recover from culture shock in about six months; most children do it in a few days. I suppose all nationalities may get it, but Americans seem more susceptible, having grown up more isolated from other nations and languages. By the end of the first month, the excitement and magic of arrival have worn off, yet the newcomer hasn't enough language ability to go anywhere on his own. No matter what educational heights he has achieved back home, in this new land he is a child in kindergarten, and at the bottom of the class even there. Useful occupations depend on language.

There's the stumbling block: the language. It's not a matter of learning vocabulary and how to spell, as if studying German or Spanish. In Burmese, the letters are all circles and half-circles in many combinations; vowels are added as extra marks attached to the consonants. There are no spaces between written words, and very little punctuation. Tenses, plurals, and other grammatic nuances are expressed by added syllables. There are sounds completely foreign to English. And finally, the meaning of the word may change entirely, by changing the tone. *Pyaw* (low tone) means happy. *Pyaw* (more forceful tone) means speak.

Ordinary Burmese people can't explain all this; they just speak it like they learned it. An accomplished linguist, like our teacher Daw Hnit, would pronounce carefully, make us repeat it till we got it right. She had modified the English alphabet with certain marks to indicate tone, to help us memorize the sound until we could learn to read the Burmese script.

Many people never bother to learn the language of their new country, but retreat to little enclaves of English-speaking people to spend their time playing bridge or painting their toenails by the club swimming pool, until their tour of foreign duty is finished. But our work depended on talking with non-English-speaking people, so we had to get on with it.

The monsoon weather finally came the first week in June, and we drove to Thonze in a pouring rain. Two of the missionary men drove us four, plus Naw Carrie and Naw Ohn Shwe and the new British missionary, Muriel. The men left us the red Willys pickup truck to use in getting back and forth to Rangoon, and went back with the other car.

Our new home was a huge two-story brick house, a relic of older missionary times, on the edge of town. Its eight large rooms were surrounded on three sides by verandas, upstairs and down. Wherever trees didn't intervene, rice fields stretched to a flat horizon. The house came with a gardener, who used an old five-gallon kerosene tin to catch rain water from a gutter spout, and then bailed it into a water tank in the eaves.

Our new teacher, Daw Yin, was a serious-faced fifty-year-old woman who had started a school in town and now had 68 pupils and two assistants. She taught us an hour each morning and each evening, five days a week, and we were expected to study four more hours each day. At her school recess times, the children would swarm around our house, peering in at us through the veranda's metal mesh. We felt like animals in a zoo, at first. Lois and Muriel led them in games like London Bridge, and Daw Yin's daughter sometimes brought teen-age students over to visit in a combination of Burmese and English. Trips to the local shops or post office brought limited communication; some of the townspeople tried to teach us by pointing to things. This sometimes helped with nouns (a farmer would point to the town's railroad track and say *miyahtah-lan*) but totally failed with verbs, adjectives, etc. Muriel and I joined the choir of a small nearby Burmese Christian church. The anthem was the only English part of the service, and the rest was mostly over our heads.

Susie and Patsy got along fine with Naw Carrie, played with the gardener's boy and girl, Ne Win and Lizbet, and seemed to do well except for some heat rash and diarrhea.

Slowly, we picked up words and phrases, but Thonze was not really a fun place. We went to Rangoon about every second weekend, and soon such weekends were stretching from Friday through Monday afternoon. When the mission suggested I go up to northern Burma to visit Dr. Seagrave's hospital at Namhkam, to see how a small-town hospital could be run, I jumped at the chance to get a break from language study.

Gordon Seagrave, MD Johns Hopkins Medical School, was a tough surgeon of the old breed, and had walked out of Burma to India in 1942 as General Stilwell's chief medical officer, ahead of the invading Japanese. He had built a 200-bed hospital by hand with truckloads of stones from the river bed, a hospital which had an excellent nation-wide reputation both for its surgery and its nursing school.

The plan was to fly to Lashio and meet an up-country missionary who would drive me the remaining 120 miles. Instead, I got a chance to see how well I could manage on one month's study of Burmese, after finding the missionary wasn't there.

At Lashio, the local *Union of Burma Airways* agent drove me from the airport into town and put me on a bus to Kutkai, about half-way to Namhkam. Burmese buses of that era were converted weapons carriers left over from World War II, with a single plank on which to sit on each side in back. Crates, sacks of rice, oil drums and other freight filled the aisle. The overflow of passengers hung on in the back, like firemen. Looking forward from where I had wedged my feet between two crates I could see that, at each sharp curve on the one-lane mountain road, a passenger in the front seat would touch two bare wires together to sound the horn. The man sitting next to me looked carsick and ready to throw up; I offered him a Dramamine pill, and we were able to communicate a few syllables now and then. We reached Kutkai after taking three hours to go forty-eight miles. That was the end of the day's run, and the driver helpfully delivered me to the mission gate. The missionary couple were in America now, but after trying my Burmese unsuccessfully on the cook/house-sitter, I discovered she spoke fluent English.

Next morning a Volkswagen minibus took me to Namhkam, where I arrived about three, and stayed at the home of Dr. Albert Ai Lun, Seagrave's associate. He took me to meet Seagrave, who looked old and ill, and was in fact suffering a spell of malaria as he sat at his desk. Dr. Seagrave didn't even look up, but made some grumpy remark about damn tourists. I mentioned that he had stayed at our house in Syracuse some years before, and he then turned to me with a crooked grin on his tired face and growled, "Well, why didn't you say so?" From then on we got along better.

During the next four days I looked at everything from kitchen to operating rooms, learning their record-keeping system, pharmacy management, nursing classes, and sanitation. The hospital itself was four stone buildings of two-stories each, housing a total of 250 patients, surrounded by nurses' dormitories, repair shops, houses and a church. I listened to Seagrave teach, as he sat slumped in a chair, his chin jutting out, questioning each student, trying to get her to think instead of just memorize. Class over, he would trudge up to the operating room to kibitz, or see outpatients in the clinic.

Many doctors visited the Namhkam hospital each year, and Dr. Seagrave made each one scrub in on some surgical procedure, no exceptions or excuses even for internists or psychiatrists. My assignment was a difficult delivery. He applied obstetric forceps and then stood back to puff on the cigarette always held lit and ready by a nurse. "Deliver the baby, Doctor," he said.

I gave an experimental pull; the baby's head was jammed tightly in the woman's small pelvis. "I don't think this is a case for forceps, Dr. Seagrave," I said apologetically.

"Pull, dammit!" he said.

With misgivings and considerable physical effort, I extracted the baby, who was obviously in shock. I spent maybe fifteen minutes trying to resuscitate, as the nurse stood by with an "I-expected-this" look on her face. Dr. Seagrave had left the room. Finally, having failed to restore any sign of life, I pronounced the child dead.

Dr. Ai Lun was furious when he heard. "I told Dr. Seagrave that patient had already lost three children in childbirth and that she needed a Caesarian section, and he said there wasn't time!"

I had mixed feelings about the old doctor. He must have been smoking three packs a day, and heart disease required him to ride a car between hospital buildings, yet he scorned all advice that he needed to rest. He still supervised the weekly baseball game that he required all student nurses to take part in. In a nation where typical medical care was a shot of intravenous calcium gluconate for almost any complaint, people came 600 miles from Rangoon to have their surgery at his hospital. He graduated twenty or twenty-five nurse-midwives annually from a four-year curriculum, each of them capable of carrying on alone in the absence of a doctor.

A verse of a hymn the congregation sang that Sunday seemed appropriate:

And the work that we have builded,
Oft with bleeding hands and tears,
Oft in error, oft in anguish,
Will not perish with our years:

It will live and shine transfigured,
In the final reign of right;
It will pass into the splendors
Of the city of the light.

I copied it on a scrap of paper and carried it in my wallet for ten years or more. That was my memory of the Burma Surgeon. A year later, he sent two excellent nurses to work with me at Kengtung.

When I got back to Rangoon, I found my wife had turned bright yellow with hepatitis. She and Muriel and the children had taken the train from Thonze to meet me, thinking she was "just coming down with the flu." They had chosen to ride third class, assuming that was the proper thing for missionaries, and I guess it was the trip from hell: in hot, crowded cars. We stayed in Rangoon an extra day or two to let Lois rest, and then drove back to Thonze with her on a makeshift bed. Language lessons continued, but in our bedroom.

Altogether, we spent five and a half months in Thonze. We made some progress with Burmese, gained some friends and experienced small town life, but never became fluent, lacking the intensive opportunity we would get when we began learning the Shan language in Kengtung.

18

The Golden Triangle

Kengtung, in the so-called "Golden Triangle," the source of Burma's opium was the capital of the East Shan States, bordered by China, Laos, and Thailand. Separated by two hundred miles of bandit-infested road from any other Burmese city, Kengtung was a land different from the rest of Burma, and had been ruled for some six hundred years by the Mengrai dynasty of Shan rulers or Sawbwas.

On December 12, 1957, an old DC-3 plane set us down on the Kengtung landing strip. Again, soldiers with rifles at the ready scanned the perimeter, watching for any surprise attack by insurgents. Our nanny and cook were farther from home than they had ever been, and perceived Kengtung as beyond the last outposts of civilization, but Lois and I were in our element. The climate was cooler, the mountains looked like home, and the men wore pants instead of the Burmese wrap-around long kilt, or *longyi*. And we were finally in a home of our own, where we could unpack and live and work.

Paul and Elaine Lewis, our colleagues from Pangwai, were there to meet us and stayed two days to introduce us around town. All the freight we had packed ten months before was waiting for us. The first thing we did was uncrate and set up our mattresses until we could get furniture made.

Our house was of brick with 13-inch-thick walls, newly whitewashed inside, and had a clay tile roof. There were three bedrooms, a living-dining room in between, and a cookhouse out back. We had two bathrooms, for dipping and pouring cold water over ourselves from large clay water pots. The house had a garden with a row of pineapple plants, papaya, avocado, and custard-apple trees, and in front of the house, a white-flowering frangipani tree. Between us and the church was a deep well, shaded by towering banyan trees.

Our outhouse was way back behind the cookhouse and surrounded by eight-foot tall poinsettia bushes in full bloom. It also had the largest orange-and-gray tocktoo lizard we had yet seen, living in the rafters. The lizard never bothered us, just ate mosquitoes and other insects, and occasionally called "Tock-too! Tock-too!" loudly in the night.

The mission compound had three houses and a brick church in the several acres on our side of the road. The Lahu congregation's pastor and his large family lived next door. Beyond them lived John Po, a retired Burma army major who was mission manager and school headmaster. Across the road were the hospital buildings, plus a small dormitory for about twenty healthy children of leprosy patients, and several more houses. Just beyond was the 9th Burma Regiment army camp. Our own backyard was bordered by the ten-feet-high city wall, a large earth and brick embankment with a dry moat beyond it. The wall was a great place to view the whole valley stretching northward toward China, sixty miles away.

On one of our first days in our new home, I was raking leaves in the chill morning fog. It was so good to feel cold, and to have physical work to do! I heard tankling cow bells, and soon a turbaned Shan man appeared out of the mist, leading a train of five pack-oxen. He paused to regard me in surprise. "Kha," he greeted me.

"Kha," I responded.

He fired off a few Shan sentences, and I answered with the only Shan I had learned so far, "I don't understand Shan." We looked at each other in friendly silence a few moments, then he and his animal train moved on and disappeared into the fog. I realized that even though I had had six months of language study, it was now time to start all over again with this new tongue.

But Shan was much easier for me to learn than Burmese. The alphabet had only seventeen letters (plus vowel marks), the sentence structure was more like English, and we were soon compiling a dictionary on little slips of paper filed in a box. Our teacher, U Hsai

Kyiao, was a Shan in his forties, sort of a jack-of-all-trades. One of his daughters would teach in the new school. He seemed to know everyone and everything in town.

Kengtung's cosmopolitan air made us feel more at home. People spoke many languages in the bazaar—Shan, Burmese, Chinese, Lahu, Kachin, Ahka, Karen, Hkuen, Hindustani, Lisu, Wa—no one spoke them all, so everyone accepted the need for translators. Kengtung's main industries appeared to be rice and vice. Opium could be had for about twenty-one cents a pipe at state-run shops that kept a list of legally registered addicts. (The government wanted to ensure that addicts bought from legitimate shops and therefore paid the state tax.) Festivals featured rows of opium booths, gambling, prostitution, and dime-a-dance arenas, along with the food sellers, balloons, and hand-operated rides for children.

The Shan States were a loose federation of territories in the eastern part of Burma, governed by sawbwas. Like the rajahs in India, many sawbwas were educated abroad and had new ideas for improving their people's education and economy. Sao Sai Long, the Sawbwa of Kengtung, was a pleasant man about thirty years old, with a university degree from Australia. He had an ornate palace with pillars of red and gold in the center of Kengtung town, which he used for government functions. His home, however, was modern ranch-style single story, where he lived with his wife and two children. His wife was active in several social improvement committees, and one of his aunts was headmistress of the city's high school. Although many ancient traditions remained, school textbooks used a simplified, easy-to-read Shan script. Commercial orange groves flourished, twice-weekly air service connected Kengtung with the rest of Burma. A new hospital in town definitely had the Sawbwa's approval, and we were therefore welcomed by the business community.

Lois and I studied Shan in the mornings. In the afternoons she oversaw the housework and I measured the hospital rooms and consulted with Hsai Kyiao and his crony, a Chinese building contractor named Lu Su Fu, about furniture and building repairs.

The mission school (kindergarten through junior high) would continue to meet in the empty hospital buildings until the new school building was completed. Since we needed several months to clean, and install electricity and running water in even the out-patient clinic building, this was not a problem. By February the hospital had a four-stall outhouse and we had begun work on the water supply.

Lu Su Fu, the contractor, would listen to the language teacher's impression of my needs, and would then squint his eyes shut and murmur Chinese to himself to figure what price the traffic would bear for each item. What came out was heavy, rather clumsy, and often painted green, but resembled what I had in mind. The contractor couldn't understand why we didn't just run hospital sewage into the street gutter like almost everyone else did. I tried to explain to him about transmission of typhoid, hepatitis and dysentery, but his final understanding was, Americans are odd.

I had already discovered that a simple hole filled with gravel wasn't enough to handle even bath water run-off at my house—soap deposit clogged the soil's pores, I guess. Our solution for the hospital, surrounded by houses on all sides, was to run waste water (but not toilets) into the existing well on that side of the road, which was deep enough to provide a head of pressure to let the soil absorb the water. We would dig a new well up-slope at a safe distance, and use an electric pump to lift water into a tower, providing gravity flow. To do this, we had to dig the well, build the tower, provide plumbing, get an electric generator, and wire the hospital.

I didn't have to do all this alone. Dr. Dick Buker, the pre-World War doctor, had trained several medical assistants who now had practices of their own. One of them had a son in his twenties, Stephen Yawshu, who was highly intelligent, fluent in English, Burmese, Shan; and Lahu. He aspired to a practice of his own someday, and came to work for the hospital. Together we learned how to cut threads on steel water pipe and lay out insulated electric wires and wall switches in the rooms. Meanwhile, a team of local builders dug a new well, lined it with brick, and built a sturdy brick water tank two stories high.

19

My First Office Practice

Many of Kengtung State's 300,000 people took their ills to self-trained "medicine men", with results ranging from satisfactory to disastrous. Foreign medicine, especially injected medicine, was held in great esteem. Patients appeared at our door almost from day one. I would see them in our home after the daily language lesson, with Hsai Kyiao staying after class to translate.

This worked all right as long as there were only a few. I examined people as best I could in our living room. Shipments of medicine from Rangoon were alrady arriving; we dispensed oral medicines in little envelopes and bottles. Lois sterilized a few wrapped syringes and needles in our pressure cooker for injections.

One of the first to come was a Chinese young lady with a midline lump in her neck. She spoke English, as well as Shan and Chinese, and said she had had the lump for years. I suspected a thyroglossal cyst, told her that surgery was optional and not urgent. She reappeared sometimes over the next few months to translate for other Chinese, and eventually asked for a job as a nurse-aide and translator.

Sometimes I was able to give good news, sometimes not. The family who roared up to the door in a jeep one night with a young man calling, "My wife, Doctor! Her heart!" was assured, after examination, that his wife did not have heart disease as they had supposed, but an apparently healthy three-month pregnancy. This news stunned the young husband.

But another lady, with chronic cough, continued to worsen even on the latest tuberculosis medicines (streptomycin, INH, and PAS in those days.) After many return visits she finally died with TB pericarditis.

During this home-based practice period, Dana Albaugh, a senior mission executive from New York, came to inspect our progress. During his three-day visit, he stumbled on a loose brick in the path to the outhouse and injured his ankle. I splinted the leg and provided a pair of crutches, but had no way to X-ray it. At his next stop, in Taunggyi, the hospital there found a fracture, and the doctor put him in a full-leg cast. After he had returned to New York, the Mission notified me that we could expect funding for a portable X-ray and power source. Had I known where to find a bronze memorial plaque, I would have fastened it to the X-ray, dedicating the machine to Dr. Albaugh and his ankle.

The long-stored U.S. navy surgical equipment in the hospital included a big steam autoclave, an operating light and table, and basic laboratory equipment. Several crates of medicines, now fifteen years old, had mostly unreadable faded labels. The mission's White Cross organization shipped crates of bandages, sterilization wrappers, and hospital linens. I had visited medical supply import firms in Rangoon during our Thonze stay, and was now ordering medicines from their catalogues. But Lois was growing increasingly tense about all the sick folks in our living room, and the safety of our children. She was also several months pregnant again. She would turn almost purple when some patient forgot where he was, cleared his throat, and spat on our hardwood floor. One of our first local purchases of hospital equipment was three spittoons. There are lots of details to establishing a hospital.

Lois summed up home office hours in a letter to her mother:

"Our house is again invaded. The compound is full of trucks and cars, the living room is full, as is the veranda. Our language lessons are hopeless because there are so many patients waiting all the time. I really don't see how Keith can keep up with them all—especially since we are not officially in business till July 1st. I help with the female patients but right now he is examining a fellow with a spleen or liver that fills his whole abdomen. The guy probably has one of these odd-ball tropical parasites … In my spare moments I am trying to get a nursing procedure book ready but I can't type while Keith is using his stethoscope, so I figured I'd write."

The last straw for her was a man with a rash, whom I proposed to examine in the privacy of our bedroom. Lois exploded. "I don't care what diagnosis you need to make," she said. "Syphilis or measles or whatever, you're not examining him in our bedroom!"

By June of that first year in Kengtung, we still had no electricity or running water, but the five-room outpatient building was clean, and the inside walls had been whitewashed or painted. Lu Su Fu had produced enough examining tables, desks and chairs so that we were capable of opening, even though water still had to be carried from the well.

We still had no nurses except Lois and Daw Thein Tin, the midwife, but her husband, the schoolmaster visited us one evening saying he had a couple of young men, high school graduates, who wanted to work in the hospital. After interviewing them, I hired one, Maung Pan, as hospital clerk and the other, Abela, as lab and X-ray technician, and included their training in my daily schedule.

On June 27, the Christian community held two dedications. The morning one was for a second dormitory for healthy students of leprous parents. It was a simple one-room building with a cooking space. But with most of the twenty students now in their teens, we needed to provide separate quarters for boys and girls.

That same afternoon there was a dedication of the outpatient building, which would open for business the following week. It was a multiple translation ceremony, Burmese to Shan to Lahu to Chinese; kind of long, but it was nice of all the people to come in the pouring rain. At the close, the Chinese congregation presented the waiting room with a fine new wall clock. It had Chinese writing on the clock face, and I knew of no tactful way to ever ask whether it was a Bible verse or something like "Buy at Chung Foo's."

On the following day, all of us: Lois and I, the hospital gardener, the cleaning lady, Steven (my translator for Shan and Lahu), Lily (translator for Chinese), Maung Pan, and Abela, moved all the supplies from our house to the newly furnished building across the road.

Language lessons continued—I had a Shan vocabulary of about 1,500 words in my makeshift dictionary, if not in my head. I picked up a little more Burmese from the army wives in the camp beyond the hospital, who would bring their children to us rather than walk all the way across town. Steven and I continued to lay pipe and electric wiring while waiting for a generator. In spare time, I taught the clerk what I had learned about hospital records from Dr. Seagrave's hospital, and taught the lab tech the basics of X-rays, microscopes, and blood counts. Lois handled mission correspondence and thank-you letters for donors back in the USA, and sometimes had eighty or more letters waiting to be answered. The kids were not old enough for home schooling yet. We were grateful for Kengtung's lack of night life, and spent our evenings at least in the same room with our children.

Nurses would appear in God's own good time. For the present, Daw Thein Tin weighed patients, took blood pressures, and assisted in pelvic exams, with Lois's occasional help.

It would be another six months before we had the whole hospital ready, but working in the dispensary building was much better than in our home. Maung Pan presided over patient records in the front waiting room, assigning a number to each patient, and keeping a large ledger of procedures done and fees received. We knew we wouldn't collect full costs, but most people would pay a little, and the merchants in town paid for their families' care in full.

Abela set up his laboratory in one room, the big storeroom became the pharmacy, one back room was central supply and sterilizing, while I and my translator used the other as exam room and office. I still needed help to be sure the patient and I understood each other even in Shan. Of course, some spoke Lahu, or Chinese, and others would have to bring a neighbor who could translate from Lisu or Akha into something my translator could savvy.

In early November, the hospital Jeep arrived, driven overland by Bill Hackett, one of the missionaries from near Taunggyi. A snub-nosed, fire-engine-red pick-up truck, its arrival meant release from dependence on Paul Lewis's Power Wagon. Eventually it proved to be a lemon, the only vehicle I ever saw that could start cold on a hill-top and have its radiator boil over by the time it reached the bottom. But now we could haul our own drums of fuel, sacks of rice, and sick patients.

20

Family

By October, 1958, Lois was ready to deliver our third child. The hospital was not yet open. She and I talked at length about whether she should go down-country to deliver. But she had already had two normal deliveries, and said she didn't want to travel 600 miles to deliver with a strange doctor when she had an obstetrician at home and a midwife two houses away. I was already stocking the pharmacy with medicines and sutures. I had even done my first home delivery, when the wife of the airline agent had her tenth daughter, feet first, a few months earlier.

Lois went into labor the evening of October 12. At about 1 a.m. it was time to call Daw Thein Tin. Lois had a pain shot, and with local anesthetic, our son John was born. Daw Thein Tin bathed him from a basin of warm water as she sat cross legged on the floor, holding him in her lap, so that I could attended to the afterbirth.

Lois and I both were glad all this happened in the middle of the night while our other kids were fast asleep. Next morning, they chinned themselves on the edge of the crib and were delighted to see him. "That's Martha, isn't it?" Patsy said, looking up at me.

"Well, yes, but we think we'll name him John."

We sent a runner to the Lewises in Pangwai with news of John's arrival, and Elaine came down to help for a few days.

Having a well-stocked dispensary at hand gave us some reassurance in raising our children. Some missionaries were far from medical help at a time of crisis. But in spite of the comfort of a near-by hospital, I didn't feel up to removing my own daughter's tonsils.

Patsy, at age two, had to snort with almost every sentence to clear her adenoids. When we went on vacation to Rangoon in January, 1959, for the Burma Medical Convention, and to visit all the ice cream shops in town, we had Patsy's tonsils and adenoids removed. It is not a common operation for doctors in the tropics; the surgeon didn't take out as much as he should have. It had to be repeated in Denver three years later, but Patsy obviously got more oxygen with every breath even after the first procedure. (Too *much* oxygen, we sometimes thought, when she got into mischief.)

Naw Carrie and Naw Ohn Shwe, our on-loan nanny and cook, had gone back to Rangoon in May, when their former employers returned. We hired Shan help to free up Lois for other tasks and to give us more practice with the language. Susie and Patsy, now age four and two, adapted to Third World life with enthusiasm. At first, we tried to make Susie wear shoes when she went outside. She saw no purpose. "Well, none of my friends do!" was her reasoning. She had a whole collection of neighborhood kids who were in and out of our house most of the day, and when school broke for recess she and Patsy were right out there with the students, spending their allowance at the food sellers in the shade of the banyan trees. Once, when calling Susie to come to dinner, I met her coming out of the neighbor's house next door, a half-eaten locust in her hand. "What's it taste like?" I asked her.

"Needs salt."

Some of the things we experienced in Kengtung were unforgettably beautiful. I especially remember our getting invited to watch *The Dance of the Animals*, a night celebration at the close of Buddhist Lent in October, when the rainy season ends. As we went down to the city sports grandstand, the usually pitch-black night was as bright as daylight, with telephone-pole-size pitch pine torches blazing on the street corners over the heads of the festive crowds. Dancers costumed as animals—tigers, oxen, elephants, crocodiles, etc.—performed expertly, expressing their joy at the end of the rains. Then the fireworks began, in this town that had learned the art from the Chinese more than seven hundred years ago. Not just sky rockets, but full-size water falls of fire, huge pinwheels, lights bobbing like fruit on a tree. Some were so intricate that I can't imagine how they were managed.

Not all of life in Third World countries is grim and hardscrabble. Even the Burmese soldiers sometimes performed impromptu costumed dances on the streets (before the dictatorship, at least), usually a good-humored lampoon of Burmese high society or foreigners. When circumstances permit, the Burmese dress well, eat well, and enjoy their holidays.

About the time John was born, Uncle Laurence Stenger, age 78 and Aunt Effie, age 73, came out from Denver to visit us. She would help Lois with the new baby and Uncle, an electrical engineer, would bring the electric system to life.

Repairing and equipping the whole hospital cost the mission something like $50,000, and the X-ray and its electric generator were a large item in that. We had located a used eight-kilowatt diesel generator from somewhere for 10,000 kyats (about $2,000 then.) It weighed two tons. When it arrived in late November, the truck driver had no idea how to unload it. We finally slid it down inclined timbers on sections of steel pipe for rollers, and it sat in a small shed out in back of the hospital awaiting completion of its concrete base. The army had a mobile crane they were kind enough to lend us one morning, and it took only about five minutes to lift it into place. Then a crowd of kids and a few adults stood around for two days while Uncle Laurence, Steven, and I looked perplexed, tried this lever and that, and vainly cranked the beast. It just wouldn't start.

The man from the local electric board gawked a while and said the Shan equivalent of, "Gee, I never saw one that looked like that before!" We finally found another mechanic whose opening statement was a confident, "If it's a diesel, it'll go." He proved it after working two hours to get dirt and air out of various tubes where it had collected on the six-day road trip to Kengtung. Then he cranked it, and it started with a gratifying roar that scattered children right and left. Shouting in my ear over the noise, he said a machine like that would cost four times our price if bought new, so we felt lucky to have it, even though it used more fuel than we planned.

But it wouldn't make electricity. Three weeks later, after the company in Rangoon sent a replacement part by plane, and Uncle Laurence had the whole machine back together again, we cranked up the engine. It started, but the dials on the switchboard still said zero. According to Steven (I was busy with a patient) Uncle did some more tinkering and finally threw up his hands and said, "I give up!" and the needle on the power dial immediately swung up to the required 250 volts. Some clergy might use this as a sermon illustration of the Power of God When All Else Fails. My agnostic cousin Phil Dergance might have suggested that the friction of the graphite brush against the rotating commutator ring finally wore through the tarnish and dirt, and perhaps both would be correct.

The machine still didn't function perfectly, but Uncle worked out the remaining glitches. The water pump in the new well worked beautifully when it was switched on, and our new brick water tower slowly filled up, ready to supply the needs of the clinic building.

My trouble at this point was mainly Uncle Laurence himself. He insisted on being his own lineman, climbing all over to string the wires instead of leaving it to Steven, with whom he could easily talk in English. Shan culture prevented Steven or me, being much younger, from giving him any orders. I was terrified that my 78-year-old, diabetic, half-blind uncle would fall and break his hip, an injury for which we were totally unequipped.

Steven called me out of the examining room one morning. "Uncle is up on the water tower; he won't let me do the work for him."

I strode out into the hospital's back courtyard and, hands on hips, squinted up at the twenty-five-foot-high brick tower. Uncle Laurence was perched on the top iron rungs of the access ladder, adjusting an insulator carrying the power line from the generator shed. "Uncle! Let Steven do that." What if my uncle lost his grip up there?

"Keith, you go back and do your work, and I'll do mine." He could be very single-minded.

I marched across the road to my house to appeal to his wife, slamming the screen door as I entered. "That would be Keith," I heard Aunt Effie say calmly to Lois.

"Aunt Effie, he's on top of the water tower and he won't come down. How do you get him to *listen*!"

95

"Well, Keith, I learned long ago to just leave him to the Lord, and it's worked so far." Aunt Effie always spoke quietly and with common sense. Do what you can and let God handle it from there, was her philosophy. As she pointed out, her strong-willed husband was still alive in spite of himself. I went back to work.

They stayed with us four months and really were most helpful. My cousins back in Denver had thought the adventure ill-advised, and predicted they would never see their parents again. Actually, the elderly pair lived another ten years after their return home, and promoted overseas mission work everywhere they went.

Life in a war-impoverished country is difficult to describe in well-provisioned America. Most people re-use every scrap of trash. The only affordable canned food is an occasional small tin of condensed milk for their tea; the empty tin is used to measure rice. They save empty bottles to store stuff on the small shelf above the cooking fire in their bamboo and thatch homes. An empty kerosene tin is refashioned into a dustpan for cleaning the bare-dirt front yard.

The hospital's running water was an innovation; most drew water in a bucket from wells. The only household fuels were wood (for cooking), charcoal (to keep the flatiron hot), and kerosene for lamps. Natural gas was still in the future, as was refrigeration. We used a kerosene-fueled refrigerator made in Sweden, but most people bought what little meat they ate fresh-killed at the morning market. before the heat of the day or the flies could spoil it. Vegetables and fruits were seasonal and bought fresh. We made peanut butter by shelling, roasting, and grinding the peanuts. Our Shan cook failed to master the process: when he set his first jar on the table one morning, its cover had risen above an expanding mass looking like an old-time milk bottle frozen on a winter doorstep back home. Tasted sour. As it turned out, he had added water instead of peanut oil, and the mixture had fermented.

When our children reached school age, we divided their day into morning attendance at the Burmese school next door, where their friends went, and afternoon home schooling with Lois, using the Calvert Course sent out from America. They grew up multilingual, from playing with the neighbor kids, and Susie much preferred school in Burmese, where English as a second language was only a minor subject. ("No, Mommy, Teacher says it this way: 'Thees ees ay pin!'"

Patsy desperately wanted to go to Burmese school, but was always shooed away by the teachers. "You're still too little, Patsy." When she finally reached age five, David Hsam, the headmaster, was waiting at the door to greet her. "Welcome to your new school, Patsy." Her eyes glowed with joy.

She came home after her first day to tell us about it and added proudly, "And I got a zero!"

Church services were also a little mixed up for our children. If we attended Shan church in Kangna village down the road, the service was Shan and Burmese. If we went to the church on the compound, the language was whatever the preacher of the day used, proceding then to translation into the other three of Burmese, Shan, Lahu, and Chinese. Our kids grew up fluent in all except Chinese, and understood that people of many languages could all worship one God.

We spent evenings at home; Kengtung rarely had any night life. We made sure our kids were in bed by seven o'clock, to give Lois and me a couple of hours of adult conversation, or writing letters or reading, at least on nights when the hospital did not call me back for some emergency. That worked well in Burma, but when we returned to America on furlough, and they discovered that all their cousins stayed up until nine or later, we had some explaining to do.

21

The Army I Remember, 1958

"CHA!" shouted the class of soldier recruits on our front lawn, lunging forward with their bayonets. Our two girls, Susan and Patsy, ages four and two, watched from our small porch as the master sergeant rapped one recruit on the head who had done it wrong. "CHA!" again; this time everyone apparently got it right. In the hot sunshine farther off, a half dozen soldiers gathered around a dis-assembled Bren gun, preparing to put it back together. Over by the well, four student buglers practiced assembly call in dismal cacophony. Business as usual for the Fourth Burma Regiment.

Although I was a pacifist, I learned a lot about the military and it's function of protecting a country, during those five years in Burma. Burma's army nowadays has changed greatly, into an instrument for keeping the Burmese themselves under strict control, but in the 1950s the country was still run by an elected premier, U Nu.

Kengtung was base of operations for a division of troops that guarded eastern Burma from the incursions of the Chinese KMT troops and assorted rebel armies and bandits. The Fourth Burregt and their families were quartered in a large grove just beyond the hospital, and more or less assumed, without asking, that they could use the grassy mission compound as a drill field. The Fifth Kachin Rifles and Division Headquarters were on a hill a half mile away. Several fighter planes nested in revetments along the town's airstrip.

Although my wife and I didn't really care to have our daughters watch this daily show, and although we ground our teeth and held our ears as we tried to shut out the bugle beginners, the soldiers were good neighbors in those days. Besides loaning us their crane to lift our generator, one day a non-com and his squad hurried to the aid of four hospital workers who couldn't manage on their own when lifting a vertical forty-foot section of iron pipe into the new well. And another day, when a civilian patient needed an uncommon blood type for transfusion, we were overwhelmed with volunteers from the army camp.

We in turn took care of their women and children. There was a military clinic across town, which took care of the battle casualties, with the help of the government civil surgeon. What we got, at first, were soldiers' wives bringing their children. "*Nah nahdeh, Bogyi,* [His ear hurts, Captain]" a mother would explain, assuming a foreign doctor rated at least top company-grade rank. Or maybe it would be a kid with swollen glands, or a wife with a miscarriage.

The turning point came when a sergeant came in carrying an underweight four-year-old in his arms. His son had not been doing well ever since he had a fever some weeks ago. I looked him over, thumped his chest, listened with my stethoscope. Dull sound to percussion, and absent breath sounds on the left. Low grade fever. The kid didn't look well. The father was gratified when I ordered a chest X-ray. I held up the film, pointing out to him the whited-out left chest, where air-filled lung should have been.

"I think he has an empyema—pus in his chest," I told the sergeant. "If we can draw the pus out, and give him medicine, I think he'll get well." This was worse than the sergeant had feared, but he gave permission. We did not yet have surgery or anesthesia, so I had the father hold the boy in his arms, painted his back with antiseptic, and inserted a large needle into the left chest cavity. As I drew back on the plunger of the fifty cc syringe, I was rewarded by a flow of greenish-white pus. His chest produced several hundred cc, which a gram-stain in the lab showed to be a probable staph infection. This was before the in-patient hospital opened, and we didn't yet have much that was suitable for injecting into the chest cavity. We did have some samples of an obscure antibiotic called oleandomycin, and I used all our supply on him over the next week. The father was impressed.

Every two days he would bring his boy, and because soldiers at that time were never far from their weapons, he would lay his Thompson submachine gun on the table so he could hold the child with both arms. Each time, I withdrew pus. The child was too weak to put up much of a fight, but he gradually improved, starting to walk and gain weight again. He was left with a thick layer of scar tissue surrounding the lung, but he survived. The mission hospital was fully accepted by our soldier neighbors after that.

As neutral medical workers, trying to maintain credibility with both the Shan villagers and the townspeople and government, we sometimes had to walk a fine line. I never went out on house calls to treat sick or injured rebels, but I let it be known that anyone who came to the hospital would be treated impartially, without unnecessary questions asked. On the other hand, I could not prevent army people entering and inspecting the hospital. When an officer told me I must report all suspicious people who came for treatment, I had to tell him I couldn't do that; if he wanted such reports he would have to send soldiers to do it. And one day when the new division commander, Colonel Tun Sein, visited us and I tactlessly referred to "our[i.e., the mission's] leprosy villages," he testily told me that he understood what I meant, but I had better never forget that they were not *our* villages, they were Burma's. He was right, of course, and I watched my conversation more carefully after that.

The Army did indeed have some battles to fight, and sometimes had serious casualties. When the Chinese Kuomintang teamed up with the Shan rebels, the Burmese regiment known as the Kachin Rifles moved up near the Chinese border, returning from battle just in time for Christmas Eve services (the Kachin ethnic group is mostly Christian.) And the Shan rebels shot up our compound one night to draw the army away from the government hospital on the other side of town, while the rebels killed an informer who was a bed-patient over there. Our area of town, Nawng Hpa Quarter, was featured in the nation's newspapers next day as "the center of fighting". Sounded like it, too, at the time.

One day, I had to go to Division Headquarters to fill out some papers. As my car entered the gate I heard someone roar out the Burmese equivalent of "Ten-HUT!" and a row of soldiers sprang to present arms. The colonel and his staff immediately appeared, expecting to find at least a general arriving. "Why, it's only the mission doctor," I heard one say, and they went back to their conference. But at the head of the line of soldiers standing rigidly at attention, the sergeant—father of my little empyema patient—grinned and threw me a salute.

22

Opening the Hospital

Peggy Smith, BSN, arrived about the same time as my uncle and aunt. A child of missionary parents herself, she had been working at the mission hospital in Moulmein, but now would be our head nurse. She stayed in our guest room (our remodeled cookhouse. The kitchen was now inside the house in the former second bathroom, with a sink and kerosene stove installed.) We planned to complete a nurses' dormitory the following year. Already fluent in Burmese, she would now study Shan.

We were slowly gathering equipment and unskilled young people whom Peggy would train to be nurse aides. The new hospital had caught the attention of Kengtung society, and having a daughter "learning nursing" became a social plus, rather like being a member of the Kengtung Maternal and Child Welfare League. (The League passed out powdered milk to pregnant women and met every month or two to drink tea and take minutes.) But like with the League, few of them expected that nurse aide school would involve any actual work. One young lady quit after the first morning because she hadn't learned enough medicine. "They wanted me to make beds and sweep floors," she sniffed to a friend.

In mid-January 1959, we took a working vacation trip to Rangoon for a last round of shopping for equipment—self-wringing mops for the floors, kerosene burners for the steam sterilizer, the latest intravenous equipment by McAllister Bicknell Co. etc. (The latter were glass blood transfusion bottles with stainless steel tops attached to rubber tubing and a steel needle.) We located snake-bite antivenin, blood-typing serum, diphtheria antitoxin, and a host of other last minute items, with ice chests to carry them in.

We set up an operating room, planning to use spinal anesthetic or inhalation ether. Ether's boiling point was about the same as the outside temperature on hot days, but the hospital's brick walls kept the room cool enough to make it usable. My daughter Susan says one of her childhood memories is the smell of ether on me when I would kiss her good night.

With no central heating in cold season, the OR was warmed by charcoal braziers, which had to be removed from the room before anesthesia began, to reduce risk of explosion. During this gathering of equipment, the nurse's dormitory also was under construction, a two story brick building for up to eight nurses, including Peggy.

And now real nurses were drifting our way. Sir San C. Po Hospital, a two-year school in the Irrawaddy Delta, sent us two Karen graduates, Naw May Paw and Naw Htoo Paw. Two Lahu four-year graduates of Ellen Mitchell Memorial in Moulmein appeared about the same time: Rhody Daniel, daughter of another of Dr. Buker's pre-war medical assistants, and Kham La, both natives of Kengtung. And Dr. Seagrave, with typical lack of preamble, telegraphed us that two graduates of Namkham Hospital were en route: one Kachin, Lu Seng, and one Shan, Shwe Yin. Together with Peggy, Daw Thein Tin, and Lois, we had enough staff to begin. The hospital committee set an opening date of February 1 for the maternity ward, to accommodate several pregnant patients coming due about then. Medical and surgical services would follow as soon as possible.

With the generator now providing adequate 220-volt power, the lab tech inaugurated our new portable X-ray machine with a picture of his own hand. We then took a chest X-ray of each worker, to be sure we had employed no active TB cases. With a year of outpatient practice behind me, and already more than one thousand registered patients, I was beginning to think that about five per cent of the whole population had tuberculosis.

Peggy Smith deserved most of the credit for getting the hospital going. She was supposed to work at the hospital in the mornings and study Shan each afternoon. Actually, she worked all day at the hospital, spent an hour after supper with her language teacher, and then went back to teach classes at night for the nurses and aides.

In mid-February, we had a mock surgery case as a drill. It was terrible. The two Karen nurses from down-country had never been in an operating room before, and had to learn from the beginning how to scrub their hands and arms and avoid contaminating their sterile gloves. But when the first real case came in the next day, everyone did just what they were supposed to do. It was a C-section patient, bleeding in late pregnancy. Rhody was the perfect surgical assistant, though she had only seen six major cases at the hospital in Moulmein, and Htoo Paw was a good scrub nurse, though she had never seen any. And the patient and her baby both came through it well. Uncle Lawrence had just finished the wiring, and the OR was like daylight inside (so bright that we later learned it had attracted several spectators, outside the window.)

By March that year,1959, the whole hospital was open. We started with a series of misfortunes.

Some were no one's fault, like the retired judge with a heart attack who arrived and immediately died. Others were slip-ups in care: a new nurse left a baby who had died of meningitis in the room a long time after death, causing the mother of the other child in that room to take her baby home without treatment. An old man fell from a second story window which had not yet been screened. He had multiple injuries and died on the operating table.

Others problems were cultural. One weekend, I happened to be the only doctor available in town. The chief Buddhist Abbot of all Kengtung "fainted" in the temple downtown, and arrived at our hospital with a stroke and uncontrolled high blood pressure. We put him in our best private room (we had two.)

The hospital resembled a Buddhist monastery for several days, with all the saffron-robed monks milling around in the hall, and young acolytes hanging out the windows. Cars drove up at all hours of the day bringing local gentry to inquire about his health. Even mustering all the formal Shan I could remember, I couldn't get his attendants to bathe him or give him drinking water. (Even to touch him showed disrespect for such a revered person.) Nurses, being women, were barely tolerated in the room. When any of the nurses tried to give him decent care, he would snatch his yellow robe around him, bristle his close-cropped mustache, glare, and puff his paralyzed cheek at them, while twenty visitors crowded into the room to watch in passive disapproval.

Lois and Peggy saw that he was getting dehydrated. I suppose they could have given water intravenously, but he was fully conscious. Unthinkingly, Lois lifted his head and gave him water to drink. The visitors were shocked at this foreigner's indiscretion. *No* one touches a monk's head, and especially not a *kala hpuek* foreign woman! After several days, when he was out of danger (but still paralyzed on one side) I thought he might as well go home, since none of his attendants were taking care of him. But a committee of visitors, including the magistrate, the town's leading pharmacist, several senior monks, and the Princess Sao Bo Sawan all thought he should stay. So he stayed a few more days.

Three months later, his determination had produced a better result than I could have imagined. I had made occasional house-calls at the temple, and we developed a mutual guarded respect for each other. At the last visit, I found him sitting cross-legged on his dais. He stood up and walked across the room unassisted. He could talk, though I noticed the younger monks, as well as I, were having trouble understanding him. He couldn't find the blood pressure medicine I had given him, but on learning that his BP was 220 again, the other monks said they would see that he took his western medicine along with the Shan remedies. He died several months later, but at least he survived "western treatment."

23

No Consultants Within 300 Miles

In non-secure border areas like Kengtung, two-way radios and airplanes were strictly forbidden to all except the government, and telephone lines had not yet reached the city. With the nearest medical center four days travel away, few of my patients were able or willing to seek specialist care outside of Kengtung. I can remember transferring an elderly woman with a broken hip, and a man whose bone marrow was making no blood cells at all, and that's about the total during four years. I was thankful for the two years of obstetrics and surgery training I had had, and my constant prayer was for God to help me remember what I had learned. But isolated doctors must attempt operations beyond their experience, with only a text book to guide them.

Cataracts were a common cause of blindness. Under local anesthesia, using a narrow-bladed Graefe knife, I learned to carefully incise the cornea, expel the clouded lens from the eye, and close the cornea with a few stitches. One of my most rewarding moments was removing the bandage from my first cataract patient, and see him smile radiantly and exclaim in Shan, "Doctor, I can see!" I wish every operation were that successful.

A village near Kengtung raised mules and horses, whose dung is a good breeding ground for tetanus germs. When the village midwife cut the umbilical cord with dirty scissors, a baby would sometimes develop tetanus a week later. I learned to diagnose the clenched-jaw cry of tetanus even before the baby entered the room. If the parents brought the child soon enough, large doses of tetanus antitoxin might save him.

Another common ailment in that part of the world has something to do with the water supply in certain villages. The diagnosis of stone in the urinary bladder was not difficult: pain, bloody urine, and the typical oval shadow of the stone on X-ray. I did the operation on about forty patients of all ages, with good results, even when patients didn't follow post-up orders as closely as I would wish. I remember five-year-old Yawba, a nephritis patient, trotting across the hospital yard to where a cookie seller had set up temporary business in the shade of a tree. Yawba was supposed to be at bed rest, but it was hard to scold him when he happily returned with a large cookie in each hand. Suddenly, seven-year-old Seng Tan, three days post-op from her bladder stone surgery (and supposedly still hooked up to bladder drainage) came racing down the stairs. As she met Yawba, he handed her one of the cookies and they went back up the stairs together.

I did a few cleft-lip repairs, babies or adults, with ether anesthesia. We had a small curved copper tube to hang in the corner of the sleeping patient's mouth. The nurse giving anesthesia would attach the tube to a bottle of ether connected to the exhaust side of the surgical suction pump, and control the air-flow bubbling through the ether with a finger blocking a diversion tube. That anesthesia technique also worked well for a man whose face had been re-arranged by a hostile bear. His mouth had healed as a gape where his right cheek should have been. Surgery was basically identifying pieces of the face and putting them back together correctly, like a jigsaw puzzle. Afterward, he still had visible scars, but looked human again.

With diphtheria emergency surgery, however, there was no time for ether to take effect. A father came one day carrying a blue-lipped, semi-conscious child, her head thrown back, gasping for each breath. I could see a thick white membrane coating her tonsils and throat, partially blocking her airway. As I studied the bacteria from her throat under the microscope, all the doubts of an inexperienced young doctor swept over me. Are these really diphtheria bacilli I see, or something less dangerous? Can I get by with a steam tent, or must I open the windpipe to bypass the rapidly closing throat? The only other one I tried that on had died. Whatever I decided, there would be no second chance. After a moment, and with the parents' consent, I took her to the operating room. Inhalation anesthesia is too dangerous in this situation. Local injection of lidocaine must be enough, plus a towel over her eyes so she didn't have to watch.

Left thumb and middle finger pushed the neck veins to each side; her lips turned bluer with the pressure. I prayed as I cut, "Lord, at least keep me from doing her harm." Left forefinger found the windpipe; one more cut and air hissed sharply in and out as she breathed. I slipped a child-size silver tracheostomy tube in, and her gasping changed to a spasmodic cough. I lifted the tube a fraction of an inch, and for the first time her breathing was quiet and regular. An hour later she was sitting up in her crib, trying to tell her father about the steam kettle by the bed, but no sound came from her mouth, only the sighing of air from the tube in her neck. It was a week later before the tube was removed and she could howl at the doctor properly.

Sometimes the mistakes I made were plainly stupid. A blind man was led into my office, his eyes brimming with pus. The translator reminded me that I had seen him several months before at a Lahu village clinic, where I had drained an abscess of his ear lobe. "I don't remember seeing a blind man at that clinic," I said.

"He wasn't blind then."

That has haunted me ever since. I had failed to prescribe an antibiotic, paying attention only to the rule of an earlier generation, that an abscess will heal if it is drained. He had rubbed the pus into his eyes, and now it was too late to treat; the infection had destroyed both eyes.

Appendectomy, Caesarian section, and gunshot wounds became fairly common. Sometimes I would try something more daring if I thought I could get away with it.

Gastro-enterostomy—making a new connection between stomach and intestine to bypass an area blocked by an ulcer's scar tissue—restored nutrition to a couple of gaunt patients.

A government clerk, with a hoarse voice from tuberculosis of his larynx, also had a chronically abscessed knee from TB; he could walk only with great difficulty, and hadn't been able to work for seven years. On X-ray, the bone looked fine on either side of the joint. Following a textbook description, I opened the knee, sawed away the infected joint, brought the clean ends of the thigh and leg bones together and immobilized them in a cast. I put a metal pin through the bones above and below the bone fusion and applied turnbuckles to tighten the pins and keep the bones firmly against each other. A year later, he could walk quite well and without pain, though that leg was two inches shorter than the other.

One morning a woman was brought in with no blood pressure. The entire upper half of her body was swollen, her profile resembling an American buffalo. She had a small wound on her left shoulder with watery pus; microscopic exam showed chains of long bacteria, like a train of boxcars. She soon died, before treatment had time to work, but when I looked up a description of "malignant edema," I suspected that she died of an especially severe anthrax infection. I later saw another case, much less advanced, that responded to penicillin.

Smallpox has no cure, and when a half-dozen cases appeared from one village, we could only isolate them in a temporary hut and give supportive care. The Burmese public health people periodically sent vaccinators around the countryside, so most people in Kengtung were immune and our mini-epidemic did not spread.

Leprosy was a scourge of the Shans and Lahus. The Akhas rarely got it. Father Columbo, a big bear of a black-bearded Catholic priest from Italy, and a recognized authority on leprosy, ran a six-hundred-bed sanitarium outside of town. I was nominally in charge of over a thousand more cases living in designated leprosy villages out in the hills, but they were inaccessible most of the time, in territory occupied by Chinese or Shan rebels. A man made occasional visits to the villages to take them medical supplies and to record the census, if a truck was going in that direction. Or several men from a village might travel into Kengtung for their village supplies, braving the rejection they often received from other travelers because of their deformed hands and faces.

Leprosy, also known as Hansen's Disease, is caused by infection from a bacillus related to the one which causes TB. It damages the nerves so that often the person is unable to feel anything, even pain, in hands or feet. So if a barefoot farmer gets a wound in his foot, he continues to walk on it because it doesn't hurt, and the sore gets bigger, and can even destroy the foot. Or the patient may use his bare hands to poke the embers in his cooking fire, not aware that he is destroying his hands even though he feels no pain. Fingers do not "drop off," but if there is enough chronic damage, the fingers are eventually destroyed, or may be paralyzed because the diseased nerves no longer control the muscles.

Nowadays, leprosy is no longer so terrifying because we have medicines to destroy the leprosy bacilli, such as Rifampin, Lamprene, and Dapsone. But in the 1950's there was only Dapsone, and the bacillus usually became resistant. We did what we could to treat the sores and paralysis. I experimented briefly with making special shoes to protect the feet, and with tendon transplants to re-attach finger tendons to a different muscle that still worked. But neither Father Columbo nor I had the time or skill it took to develop such treatment on a large scale.

The hostel for children of leprosy patients was another experiment to limit the spread of the disease and at the same time educate a few of the leprosy villagers' kids. Before the World War, Dr. Buker had bought some rice fields and rented them out to farmers, for several ox-cart loads of rice per field per year. The rice of the rent payment fed the hostel students.

Hsai Kyiao, my language teacher, was in charge of this program, and after a couple of years I became aware that he was using some of the hostel rice for his own family. When confronted, he said it was only a little bit and didn't really matter, and after a few days of standoff, I finally asked for his resignation. I tried collecting the rice field rents myself with the help of John Po, the schoolmaster. The farmers had no difficulty in painting us as absentee landlords oppressing the poor villagers, never mind that we used the rice to feed poor children. I will never again get in the position of being a landlord to anyone.

24

Brush War

Red China supported the Burma Communist Party and its armed rebels. Taiwan backed the Kuomintang (KMT) forces—remnants of Chiang Kai Shek's Chinese army that had fled into Burma and now lived off the land, robbing the local villages. Some of the Shan insurgents wanted to secede from Burma. The Red Lahus were a smaller rebel group struggling for their own turf, and then there were assorted bandits called *dacoits* who robbed the truck convoys to Kengtung whenever they could. The Burmese army division stationed at Kengtung had a lot to deal with.

Kengtung's ruler, Sao Sai Long, rarely declared his position publicly in all this political tangle, but I recall one morning when he used me to do it. Once a year, all the villages in the state sent delegations to reaffirm loyalty to him. He held court in a large tent at the festival grounds not far from the hospital. Each village group came singing and bearing, on the shoulders of three or four men, a huge sky rocket made of bamboo. Gunpowder filled the four-inch diameter barrel; they were launched from a frame the size and shape of a ski jump. The villagers cut notches in the narrow bamboo tail to create a warbling sound as each spent rocket fell from the apex of flight.

Fewer patients came to the hospital during the week of celebration, and I took the opportunity to go to the fairgrounds and see the ceremonies. I stood at the edge of the crowd around the Sawbwa's tent, where a group of children were performing a dance in front of the platform where Sao Sai Long sat. He was reading a newspaper, totally ignoring the performers. I felt a hand on my shoulder. A court official informed me, "He wants you to come up." I modestly protested that I could see all right from where I was. "My lord wants to talk to you," said the official, and I followed him to the front of the tent and up the steps.

The Sawbwa put aside his newspaper and became his usual gracious self, spending perhaps five minutes in random small talk. The dancers ended their performance about the time the court steward ushered me back down the steps.

I asked him, "Who are the dancers?"

"Oh, they are students from the Chinese Communist school," he said, and I realized that the Sawbwa had talked with an American during their performance as a way of thumbing his nose at the Communists.

The government kept close track of us and our visitors, especially through the police division known as "Special Branch 2" and army intelligence. Dr. Seagrave had once been arrested for "treason," several years before, when Shan rebels took some of his medical supplies at gunpoint. He had been under house arrest until exonerated in court. For about a year we kept much of our antibiotic stock hidden up in the hospital rafters to avoid a similar situation. I did what I could to maintain neutrality and make medical care available to all.

The battles taking place were real. In May of 1959, the KMT's and the Shan insurgents reportedly made an alliance, and threatened to invade the city. Burmese army and air force troops poured into the area, and were rumored to have captured a main KMT camp near the border. Burmese Army Major Periera, returning from inspecting troops in the north was ambushed. He was the only one in his small convoy to immediately take cover and return fire, and he was killed. Another rumor (from more than one source) said the army later arrested the State Chief of Police and accused him of sending four men to kill Periera.

In 1961, the Shan rebellion really heated up, and few roads were safe to travel. Our thick-walled brick house sheltered a number of our neighbors one night, when Shan rebels came and told the night watchman, "Go home, old man, we are going to shoot here for a while," and proceeded to do so. I remember, during a lull in the shooting, hearing a voice outside in the dark calling softly, *"Sayama! Sayama!"* (the word can mean either nurse or teacher.) We debated whether someone was calling for medical help, or whether a Shan rebel was trying to get us to open the door by speaking Burmese. We finally chose to stay silent.

One afternoon in February 1961, an observation plane spotted an airdrop set-up in the forest, and notified the Burmese fighter squadron at Kengtung. The three-plane patrol found and challenged an unmarked aircraft coming up from Thailand. The intruder fired on the squadron. In the ensuing battle, the Burmese shot down the intruder and lost one of their own, both planes crashing in Thai territory south of us. Another of the Burmese planes returned to Kengtung airstrip with part of its tail shot away, and parked there for the next year. The Voice of America Broadcast that night said that Burmese fighters from Kengtung had fired on an "unarmed plane bringing aid to Chinese refugees." With the Burma Airforce fighter lying by the Kengtung airstrip as evidence that the intruder was armed, I thought VOA was either naive or lying. Taiwan later acknowledged sending the plane, and said that such flights would continue.

To tell its side of the story, the Burma Air Force flew the military attaches of India, Indonesia, United States, and Thailand to the Burmese town of Mong Paliao near the Laotian border. They had recently captured a KMT base there, replete with weapons, ammunition, radios and other supplies, all bearing United States markings. A Rangoon newspaper, *The Nation*, printed a photo of one label originating at the Erie Ordnance Depot, Port Clinton, Ohio. A Burmese news reporter noted that the American officials paid the closest attention to equipment several years old, saying it could all be bought by anyone at any army surplus store. The reporter said the Americans made no comment on the items manufactured within the past year.

Both sides in the fighting grew more surly. The rebels deposited three headless bodies on a lawn downtown one night. Another night, unknown persons abducted our former cook, Ai Hsai, and slit his throat. No one would say why he had been killed. At his family's request I drove out to pick up his body and take it to the cemetery. At the burial service, the Shan Christians sang "Safe in the Arms of Jesus."

I knew what they meant, but I thought how alone he must have felt, with no one to help him in his last hour.

The week before we left Kengtung for our furlough in America, I stood on the Kengtung city wall next to our house, watching Burmese soldiers advance across the dry paddy fields surrounding Kangna village, a half-mile away. Even at that distance, the machine guns and mortars sounded loud enough to be next door. I wondered if my family and I should be taking cover from stray bullets, but I noticed none of our neighbors doing that, so we stood there with them and watched. It was not as though we were strangers to war, after five years in Burma's Shan States. That week I had an eight-year-old boy in the hospital, who had run in front of a machine gun, resulting in two bullet wounds and a compound fracture of his femur, and I had seen many before him.

A quarter of Kangna was now in flames. My neighbor standing beside me said the army was clearing out snipers who had fired at a passing military convoy from the village brewery.

I stood there wondering how I, a pacifist from the age of ten, ever got into a situation like this. I began to realize that sometimes farmers have no defense when their guns are gone. The dilemma is, if they use them, hostility and violence escalate. If they don't use them, they are at the mercy of their rulers. And rulers or rebels, either one, typically have no large supply of mercy or common sense, as history demonstrates, year after year. Life was simpler when I was a kid.

I had been a pacifist all my life, but my experiences in Kengtung, watching the behavior of both the Burmese soldiers and the Shan rebels showed me that when there is no way to defend one's self, those with the guns can do anything they like.

I have never felt any shame about my draft status or my stand against war. I figure my fifteen years overseas gave me as much experience in war as some military doctors have had. War, either pre-emptive or defensive, is a futile response. But the events in Kengtung modified my attitude during the Vietnam years that America was now about to enter.

25

"How Many Souls Did You Save, Doctor?"

Sometimes, I hear the above question aggressively asked when I speak about missions to American audiences.

The answer is, "How many did I save? None. Jesus saves souls. But I hope I sometimes helped him."

American Christians who have never been outside their homeland often assume that the missionary is the star performer on the foreign field. For the pioneer in an area never before touched by the Christian message, that may have been true. There are few more heroic tales that those of William Carey in India, or of Adoniram and Ann Judson in Burma, who labored for seven years before even one person believed their message, and who lived to see thousands accept Christ.

But even then, the goal was to teach people of the country to tell the Gospel story in their own language and cultural view. That is even truer now, when in Burma, for example, there are over one million Christians—Baptist, Roman Catholic, and others.

There are still foreigners who become expert communicators. Among my close colleagues, Paul Clasper and Emily Ballard stand out, each completely fluent in conversational Burmese; Paul and Elaine Lewis in Lahu and Akha, and Don and Janet Schlatter in Lawa. But they are far outnumbered by citizens of the land who have given their whole life and effort to telling their neighbors about Christ.

Sala Ai Pun, headmaster of the Lahu high school at Pangwai, felt called to resign his post and devote the rest of his life to the leprosy villages. (I had nothing to do with this decision; I was as dubious about the idea as anyone else.) The Lahus were aghast, protesting that he was needed at the school and, moreover, he was in his sixties, diabetic and almost blind. He replied that this was what God wanted him to do. He and Yakop (the young man who had visited the villages for years) made an unlikely pair, walking the mountain trails. The younger man limped with a deformed hip and had a heart defect; the elder was too blind to see the single-log bridges clearly that spanned rushing mountain streams. He had to crawl across them on his hands and knees, guided by his wife.

For the next several years Ai Pun visited leprosy patients, giving them the personal attention and spiritual guidance that no one had offered them in twenty years. At first I was concerned about his diabetes, because he never had any refrigeration for his insulin. But for him, the insulin always seemed to work. He and his wife are long gone now, but today most of their eight children are college-educated leaders in the Lahu community.

Sala Yawtha Chang was my next-door neighbor in Kengtung, and a leader of another group of Lahu Christians. I differed with several of his theological and medical beliefs, but I'll never forget that even though he believed that blood once lost is gone forever, he still gave a pint of his own blood three times to help a man I was treating for recurrent internal bleeding.

The pastor of the Shan church at Kangna once came to me with a sore eye. I diagnosed dendritic keratitis, a viral infection that never responds to bacterial antibiotics, and that can destroy the eye. I painted his corneal ulcers with a special iodine compound repeatedly, with eventual success. The Kangna congregation, fifty or a hundred people in the 1960s, now numbers around a thousand. The pastor must have continued to do good work. And the pastor in 2001 is a former hospital night watchman, on whom I performed an emergency appendectomy forty years ago. So even though I am not a prolific preacher, God has enabled me to be instrumental in other ways, as he can with each of us.

Some of God's servants are cultivators, some are harvesters. I perceived my work as preparing the ground. Or, if you prefer, I was the salesman with a foot in the door, offering a product (medical care) to which the householder could relate, until he realized that God had something even greater to offer.

Lois and I were sometimes parental surrogates to some of the nurses whose own families lived hundreds of miles away. Inevitably, these young ladies attracted suitors, and marriages took place. Fascinated by Western wedding customs, and seeking an exotic touch to the ceremony, they would ask me to give the bride away, or Lois to make a wedding cake, or blonde Susie to be one of the flower girls.

Lois was also able to assist others in bringing God's word to those who had never heard it. For about a year, she went weekly with a Shan friend to Wan Mai, a village of new Christians, to teach reading and Bible. When a group of armed insurgents demanded a ride to a village farther on, the Shan girl told them, "We are women, we can't do that." This was apparently an acceptable answer. For a couple more weeks, I went with them, once passing a truckload of young men with rifles sticking out of the vehicle at all angles. Soon after, the Burma army shut down local travel outside the city. Lois often drove the hospital jeep truck to pick up market supplies or to drive a patient home. Even with no overt evangelism, small-town girls saw a woman actually driving a truck, and perhaps caught a vision of what might be possible for them some day.

26

To Thailand

On March 2, 1962, General Ne Win seized power in Burma, deposing U Nu's elected government. In Kengtung, the coup took place quietly. I was making an early morning house call to a family just outside the west city gate. Soldiers at the gate politely told me I must leave the car at the gate, so I walked the remaining short distance. As I returned, a Shan policeman was coming to work on his bicycle. Soldiers sat on the brick arch above the gate, their rifles in their laps. "No work for you, today, man," one told the policeman. "Go home and take a holiday."

Sao Sai Long, the Prince, was in Rangoon at the time and was detained there, under house arrest. Now, more than forty years later, the Army is still in total control of Burma.

As it happened, the following month marked the end of Lois's and my first term in Burma. Missionaries typically stayed about five years and then were rotated back to the States for a year to provide time with family, for speaking and raising funds for the mission, and for updating professional skills.

My relief doctor, Salai Aung Thaik, a young physician from the Asho Chin area of Burma, had arrived in Kengtung two months before we left. He and I worked together in surgery and general medicine, installed a new, more efficient electric generator, and John Po taught Aung Thaik to drive the cantankerous hospital truck. My family and

I had plane reservations in late March for Heho airstrip, where we would get a train to Mandalay and attend annual mission conference in Maymyo.

On Monday, our departure day, Kengtung had too low a cloud ceiling, so the plane returned to Rangoon without landing. All of our household goods were already stored for our return in a year, so we lived out of our suitcases until the next plane. The mother of the pastor of Kangna Church became very ill that night, and I assisted Aung Thaik in removing her acutely inflamed gall bladder. He did a good job.

Two days later, the plane landed uneventfully. I had expected the Customs officers to examine our luggage thoroughly, but was surprised to see their attention focus on my account book and letter files. They found nothing incriminating, and we were allowed to depart.

We spent that night at Kalaw. It was so relaxing, going for a walk at the edge of town with no patients to worry about, no meetings, and no insurgents. I flinched at the sound of a gunshot, then realized that here it only meant someone was hunting. We arrived late at the mission conference in Maymyo, then left for Rangoon by train when it was over.

Since our arrival in Burma five years before, the British Overseas Airways inaugurated jet plane service with its "Whispering Giant", soon to be followed by Pan American's around the world flights, and long ship voyages thereby became a thing of the past. We flew Pan-Am to Bangkok, and onward to Hong Kong, Tokyo, Honolulu, and Los Angeles.

Our three children saw many things for the first time in their memory. Seven-year-old Susie stopped in front of a TV as we entered the hotel lobby in Hong Kong. "What's that? Wait a minute, I want to watch." Later that afternoon, all three were seated on the floor in front of our room TV, eyes fixed on the motionless station logo of a channel that had not yet opened its evening program. Three-year-old John slipped and cracked his head twice during his first experience with a bathtub (in Burma, bathing is dip-and-pour from a large water storage jar.) Elevators were a new phenomenon. So was the ocean. ("Well it's certainly a very *big* ocean," Susan remarked, after the plane had been over the water for ten minutes.)

Lois became acutely ill on the flight from Hong Kong to Tokyo, and showed symptoms of overactive thyroid, confirmed when we stopped off in Denver for a few days. Perhaps it was a stress reaction to the kind of life we had been living for the past year of bridge bombings and restricted travel. Visions of having our free time in America cut short by surgery were allayed when the radiology department assured us that a single drink of radioactive iodine was all she needed.

Lois and I experienced reverse culture shock at the abundance of food in our first American grocery store. Here were whole aisles of superfluous packages of Froot-Loops and Sugar-Frosted Flakes, when most of our neighbors back in Burma had trouble just buying rice. We hadn't seen cottage cheese in five years, and we realized that we could now eat lettuce without fear of amebic dysentery.

We went to family reunions, and spent part of the summer of 1962 as "missionaries in residence" at Green Lake, where both of us had worked on the staff nine years before. Our duties were light; we were to be available for interviews and conversations about missions, and occasionally spoke in public. The rest of the time we were free to enjoy the swimming, children's activities, crafts, and other amenities of the Conference Grounds.

In September, I rejoined the house staff at Denver Presbyterian Hospital as a second-year surgical resident until time to return to Burma the next summer. I found it difficult, after four years of surgery on my own, to be micro-managed in the post-op routine care of other doctors' patients, but the added experience was good for me.

Toward the end of May, we moved to Bridgeport, NY, to stay with Lois's mother until our return-visas for Burma came. By August, we were getting anxious. Lois was six months pregnant, and mission policy at that time was to not travel between seven months gestation and three months after the baby's birth. After many phone calls to the new mission headquarters in Valley Forge, PA, the mission executives suggested we wait for our Burma visas in Bangkok, Thailand, the closest mission field to Burma, and the location of a large modern mission hospital.

While we waited to board Pan-Am's "around-the-world-flight" at New York's Kennedy Field, the Pan-Am ticket agent eyed my pregnant wife and beckoned me aside.

"That your wife?" he asked.

"Yessir."

"You know, this is a very long flight, without medical facilities on board. We can't accept her without a doctor's certificate.

"I'm a doctor; do you have a piece of paper?" I showed him my credentials and wrote, with tongue in cheek, "I am responsible for my wife's pregnancy," and signed it.

The man wasn't happy about it, but it was boarding time, we had three sleepy and fretful children clustered around Lois, and he let us aboard.

We had overnight rest stops in Paris and Beirut. John was sick with strep throat in Paris and most of our time was spent in our hotel room. Lois and I each had about ten minutes outside for a distant view of the Eiffel Tower as our tour of France.

Burma allowed us a 48-hour transit visa. We saw a few friends in Rangoon, and arranged for the ongoing care of our house and stored goods in Kengtung. The next day we arrived at the mission guest house in Bangkok.

The Burma visas never arrived. We were the first returnees to be affected by General Ne Win's new "Burmese Way to Socialism" policy of expelling all citizens of other countries (even some from India who had lived in Burma all their lives.) Within two more years, all missionaries and other expatriates were gone from Burma. We would not see that country again for another thirty-five years. The embarrassing good news was that the Christians in Burma multiplied at twice their former rate, after all the foreigners left.

Even before the final word from Burma's Foreign Office, the Thailand Baptist field secretary, Cecil Carder, told us we might as well occupy our time with Thai language study. He helped us rent a small house in the Saladaeng district of Bangkok, and enroll our kids in school. When the final "No" on our application for a visa came from the Burmese Foreign Office, the Lewises (still in Burma) arranged for shipping our beds, blankets, pots and pans, etc. to Thailand. The shipment never arrived; the export permit reached the customs office on the Burma-Thai border at Tachilek a day after its expiry date, and our possessions evidently just stayed there and rotted.

On October 17, our youngest daughter, Nancy Lynn, was born at Bangkok Christian Hospital. It was modern, by Kengtung standards, but after delivery no nurse checked Lois for bleeding the whole night. In the morning, the American head nurse stopped in to visit and remarked, "If I were you, I'd take the baby home. There's thrush in the nursery."

We lived in a pleasant compound, shared with Finnish and Philippine neighbors, not far from the language school. Beginning at kindergarten-level again in another new language was not a pleasant year. Union Language School, open to all foreigners, was larger and better organized than our study in Burma, and taught us modules of language intended for our particular work, plus general topics and reading and writing Thai.

We would be assigned to the northwest border area of Thailand, among the Karen hill people, who had long desired a hospital of their own. After considering several sites, the mission settled on the town of Mae Sariang, in Mae Hong Son Province, already a center for mission work. Mae Sariang had little access except an airstrip, but paved highway construction would reach it in 1965.

Christmas in 1963 was a bleak day in a rented bungalow on the ocean beach at Cha-am. We had a green felt outline of a Christmas tree taped to the wall, and a small canned ham to celebrate with. That afternoon a telegram from the mission office in Bangkok came, telling us that Immigration had given us a 48-hour notice to leave the country. We cut our brief seaside trip short and returned to Bangkok. Somehow Lois lost her passport during the trip and we spent our allowed 48 hours at the American Embassy and Thai Immigration getting a replacement. But apparently the new passport and visa allowed us all to stay in Thailand two months longer.

Immigration made us physically leave Thailand twice during our year of language study in Bangkok. We could turn around and come right back in, with a new tourist visa, but we did have to leave. Permanent-stay permits were given to few Americans per year, based on USA's equivalent treatment of Thais, and most of these were snapped up by the big trading companies for their employees, or by others willing to pay something under the table. We would exit to Penang, Malaysia, stay a day and return.

Meanwhile, we buckled down to learning Thai language. Our schedule started at 6 a.m. because the kids' carpool had to leave by 7 to be at school by 7:30. Lois and I left at 7:30 and had classes from 8 to 12. We finally found a morning pre-school for four-year-old John in the Montessori system that promised us that he would be able to count to twenty after the first semester. (But he could already do that in four languages in Burma.) The girls got home around three, and Lois and I had to put in two to four hours daily at homework.

The teacher assigned to Lois came to our house to teach her after the baby arrived. Lois was having general discomfort from being in a hot climate without much adult company she could converse with, and was trying to manage four children plus Somphawn, who cooked and went to market, and Ah Nong, who came in to do the laundry and cleaning. At the same time, Lois was struggling with new pronunciations and yet another language. The teacher was new to the job, too, and concluded that Lois would be a slow learner, maybe not worth too much effort. Meanwhile, I was having trouble of another kind, in my class.

27

Gearing up for New Work

Thai is a tonal language. Westerners use tone of voice to indicate a question, or anger or other emotion. But in many oriental languages, using a different tone changes the meaning of the word itself.

As a beginner in Thai language school, I mystified my language teacher and the headmistress by getting the tones all correct from the start. Very politely, the teacher asked me, "Please tell me how you know the tones," thinking perhaps she was on the verge of discovering a new teaching technique. I confessed that I had used the Shan language for four years and that the tones are about the same in both languages. From then on, she expected me to comprehend everything automatically. Another man (who had studied Thai in America) and I were put in an accelerated class. I was a terrible student in vocabulary, not to mention my depression about starting language study all over again.

Having been through this trauma of adjustment once before, Lois and I took interest in watching its symptoms develop in our language school classmates. Most of them were newly arrived in the tropics, with all the attendant problems of delayed baggage, kids without playmates, neighbors they can't understand, high prices of the foods they used to eat back home, etc. One Swedish girl in Lois's class would sit for three or four minutes before mustering a reply to a question, while an American housewife in my section would respond immediately to any questions with an aggressive, "I'm sorry, but I just don't understand it!" We felt pretty hostile ourselves, some days, but at least we knew that things would get better. Moreover, five years' contact with tonal languages really did make learning Thai easier. The teachers were very patient with all of us, and most were experts at this kind of teaching. The head teacher, Achan Noree, had studied at the University of Michigan, where she had to study Mandarin Chinese solely to learn how it feels to be a new student.

After three months I also began to study for the Thai medical exam. Although a license to practice medicine in Thailand is good for life, the exam for foreign graduates is designed to eliminate those with substandard preparation (and those who plan to compete with Thai doctors in the cities.) Twelve of us foreigners took it. The examiners were pleasant but tough. Four of us were medical missionaries from several groups, and compared notes afterward. An examiner asked one of us about diagnosis of vaginal bleeding. After several minutes of discussion, the examiner asked, "Wouldn't you like to do a pregnancy test?" My colleague mentioned several types of test, but the examiner wanted to talk about an old one where patient's urine was injected into toads. If the woman was pregnant, the urine would make the toad produce sperm. "What do toad sperm look like, Doctor?"

He had no clue, but said, "The head is a little broader than that in human sperm."

"No, Doctor," said the examiner, as if the answer should be obvious, "they have two tails."

They asked us about "anchovy paste" sputum (a sign that an amebic liver abscess has ruptured into the lung), about patients with tetanus and anthrax, asked us to name all the types of abdominal hernia. Fortunately, we could take the exam in English in those days. Now both written and oral parts are given in only Thai language.

A month later, the Ministry of Health awarded each of us an impressive document inscribed with a mythical winged Garuda and the declaration that we were licensed to practice modern medicine, class one, according to the laws and regulations of Thailand, dated in the Buddhist year 2507 [A.D.1964].

A medical module in the Union Language School gave me the words for abscesses, contusions, abrasions, various bandages and the common diseases. A sociology module presented vignettes of Thai life, interaction of Thai teenagers teasing siblings, a postman's recollections of his job, a man's sensations while going into allergic shock, etc. (Where westerners "turn blue," Thais insist that they "turn green," I learned.)

When the curriculum turned boring one day, I bought a set of Thai public health regulations from a shop down the street, and laboriously translated them, referring to my Thai-English Dictionary for almost every second word. I learned that the mission's design for the proposed hospital in Mae Sariang did not meet government requirements, and would be inspected before being granted a license. With only a single doctor, ten beds were the maximum allowed. Two doctors on staff may have up to 25 beds. Moreover, hospital rooms must have a certain number of square feet of floor space, and cubic feet of ventilation, per bed. No one in the Baptist mission had known that, and if the larger Presbyterian mission hospitals did, they hadn't bothered to pass the information along.

We changed the hospital design accordingly; the new design provided for two private rooms, plus eight more semi-private beds, a delivery/operating room, scrub room, storage, and bathing/toilet areas. An outpatient building next to it held a small lab, pharmacy, reception/ medical records area, examining room, X-ray, and central supply area. During the construction period, I planned to see patients in the store room under my house. Most rural houses in Thailand are elevated on posts, with area underneath for farm animals, vehicles, hanging laundry, or other needs.

The mission building committee made some amused comments when the first building erected was a small shed labeled "morgue." Actually, we used it for storing building supplies, but if anyone did die, I didn't want the body waiting at my house for the relatives to claim it.

Our next-door neighbors were Bob and Pat Coats, missionaries to the Sgaw Karen people. They had five children about the ages of our own four. One other American family lived across town in Mae Sariang at the New Tribes mission, Don and Janet Schlatter and their five children, working with the Lawa language group.

Bob and Pat eagerly welcomed the new medical work, and oversaw the early preparations while we were still in language school. Lois and I never saw our new home site until we had completed a year of language study and had moved out of Bangkok to continue study in the northern city of Chiangmai.

We moved north at the end of August, 1964. We enjoyed the more laid-back attitude of the Chiangmai Language School. Life in crowded, traffic-jammed metropolitan Bangkok had really been getting us down—I hadn't realized how much until we were free of it. The kids all liked their new school and all found friends nearby so they weren't always begging to be driven to some friend's house several miles away like in Bangkok. Lois did her own cooking again, which pleased both her and her family.

My own spare time was filled with odd jobs connected with the hospital. I ordered medicines and building materials, and wrote instruction manuals for the laboratory and business office. I attended ward rounds at McCormick Hospital three times a week, and spent one afternoon touring Chiangmai University's Suandok Hospital, where some of my patients would go for special treatments. I also studied medical texts and journals several evenings a week to catch up on developments in medicine.

The two older girls were delighted to be in a quieter neighborhood where they could ride their bikes or walk to school. We learned from our North Thailand colleagues where to buy groceries or building materials, where to eat out, which cinemas had a special room with an English sound track, etc.

Moving our family to Mae Sariang, in late October, Lois and I experienced our most hellish ride yet. When the road was dry, a car might average thirty miles per hour, but it had rained heavily the day before. I was glad our experienced neighbor, Bob Coats, was driving and not I. The first 110 miles went well, but then we came to a landslide that filled a rock cut. A bulldozer was working there, and dragged us through the mud and rock with its cable. A few miles farther on, a really massive slide had collapsed the road, and we had to use a temporary detour. The mud was so slick that we slid down the steep grade for about a quarter mile out of control, with a drop-off on one side. And after the construction camp at the bottom of that grade, the road became still worse. We bounced into potholes that showered the windshield with opaque mud, then skidded toward the edge of the road, trying to maintain enough momentum around a curve to not stall on the next upward grade. Teams of bulldozers and earth movers worked some areas in endless-chain fashion. We joined the procession, trying not to bump into the one ahead on the gluey mud, while evading the maw of the one behind us.

Finally, at the top of the steepest grade, we reached the end of construction. For a few ghastly moments we thought we would have to back down the narrow, muddy slope, but Bob got us turned around and drove back a quarter-mile to where the old logging road had turned off. From there we had no trouble until within three miles of Mae Sariang, where even the lowest gear of four-wheel drive couldn't get us out of a deep mudhole. Bob slogged through the mud, carrying a winch cable, and hooked it around a tree fifty feet ahead, and winched us out. We reached Mae Sariang about dark. Pat Coats, bless her heart, had had our heavy furniture shipped ahead by truck and moved into our house so that all we had to do that night was make the beds. But both Lois and I had definite symptoms of stomach ulcer at the end of that trip and vowed we would stay put in Mae Sariang until the new highway came through.

The new house was beautiful, with silky light brown unfinished wood, three bedrooms, and a small school-room/study. The front veranda overlooked the whole valley, with the mountains of the Burma border to the west. We had an inside toilet hooked to a septic tank this time, and town electric lights from the start. We still chose to have "walking water" carried in by a couple of older boys from the Karen student hostel nearby. They earned pocket money by filling our big water jars daily.

Mae Sariang town, a dusty, sleepy *amphur* (county seat), had a population of maybe 5,000 in town, 40,000 in the area. Logging and rice-farming were the main occupations. It had dirt streets, with a few shops and a new three-story bank building downtown, a mile away. Weather was hotter than Kengtung, cooler than Bangkok. Trucks negotiated the one-lane lumber road from Chiangmai with difficulty, and transport of freight further into the boondocks often used a cow train or elephants.

"Mae Sariang Christian Medical Unit" opened for business in the storeroom (about 12 x 15 feet) under our house on October 25, only a day or two after our arrival. It started as a couple of chairs, a wooden exam table, and a shelf of medicines. By the end of November, we had seen 212 people, with a total of 300 visits. Bob or Pat Coats, or the Christian Hostel parents, Thra Ben and Thramu Lahsay, translated

Karen for us, and Lawa patients usually brought one of the Schlatter family with them.

Our first surgery was for a man with a small bladder stone that had dropped into his urethra, blocking his urine. He needed only a little local anesthesia and a small incision. I sent him home in his ox-cart with a catheter in his bladder, and made a house call or two until the catheter could be removed. A very minor procedure, but apparently the first-ever surgery in Mae Sariang, occasioning good word-of-mouth publicity in the town's tea shops. Not all our problems were behind us, however.

28

In Business

By December the road was dry, if not yet paved, and Mae Sariang became a tourist destination of sorts. Missionaries, American consular staff, doctors from Chiangmai, all were curious to see this outpost. Ten-year-old Susie even brought an American pilot home from the airstrip, she and Patsy having dashed down there on their bicycles when they heard a small plane come in one evening. He flew for Air America, bringing "supplies" to classified building sites in northern Thailand. He said he hoped we wouldn't be angry with our daughter, but she had assured him we had a place for him to stay. He was a lawyer from Texas, and entertained our wide-eyed children that evening with stories of flying the jungle.

Christmas was more fun than the previous year alone on the beach. An elderly couple from mission headquarters in Valley Forge were our house guests. The mission gardener even found us a jack pine for a Christmas tree, though he couldn't understand why we wanted it inside the house.

But Christmas Eve brought us a tragedy which showed us how primitive our medical facilities still were. A merchant in town brought one of his truck drivers from a road accident, and I could not stop the arterial bleeding from deep in the muscles of his buttock. I had no surgical equipment yet. He was going into shock in spite of all three of our bottles of artificial plasma, and his boss agreed to take him to

Chiangmai. Not only did his injured employee die in Chiangmai that night, but he himself was killed in a separate road accident on the way home. The merchant's last words to me Christmas Eve had been, "Doctor, my luck just isn't good."

Our own safety appeared a little shaky, two weeks later, coming home from the annual Mission Conference down-country. We took a plane from Bangkok, after having trouble with train reservations. Lois was uneasy with the old DC-3s that Thai Airways used for domestic flights, but everything went well during the first leg of the trip, Bangkok to Prae. We picked up about a dozen missionary kids there, who were returning to boarding school in Chiangmai. Above the mountains, ten minutes north of Prae, the kids began shouting to each other, "Look! The propeller isn't going around!"

Sure enough, the starboard prop was feathered and motionless, with some kind of fluid streaming back from the engine. Young faces shone with excitement as the plane labored onward with the remaining engine, gradually losing altitude. "Gee, wouldn't it be scary if the other one stopped too!" someone squealed. The plane barely cleared the last mountain ridge and made an unscheduled landing at Lampang. Thai Airways dispatched another plane, which also had engine trouble and failed to arrive. All of us, including three Norwegian tourists who were getting more local color than they had bargained for, stayed overnight as guests of the airline in Lampang's new hotel and traveled on, next day, on a third plane.

Even working out of the store room under our house, we averaged more patients than we ever had in Kengtung. Several days I saw as many as thirty-five patients plus making several house calls by bicycle, and most were really sick.

I spent most of one night at the home of a young man who had been illegally fishing with dynamite, after a charge exploded in his hands. I sat on one side of his mat, tending an intravenous line and picking bamboo splinters out of his face, while a native practitioner sat opposite me, blowing air over the patient's chest. Actually, most of the people in the room worked pretty well together; one of the best helpers was a young monk from the local monastery. The patient's fingers were in shreds, and I'd had to tie off the radial artery in his left forearm. The family adamantly refused to take him to Chiangmai, even when a local freight company sent a truck to their door, and would I please come every day and treat him. The trouble was, I couldn't. His home was two or three miles by bicycle, and he really needed almost constant care. I finally compromised by giving the family instructions for nursing care, after his life was out of danger, and saw him every few days. I knew from the start that his right eyesight was gone; the left eye was okay so far. I fought infection, protected him from tetanus, but could do nothing for his surgical repair.

To Mae Sariang's credit, gossip reported that the neighborhood was shocked by the family's attitude. The matriarch admitted to me later that she had refused the hospital because the police would investigate and jail him for stealing dynamite and for illegal fishing.

On a happier note, a pregnant Karen woman came in with pneumonia. Lois attended her premature labor and rapid delivery before I returned from an errand. The mother responded to antibiotic treatment, but was too sick to nurse the child. Lois kept the three-pound girl in our bedroom, using a dresser drawer as a crib, feeding her an ounce of milk every three hours. Two-year-old Nancy was delighted to meet someone smaller than she, and summoned Lois every time the baby stirred. The Catholic priest came later to baptize the baby, something that doesn't often happen in a Baptist missionary's home. I figured it would do the baby no harm, and might do it some good. The baby's aunt and father came to visit every couple of days while the mother recovered from her pneumonia.

We developed a friendship with them even though we spoke no Karen and they knew no Thai. The aunt and the baby's brother came to visit us once and he and John played with John's toy soldiers. Before they left, Lois served them ice water. Neither the boy nor his aunt had ever seen ice before. The boy carried an ice cube in his hand as they walked away down the path. When "Julie" reached three-and-a-half pounds, her aunt took her home.

I delivered another baby for the mother, when I visited Mae Sariang for a month in 1971 and Julie was age six or seven. The last I heard of them, Julie was seventeen and had a job in Chiangmai.

One day, I saw forty-nine patients in the store room and we decided to move the work into the almost-completed out-patient building later that week. One of the early star cases was an eighteen-year-old boy who had been blind for a year. My physical exam suggested that he had a pituitary tumor pressing on the optic nerves. In Thailand, this kind of surgery could only be done in Bangkok. His father felt insecure about taking him to the big city so far away, but Cecil Carder, the mission field secretary, agreed to meet them at the train and look after them during the boy's treatment. The father was one of the few, early on, who expressed interest in Christianity because of the care his son received.

Lois and the other missionary mothers, meanwhile, were looking after our children's schooling. A fourth family had arrived in Mae Sariang, the K's, with the New Tribes Mission. Mr. K had been a barber who "felt the call" when he became a Christian, and went to Bible school. Mrs. K had taught her children the previous year when she and her husband were in language school, but had apparently dropped any subject that didn't interest her children, so they had some catching up to do. Among them, the four families had about fifteen kids, although not all were of school age. Lois taught the lower grades, Pat Coats the older ones, and everybody went once a week to Janet Schlatter for art and music.

The K family headed home after three months, deciding that mission life was not for them. Perhaps a felt need for sacrifice is not a very sustaining motive. I guess they went back to barbering in America. Mr. K said there was more chance to do Christian witness there than in a foreign language, and, considering the time the latter would take, he was probably wise.

The Immigration officials began giving us 48-hour notices again to leave the country. The local officer ill-advisedly announced it to me in front of forty waiting patients, and I guess some of them told him quite plainly what he could do with his notice. Still, it was discouraging to realize that our work could be interrupted, or even ended, at any time on someone's whim. Usually I wrote an appeal, saying I could not treat the sick while traveling back and forth, and that gained me a month or two.

The day after one notice arrived, help came from an unexpected source, as an answer to prayer (or so I believe.) A new Landrover pulled up outside the dispensary, and the Deputy Governor of Mae Hong Son Province informed me that a royal princess was in the car, and wished to see our work. The Princess was a very gracious lady of 35 or 40, who seemed to take a genuine interest in every detail. Her most welcome question was, "And how many doctors do you have?" I replied, "One now, but none after next week," and went on to explain.

I didn't know how much influence she had with the Immigration Service, but I could see that the deputy governor was paying close attention to her every word. At any rate, we didn't have to leave the country any more until we went on home leave.

The hospital building gradually took shape next to the dispensary. We would soon have ten beds and an operating/delivery room, but no nurses. We had two Karen girls with a junior high school level education, plus a young Karen man with a year or two of junior college, who wanted to give up running guns across the border into Burma and settle down. The girls acted as nurse-aides, and one, Naw Tho Po, doubled as record clerk and translator. Another girl, Htu, was Lawa and could translate that language into Thai. A young man, Danny, studied the elementary manuals I had devised in X-ray and lab work, and soon could do a credible chest film, blood count, and blood typing.

These workers were of great help in running an outpatient dispensary but except for occasional student nurses from Chiangmai volunteering a month of service, we had no professional staff. Htu's mother soon demonstrated the urgent need for a hospital with surgical capability.

Htu's mother had written me a letter saying how glad she was that there was finally a doctor in the area to take care of people. She was in her fifth pregnancy, and had come several times for prenatal care, accompanied by a visiting nurse from Australia who was spending her vacation at the New Tribes mission.

A week later, the nurse called me out in the middle of the night. Htu's mother was in labor, couldn't deliver, and a village practitioner had given her an injection of Methergin "to give her uterus strength." Methergin causes very strong uterine contractions, and is given only after a baby is delivered, to treat excessive bleeding. Thai health laws specifically forbid giving it prior to birth. With the baby's head impacted in the too-small pelvis, the uterus was pushing against an immovable object, and finally ruptured, and Htu's mother died of internal bleeding while the nurse held her in her arms. The village medicine man was untrained, and unlicensed to give injections; but he said he had given Methergin "a hundred times, and it had never caused trouble."

The tragedy was my fault as well as his. I had made the error of assuming that a fifth baby, of normal size, would deliver. I should have asked if the previous four were small at birth. I should have measured her pelvis. Had I discovered that it was smaller than average, I could have sent her to Chiangmai to await labor, where surgery was available. I have managed close to one thousand pregnancies since that time and I always, since then, measure the internal dimensions of the pelvis at the first exam, whether it is a first baby or a twelfth. Manual exam is not a precise method, but it is usually enough to predict difficult labor and the possible need for Caesarian section.

Time was getting short; hospital construction would soon be complete. Where would we find nurses?

My parents, Edwin and Emilie, in their early twenties.

Lois   Lois and Keith, February 20, 1953

The mission hospital at Kengtung, restored in 1958
after being bombed in World War II

Open market in Kengtung. Shan woman (bending over) is buying food;
three women behind her are Akha tribal women in typical everyday garb.

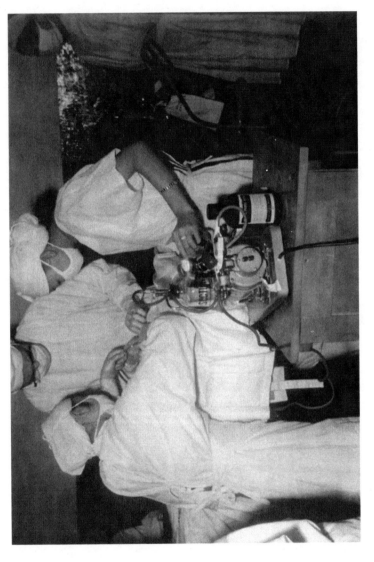

Cleft lip repair, Kengtung, 1961. Nurse Rachel Kyiao administers ether anesthetic (chapter 23). On cold mornings, the charcoal braziers had to be removed before surgery to prevent ether explosion.

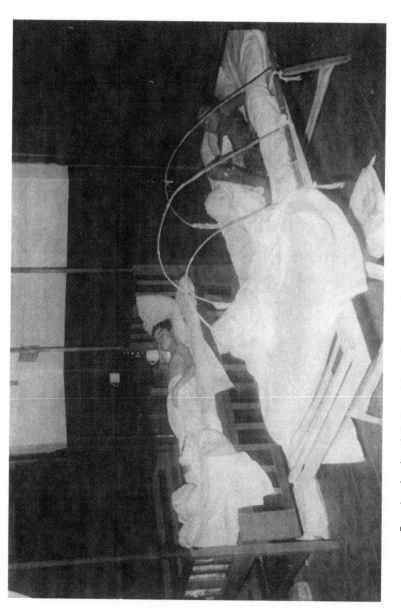

Boy in the back is in a hip spica cast for machine gun wounds of thigh; boy in foreground has body burns after falling into a cooking fire.

Opium Addict's shack, Mae Sariang. Family income less than twenty cents per day.

Mae Sariang Christian Hospital, built 1965

First graduating class of village health workers,
Mae Sariang, 1966, with their medicine bags.

Our family in our front yard, Bangkok, 1964.
l to r: Susan, John, Keith, Patsy, Nancy, Lois.

Mae Sariang team heading for Sa Kaew refugee camp. Back row, Keith, Lois, Rosa Crespo-Harris. Front, Mala, Weena.

Part of Sa Kaew Refugee Camp October, 1979
Shelters for non-hospital area are sheets of plastic on sticks

Hospital Tent #8, Sa Kaew. In foreground, a child searches her mother's hair for head lice. Papers hanging from ceiling wires are patients' medical records.

My prefab doctor's office in Pinehurst, Idaho. 1981–1993.

Memorial to the 91 silver miners lost in Kellogg's Sunshine Mine fire of 1972. The miner is depicted operating a hard-rock jack-leg drill.

Our family at 50th wedding anniversary, Post Falls, Idaho. l to r: John, Pat, Lois, Sue, Keith, Nancy.

New malaria and fever research ward at Kwai River Christian Hospital, Sangklaburi, Thailand, 2004.

Teaching about tuberculosis to group of village health workers, near Myitkyina, Burma, 1998.

Kachin village near Sadon, Burma, 1996. Village elder in foreground was age ninety-six.

Teaching village health at Putao, Burma, 1998.

Village health clinic near Ukarumpa, Papua New Guinea Highlands, 1995.

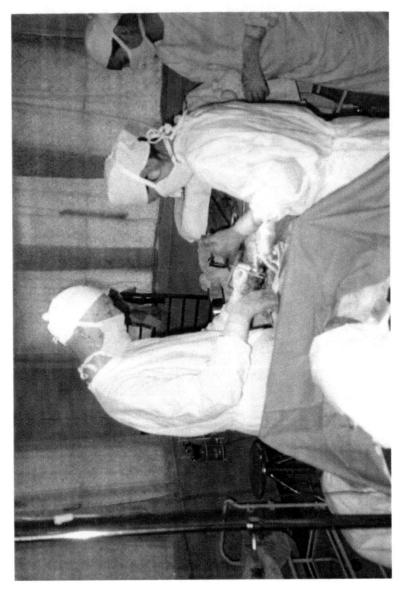

I do a Caesarian section with spinal anesthesia at Kwae River, circa 2002.

29

Mae Sariang Christian Hospital

In May, 1965, the new highway came through. For about a week we and our children hurried through supper and joined our neighbors to watch the tractors and earth movers fill in the gullies and smooth out the ridges, to make a level roadbed a block behind our house. The paving crews were still many miles back, but the roadbed was complete by the following week and the graders moved on northward.

With the increase in traffic came traffic's problems. Within a week an eight-year-old girl died crossing a street. People were not used to looking right and left first. Higher speeds brought out the defects of both the vehicles and the drivers. No one had any concept of maintaining brakes or tires on the buses and trucks that now drove eighty km/hr. No one had any practice with rules of the road at such speeds. The police continued to write up accident reports, but did not patrol the roads to enforce safety. Twenty-year-old drivers might keep to the middle of the road and side-swipe oncoming traffic. Or drive too close to the edge and have an unstable road-shoulder collapse and send their vehicle tumbling down the hillside.

Many more injuries made opening our hospital more urgent. When we admitted the first patient to our new hospital, I feared she would die. She had delivered a premature baby, then had diarrhea and possibly amebic hepatitis. I had no idea what to do for her, and chose medicine by "best guess." We had one nurse and one midwife who covered day and evening shifts, and the patients' families were on their own at night.

We had a bit of drama that week in the missionary families' weekly get-together. Someone prayed that the hospital would soon have some nurses, and the prayer was interrupted by a taxi driver at the door asking where he should leave the nurses' baggage. One of the two arrivals, Orawan, had spent a month with us earlier in the year, and was now only visiting. Her companion Yawaluk, however, became our first full-time graduate nurse-midwife. Another, Gaysala, showed up on the back of a motorcycle two weeks later, looked over the town for three days, and hired on. That same weekend, two nurses appeared from Mae Hong Son, wanting to transfer back home to Mae Sariang. Within three months of opening, we had a full nursing staff, and three or four unskilled applicants each week asking for other work.

With the new road came an influx of middle-class Thais—teachers, government servants, farmers and construction crews—attracted by the climate, the improved transportation and, we hoped, by the medical care now available. Malaria control teams sprayed our houses white with DDT, and mosquito nets were no longer needed.

The Prime Minister's son, General Senga Kittikachorn, Minister for Rural Development, arrived one day in a caravan of Mercedes-Benz and Land Rovers, for a town meeting to hear the needs of the populace. He spent a few minutes touring the hospital, with Thai reporters and TV cameramen in tow. He promised concrete pavement for the town's streets and a permanent bridge over the river. However, he also told me that Americans didn't need visas (true only for one-month tourists), which made me doubt his sources of information.

Another missionary, Esther Greenmun RN, arrived to become director of nursing. The hospital census picked up in September, after planting season was over. People began coming to us from out of town, and we had our first two major surgeries in one week, a ruptured ectopic pregnancy and a Caesarian section. Since these were the first major procedures ever to have been done in Mae Sariang, they caused a stir in the tea houses again. Among those most impressed were the hospital workers who assisted. Most of them had never helped on a real case before, although we had had some dress rehearsals. They performed without any major hitch; we were fortunate to have otherwise healthy young patients with intelligent and cooperative families. Both patients survived.

The Karen churches of the area gave an offering which was used to build a bamboo shelter to temporarily house patients' families, or people needing to stay in town for several days. It had three rooms and a cook-house, relieving our Karen neighbors, who had been feeding a continuous stream of hospital visitors in past months.

Many hill villages, however, had no concept of sending a sick patient to the hospital. Traditionally, the village medicine man always came to the sick one's bed. A man arrived after traveling all day to say that a twelve-year-old boy in his village had had a stomach-ache two weeks ago, treated with hot stones on the abdomen. The family had not let him drink any water, and he had not passed urine in six days, and now had swelling. They had made offerings to the spirits, and had let some blood out of a vein, but nothing had worked, so they would now like to buy him some medicine. I explained the idea of carrying the boy to the hospital on a stretcher made of bamboo poles and a blanket, and the man thought they could do that. I had no way of knowing whether the boy now had an infected burn of the abdomen, a ruptured appendix, or was dying of thirst. I suggested that if he was thirsty, give him water, and I sent a two-day supply of an antibiotic, and some dextrose to mix with the water to give the boy a little temporary nourishment until he could reach the hospital. He never arrived. Perhaps the villagers, in spite of my instructions, thought the medicine was the whole treatment instead of a means of tiding him over until he arrived.

The same messenger said there was a sick woman in the village who had been too weak and dizzy to get up, since having a baby five years ago. He described her as very pale, and not eating much. From past experience, I felt fairly certain she had hemorrhaged after her baby was born and now had severe anemia. Twenty-five cents worth of ferrous sulfate pills should restore her to health within a month or two, but again, I didn't know whether she took them or not.

Problems like this were frequent, and a big town like Mae Sariang was too far and too frightening to many hill people, who had never in their whole lives been more than a few kilometers from home.

Somehow, we had to find a way to induce the hill villages to trust the new hospital.

30

"Medical School in a Week"

The hospital had a governing board by the end of 1965, including several prominent local Karens. Because villagers out in the hills trusted their native medicine men, the board proposed reaching the villagers by offering to train the medicine men.

The student hostel house parents, Thra Benny and Thramu Lahsay, both well-educated Karens from Burma, offered the hostel as a meeting place and themselves as translators. The board sent invitations to villages one or two days' walk from Mae Sariang, suggesting each choose two people to attend a three-day course. Each village would get a free box of medicines, with refills at cost. I chose the contents, mostly simple remedies for fever, diarrhea, pain, malaria, anemia, and so on. We included one or two simple antibiotics.

Eleven villages accepted. For three nights after work I taught people how to use these medicines. Thra Benny translated into Karen, and copied it into simple written Karen, giving the use and dosage of each medicine.

Most of the students had never had more than two or three years of school, and knew nothing of bacteria. I introduced the topic by briefly mentioning familiar dangers in the forest like tigers and snakes. Then I scaled it down to mosquitoes, lice, and other small critters they recognized as nuisances. Finally, I taught about still smaller "germs" that could enter the body and cause some of the diseases they have in

154

their villages. I had the lab tech set up a slide of a drop of swamp water and a few stained specimens. From there, we could discuss how to prevent germs from entering the body, or how to deal with them after they had.

The talks also covered a few simple rules for treating fevers, cough, etc., and when to send a patient to the hospital despite the distance. Some of them asked intelligent questions, and taught me a bit about some of their traditional ways of treatment, especially childbirth. Others just sat there, and we had to hope they would at least do little harm.

In the daytime, I worked in the hospital while others taught sanitation, literacy, and other health topics. By far the most popular was Lois's and Lahsay's session on family planning. The students stayed an hour overtime to ask questions about ovulation, anatomy, and methods of birth control, all new topics to the Karens.

We had problems, especially the first night. Someone had to go round up a student who was still taking a bath at lecture time. One delegate could not read a word, and someone else from that village had to help. One elderly man, whom Benny introduced as "a doctor in his own right," asked my opinion of cases where the wind goes through the arms faster than the blood. Probably his question made sense to him. I tried to answer, but neither of us understood the other's terms of reference.

We hadn't time to explore all the inter-cultural confusion of ideas, but some important points emerged: (1) Don't spread cow dung on burns. (2) Don't withhold fluids in diarrhea or fever patients. (3) Try to limit bleeding after childbirth. Karens encourage bleeding, to get all the "bad blood" out of the womb. I agreed that the clots should be emptied, but showed them how to massage the uterus after birth to get it to contract. That way, blood stayed in the blood vessels, where it is "good blood." (4) We discussed blindness caused by lack of vitamin A. Benny pointed out that several green plants that Karens regard as weeds, are actually high in vitamin A, and could keep the eyes healthy if the weeds were boiled and eaten. (5) We also talked about sources of protein, and about preventing measles epidemics which killed so many children.

Altogether, everyone thought the conference a success. Some talked of another in the fall, inviting Karens from other parts of northern Thailand, and inviting Lawa villagers, with Don Schlatter to translate for them. They talked of a special conference for village midwives. They planned to send medical teams to outlying villages to give immunizations, family planning, and health teaching. All of these eventually happened.

Other organizations offered help. Soon after arriving in Thailand, I became friends with Dr. Ed McDaniel, a Presbyterian missionary obstetrician at Chiangmai's McCormick Hospital. I told him about Depo-Provera, the newly developed shot that prevents ovulation when given every three months. A Baptist layman in top-management at the Upjohn Company had donated free vials to our mission. Upjohn had already completed clinical testing in USA and Mexico, and marketed the drug in many First World countries. Ed transformed family planning in Chiangmai with this new technique, and it later spread to all of Thailand.

At the same time, Church World Service offered intra-uterine devices free to mission hospitals. The IUD became an affordable method of contraception for Third World countries, although problems arose later. Some clinics in India, for example, high-pressured patients to accept them and, without adequate follow-up some of their patients developed serious infections.

For a few months I surveyed all women patients ages fifteen to forty-five, to find out how many children they had had. Among the hill-tribe women nearing the end of child-bearing age, they averaged eight births, of which four had died at some time in childhood. I asked each woman how many more children she wanted. Those with only two often wanted a third one, especially if they already had two boys or two girls. But most of those with three or more would answer, as though I were rather dull, "How many more? Why, I don't want any more!" So much for sociologists who assume that all Asians want many children to support them in old age.

Depo-Provera became popular in Mae Sariang as well as Chiangmai, among both Thais and hill tribes, and some villages hired a bus every three months to bring their women for shots. Spacing babies two years apart improved the health of village women, and helped prevent anemia and under-nutrition. It also lowered maternal and infant death rates. Several times each year, some father would bring us a newborn whose mother had died in childbirth out in the village. With no breast milk available, he might try feeding powdered milk. But a can of powdered milk was so expensive that most families greatly diluted it with too much water, resulting in a badly malnourished baby. Now, with fewer pregnancies, more mothers survived to breast feed their children.

In the 1960s and 70s contraceptives appeared to be the answer to many of the world's problems. Voluntary limits to family size, and slowing of population growth could favorably affect poverty, urban sprawl, deforestation, public education resources, water, and other natural resources, and a host of other world problems. But many minority groups saw family planning only in political terms, suspecting it to be a means of domination by religious or political opponents. One of my friends, a black Baptist leader in USA, told me that family planning will never be accepted by African-Americans, regardless of any supposed economic or health benefits.

But in Thailand, nation-wide family planning reduced the annual population growth rate from 3.5 % to 2% over that next twenty years.

The Karen medical program had many more facets than one local hospital training "barefoot doctors." Musikee and Baw Gaow, villages in Chiangmai province, each had a nurse providing elementary care to surrounding villages. Often, they or we needed to send a patient for more advanced care at one of the Chiangmai hospitals, but most rural Karens feared the big city. The Karen Baptists hired Sally-Amo, a city Karen woman, to look after such patients. She could translate, explain what the doctors proposed to do, and arrange transport home after recovery. The mission provided a financial subsidy to help these patients survive away from home. The Karen Baptist Bible School asked for a medical training course for their student pastors. Villages asked nurses or medics to accompany evangelists and agricultural teams and provide immunizations, treatment of simple illnesses, and health teaching.

I saw the medical program as two halves—we needed direct village contact through medical boxes or traveling medical teams, to establish credibility. And the Karens needed a hospital for more severe illnesses and injuries, where they would feel welcome and could receive the same level of treatment as Thais.

But Lois and I now had less than a year until scheduled home leave in mid-1967. The mission had given no hint that any doctor would take my place when we left. Considering the time needed for language study and licensure, my replacement should already be on the field.

31

Leaving Thailand

Successful as Mae Sariang Christian Hospital was, there were a number of reasons for not returning to Thailand after the one-year home leave that would begin in July, 1967. I tried to present a balanced picture in my February, 1967 annual report to the Mission Board in America:

"The hospital's contact with about 5,000 individual patients during the year illustrates the work's potential for reaching people, if some effective means of spreading the Gospel message had been employed. As yet, only a very few patients have understood our reasons for being here. The large (Buddhist) majority assumes that we are doing all this to earn merit for ourselves, the sooner to reach Nirvana. Some others assume I am a CIA agent. Perhaps one percent have understood our real purpose, and a few have accepted Christ. A larger percentage has perhaps become aware that there is something beyond their Buddhist or Animist experience.

"Aside from spiritual matters, the work has been worthwhile in raising the standard of medical care in Mae Sariang. Our eight-bed hospital is the only place in a fifty-mile radius doing surgery, laboratory or x-ray work. Although the government has a clinic with two doctors, their clientele is not large. The hill villages are still at the mercy of spirit diviners and itinerants who inject plain water for fancy prices …

"We should consider the future of the hospital, and our mission in general, with the present visa difficulties in Thailand. As the Boards no doubt know by now, several thousand compete for the annual quota of 200 permanent visas granted Americans by the Thai government each year. Our own government also has a quota system for foreigners, so we can't really complain. As long as the present crisis in Vietnam lasts, this situation will continue and will worsen. Usually, those who are willing to bribe get the visas; the current rate is said to be five thousand baht ($250 US). Those who do not bribe must leave the country every two months. There is much controversy among individual missionaries whether bribing is necessary to accomplish God's work. I believe the two are not compatible. Too many Thais say that, after all, all religions are about the same, and they can point to missionaries who bribe as an example.

"I myself have applied for a visa for four consecutive years and still have none. If we do not bribe—and I believe we should not—there are several possibilities: (1) That the present political era is not a good time in which to evangelize Thailand by Americans. (2) That the Mission consider using missionaries holding non-US passports for the Thailand field. (3) That our missionaries come prepared to leave the country every two months (with all the attendant effects on work and personal morale), understanding that in time, even this may be impossible.

"Our own reasons for not returning to Thailand next term are related not so much to lack of a visa as to a wish to give our family some roots. I also need to discover whether I may be a more effective Christian and a more effective doctor among those of my own language and customs. While I still have a lifetime commitment to Christ, this is not synonymous with a lifetime commitment to the foreign field.

"Our mission could direct more of its recruiting toward missionaries who will come for one or two terms, and should stop implying that anyone who gives less than a lifetime career to the foreign field is a dropout. It is possible to study a language and establish a working program in a single four or five-year term, as many have demonstrated, myself included (twice) ... Our mission can turn the present-day trend of short-term mission work to advantage by emphasizing the one- or two-term missionary as the rule rather than the exception. Some will still discover a life-long calling on the foreign field. The majority, returning to their home churches without guilt feelings, will be living reminders that mission is everybody's task. This could be the basis for an entirely new outlook on missions in the home churches. The present

[1967] attitude in America is often based on ignorance, distortion, and idealization far removed from the realities of the foreign field. Possibly doors are closing on old methods in order to re-direct our attention to new paths."

The problem of medical staff for the hospital was finally solved through the pool of foreigners expelled from Burma in 1965. Dr. Bina Sawyer, previously at Moulmein Christian Hospital, would take over my job with only a short gap for language study. Peggy Smith, the former director of nursing at Kengtung, would take charge of the nursing staff. I knew both well, and had no fears for the ongoing work.

There were other more personal reasons for our decision to return to the States. Partly, it was burnout. It was great to be a pioneer doctor, to see bizarre diseases and restore health to some who would otherwise surely die. It wasn't so great to be medical superintendent, responsible for construction, maintenance, and labor problems of a hospital. We now had to compete for good nurses with Chiangmai hospitals that offered western wages, and the budget was not so simple anymore. On average, patients paid about 50% of their cost of care, but the poorest Karens, having nothing but their pride, often didn't come at all.

We had been expected to learn four languages in ten years, and we never did get seriously into Karen. A half-drunk official once predicted that I would never get a visa because I had been in Burma and was now too near rebel territory. That raised the specter of a move to another new language area if we returned.

On the professional side, there is a tendency toward stagnation and egotism when there are no professional contacts. I admire young missionaries, but I had noticed that some older missionaries working in isolated areas become set in their methods to the exclusion of anything new, and I didn't care to become one.

The final straw was what happened to our daughters on their way back to boarding school after Easter vacation in 1967. We and the Coatses sometimes hired one of the local taxis to take our kids back to Chiangmai, and it had always gone well. Sue and Pat had to be back earlier for a choir rehearsal this time and, at ages 12 and 10, were the only passengers. The taxi driver hit a cow on the road. No one was hurt, but the radiator was damaged to the point where he had to refill it at every stream or ditch. He finally flagged down another car—several Japanese businessmen—and turned the girls over to them. "I was so naïve," Sue now recalls, "it never occurred to me we could have disappeared without a trace." The men did indeed deliver Sue and Pat to the school but it could have turned out tragically different, and we thought it was time to keep our children closer to home. If we returned for another term, Sue would have to be in high school, six hundred miles away in Bangkok. Many missionary families coped with all this quite well. On the other hand, of all the missionaries sent to the field, about 50% terminated at the end of their first four-year term or earlier.

We had kept a road map of Colorado on the wall for a couple of years, with pins in towns of over 1000 population lacking a doctor. In 1967, however, we received an invitation from Dr. Bob Cordwell, my cousin Dorothy's husband, to take a look at his family practice six-doctor group in Kellogg, Idaho, where they needed a seventh man.

I also received a subpoena from a lawyer in Denver. I was named in a lawsuit for $1.1 million dollars over a baby delivered twelve years earlier by a doctor whom I had assisted as intern. The lawyer in the USA hired a Thai attorney to take a taxi to Mae Sariang and deliver the subpoena by hand.

Meanwhile, my last few months in Mae Sariang turned into quite a trauma practice. Possibly our worst traffic accident was a collision between the Mae Hong Son bus and a loaded gravel truck. The 21-year-old bus driver was hugging the middle of the road, both vehicles were speeding, and sideswiped each other. We received seventeen casualties, all in a bunch. The first load came at top speed and drew up with a screech of brakes. The injured had been piled in the back of the pick-up any old way, without any attendants to cushion them from jolting against the iron sides of the truck bed. One old woman's neck was broken, whether from the accident or the ride to the hospital, I never knew; she died a few moments later. A soldier had been taking his eight-month pregnant wife to deliver her baby in Mae Hong Son; she was killed outright. He was sobbing, trying to comfort his injured one-year-old son, and trying to unload his rifle all at the same time. Our neighbor, Bob Coats, was trying to hold the barrel of the rifle up, since the man wouldn't let go of it. The soldier removed the ammunition clip all right, pulled the trigger to demonstrate, but had forgotten the round in the chamber. I heard the gun go off while I was giving emergency aid to others and thought, he's killed himself. Thanks to Bob, we only had a hole in the ceiling.

We sewed up cuts and X-rayed bones for seven hours, surrounded by a mob of people seeking relatives, or just morbidly curious. I told one lady to come back in three days for a dressing change, and she replied, "I just can't … I'm afraid to get in a car again!"

The bus driver regained consciousness after three hours, and spent the afternoon quietly weeping in his hospital bed.

A Karen patient from far up in the hills had been sick for months, and his friends had finally carried him down toward the highway. On the trail, someone told them about the accident, and they turned around and headed back home with their patient, afraid to trust a car. He never came to see us.

The Thai police apparently did nothing to stop this carnage. Teenagers continued to hot-rod trucks at any speed, and overloaded buses had unrealistic schedules to keep. And the fat traffic police lieutenant with the Panama hat continued to bring me forms to fill out, but never made any arrests until after accidents happened.

A month later, it happened again. Two speeding cars approached each other; one drove on the shoulder, and the side of the highway collapsed. Two dead at the scene, another died on my examining table. The wife of a local business man came looking for her 65-year-old father; I said we had no one of that description. She became hysterical, saying she knew he was in that car. She drove out to the scene and found her father lying in a deep gully. She got some construction men to haul him out with a rope and brought him in. Fractured arm, collar bone, four ribs and pelvis, and a torn bladder too. We stabilized him, sent him to Chiangmai for surgery, and he recovered.

After such major emergencies I felt totally exhausted for about two days, unable to imagine anything but getting some sleep. There were other times when work was lighter and my family and I could sit on our porch after the day's work and just enjoy the quiet evening. Some days, as field medical advisor; I dealt with the health problems of other missionaries. There were plenty of them, both physical and emotional, and even occasionally psychotic. In spare time, I beefed up the hospital's dry-season water supply, helping install a deep-well automatic electric pump up on the hill with pipes to both our house and the hospital water tank. Or planned staffing for the period between our departure in June and Dr. Sawyer's arrival after her licensing exam in September. The trip home looked more attractive with each passing week.

The family and I planned to take a train to Singapore in July, sail via the Suez Canal to Genoa, invest in a VW microbus (cheaper there than in the US), drive through Europe and sail from Rotterdam to New York. We would have to pay the added cost above a straight flight home from our savings, but we could manage it. Lois's mother would make her first trip overseas, to come and see Mae Sariang and travel part way home with us. Three-year-old Nancy had never seen any water craft bigger than a rowboat, and had many questions: Would the ship come to Mae Sariang to get us, or would we have to walk? Would we get off the boat each night to sleep?

May was the busiest month ever at the hospital, with a total of 818 patient visits. Most days had no major emergencies, and the successful patient encounters were very rewarding. A young girl's TB was discovered soon enough for effective treatment. A malnourished child opened his eyes and could see, after treatment with vitamin A.

The hospital finally had a budget item for a Thai evangelist. He stayed at our house for a week or two and then found quarters downtown. Quite personable, Wichai was; I walked over to the Student Hostel one day and was amazed at the dazzling smiles from all the young ladies, till I discovered that he was walking right behind me.

We saw neither our Singapore ship nor the Suez Canal. The Israelis had another war with Egypt that summer and several ships were sunk to block the canal. Instead, we flew Swiss Air to Geneva and on to Genoa, Italy, to pick up our VW van. We toured Italy, Switzerland, Germany, and Holland on $5 per person per day, and then took ship for New York.

32

Idaho

"Welcome home," said the Immigration officer at the dock, as he glanced through our passports and noted our four-year absence.

"You gotta lotta nerve!" shouted the New York taxi driver, complaining about my $1.50 tip, after he had run up the fare by going several miles toward the wrong hotel and had to be turned around.

I had mixed feelings about our arrival in America. Lois, the four children, and I had just landed in Manhattan from the Dutch ship *Statendam*. Now, after collecting our Volkswagen minibus from the dock and heading out of New York City to visit mission headquarters and our eastern relatives, I faced as many unknowns as we had had in going overseas. Would I be able to earn a living on my own, after leaving the mission? None of us had ever seen North Idaho. What would school be like for the kids? Would I get along with my new doctor partners after years of practice on my own? Was I doing the right thing to change jobs? Was I deserting God by resigning from the mission?

We rolled across the early September landscape of mid-America and entered Montana, a new state for all of us. Butte turned out to be a drab hillside mining town where the rain poured down in torrents. After driving forty miles further through rainy darkness, we finally found a motel in the little town of Deer Lodge. Only two hundred more miles to go. Next morning, we paused in Missoula to shop for school clothes, then drove onward through an encouraging green valley, and over Lookout Pass into Idaho.

We knew the main industry in our new home-to-be was mining. Still, we hadn't expected the river to be running opaque gray from rock dust, or the valley bottom to be covered with burned tree stumps. The closer we came to Kellogg, the bleaker the landscape. It didn't look at all like the photos the Clinic business manager had sent us. We almost drove straight on through to Coeur d'Alene, but we turned off the highway at Kellogg and found my cousin's house.

Bob Cordwell was a family practitioner, age about forty-eight, who had practiced in Kellogg for nearly twenty years after serving as a major in the Alaska command in World War II. His wife, Dorothy, was my Uncle Henry's daughter, nine years older than I, who taught piano and organ. Their four children were all high achievers; two still lived at home, the youngest between our oldest two in age. We would be guests in their house until we could find someplace of our own in a boomtown housing shortage.

Kellogg was a mining company town. It had begun eighty years earlier with Noah Kellogg, a prospector from the gold mining towns farther north. He hadn't much money, but a store owner grub-staked him with provisions in exchange for one half of anything he discovered, and he moved over a mountain pass into the valley of the Coeur d'Alene River's South Fork. Prospecting is a lonely life among the pine-covered gulches and mountain slopes. Noah had no company but the jackass that carried his tools and supplies. When the beast wandered off one night, Noah was furious. He finally found the animal high up what is now Wardner Gulch and, as the story goes, picked up a rock to throw at him. It was a remarkably heavy rock, not gold, but showing a gray metallic sheen. The claim he staked in 1885 produced, over the next hundred years, three million tons of zinc, five million tons of lead, and a half-billion troy ounces of silver.

The gold mine towns of the North Fork are only a footnote in history now, but Noah Kellogg's discovery in the valley of the South Fork created a sustained rush of prospectors and entrepreneurs. They established mines for twenty-five miles along the Osburn geologic fault, and the more fortunate soon became millionaires.

The Mullan Trail, a dirt-track military road through the South Fork Valley, ran from the Missouri River headwaters in Montana to the Columbia River farther west. It later became part of U.S. Highway 10, and later still became Interstate 90, connecting Boston to Seattle. The Union Pacific Railroad built an eighty-mile branch line to carry metal and logs out of Shoshone County. The "Silver Valley" became the largest and most prolonged source of silver in the United States.

The Bunker Hill Mine, as Noah Kellogg's discovery was named, became the area's major producer, with shafts extending downward more than a mile underground, and with 150 miles of tunnels. At first a tramway of buckets carried the ore from Wardner Gulch over the hill to the mill and railroad in the river valley. In 1929, the company drilled the two-mile-long Kellogg Tunnel at valley floor level to carry trains of ore cars and the 300-man work crew in and out more efficiently. The mine, mill, lead/silver smelter, zinc refinery, and sulfuric acid plant all provided jobs for three thousand men at the Bunker Hill Co. alone. The Sunshine, Crescent, Galena, Lucky Friday, and a host of smaller mines provided well over a thousand more jobs. The logging industry's lumber and mine timbers created three hundred more in the forests and sawmills. An able-bodied man could always find work.

Arguments over the merits of mining versus logging fueled many a Friday night barroom fight in the Silver Valley. As the most junior member of the doctors' partnership, it was my lot to take Friday night call in the hospital emergency room, the busiest night of the week, Friday being payday. I remember my gratitude to Whitey's Bar, one of the noisiest, when they padded all the iron pillars in the main barroom with shag carpet. I thought it reduced my suturing tasks by maybe a third.

Miners are an independent lot, passing their skills from generation to generation. Some migrate restlessly from one town to another across the American West—Montana to Idaho to Nevada—seeking a new life, or maybe fleeing life in the last town. The strong bond between a miner and his partner, on whom his life depends from moment to moment, can never be fully appreciated by those of us who work above-ground. They have a cordial disrespect for management, and a wariness of newcomers that may take a year to overcome. But when trust is established, it endures.

The six doctors of the Clinic were almost the entire medical staff of West Shoshone Hospital in Kellogg. We met them and their wives at a reception, from elderly Dr. Staley, to Dr. Panke who was ten years younger than I and had joined the practice earlier that same year. I would work on salary the first year and then, if agreeable to everyone, I would become a full partner. Dr. Scott, the surgeon in the group, was on the Idaho Board of Medical Examiners, and arranged a temporary Idaho license till my permanent one arrived.

There was, however, that pending lawsuit in Colorado, for which I had been served papers in Thailand. It involved a woman who, at age 40+, had delivered a mentally retarded only-child. I was just the intern on duty that night, but the attorney named the hospital and me as co-defendants, along with the estate of the now-deceased doctor. He got around the statute of limitations by claiming the doctor fraudulently concealed information.

Her attorney claimed the obstetrician told her she would deliver at midnight, and I had "negligently" not moved her to the delivery room until 7 a.m. Moreover, I had "fled the country to escape responsibility" for my part in the doctor's use of forceps and his giving "rectal gas" (the attorney's innovative term for an enema of liquid ether and paraldehyde in mineral oil, a now obsolete means of sedation.)

I had no malpractice insurance—never needed any in Asia—but Denver Presbyterian Hospital stood behind its house staff in such matters. Our former pastor in Denver, Henry Croes, helped me find a defense attorney. The attorney's first advice was to just stay out of Colorado for the rest of my life, but banishment from my favorite state didn't set well with me. He then advised me to offer "no contest," since he imagined that missionaries were penniless and therefore could escape payment. I thought I had better go there in person.

Lois and I and Nancy, who was too young to be in school, took the train to Denver. We stayed with cousins Dave and Marjorie Mosconi, learned the case was continued until next year, and returned to Kellogg. I appeared again at the courthouse in June of 1968, only to learn that the plaintiff had settled out of court for $2,000—which the hospital paid—and I was out only my attorney's initial $200 fee plus my travel costs.

I began work in the partnership in November, 1967. Dr. Staley, the senior partner, at first took a dim view of my missionary experience and suggested that I be limited to insurance physicals and mining company pre-employment exams. That ended amiably when he dropped into the operating room one day. I had the patient's hand open, doing carpal tunnel surgery, and had laid out the anatomy as precisely as a picture in a textbook. He approved, and never mentioned routine physicals again.

Except for the five doctors at East Shoshone Hospital, ten miles up the valley, we were the only medical care closer than Coeur-d'Alene, forty miles west, or Spokane, thirty miles beyond that. We referred a few cases to specialists in those cities, but most of us delivered babies, did Caesarean sections, appendectomies, tonsillectomies and the like, and managed simple fractures. Dr. Scott, an excellent surgeon, covered the more complicated cases.

Altogether it was a busy practice, but much more relaxing than being alone and on call every night. Idahoans were congenial; miners and lumberjacks spoke language a lot easier to learn than the Karen tongue, and we liked having our children at home. The schools were good. Lois soon took a job as school nurse, got home about the same time our kids did, and could take the same day off that I had.

We didn't find a house of our own for a month. Finally, someone tipped us to a newly built four-apartment complex, and we rented a two bedroom unit for the six of us. Sue had to sleep on the couch, but at least we had our own place.

After six months in the Legion Avenue apartment, we found a four-bedroom furnished house to rent. The owner, Delia Schwab and her husband Charlie, lived in the same block and owned the house next door as well. Charlie was president of the Bunker Hill mining/smelting complex. After a year, Delia said we would have to buy the house or move. We could have it for $10,000, and for an extra thousand, she would include all the furniture. The latter included a forty year old refrigerator (still running now, thirty-eight years later), stove, freezer, washer & dryer as well as beds, chairs and tables. We took the offer, and went to the bank to arrange a loan. The bank told us no.

"What?"

"Sorry. No."

"But we have ten thousand dollars in savings certificates in your own bank for collateral."

"But you have no established credit record."

And that was that, to them. I saw no use arguing. We pulled our savings account, used it to pay cash for the house, and took our future business to another bank.

Schools were within walking distance. The older three children entered fourth, sixth, and eighth grades. Nancy was just under the age for acceptance in kindergarten, so Lois used her teaching experience from Mae Sariang to home-school her, the first year.

Kellogg was a rough mining town, using language often far different from that of a mission station. John's teacher, Barbara Fisher, added a dry comment to his first report card: "John has learned a great deal in fourth grade, much of it not in the classroom." Susan picked up friends as easily in Kellogg as she had in Burma and Thailand. Our kids proved to be intelligent, coped well with classroom discipline, and earned good grades. They also had enough street-smarts to not appear to be "brains"."

Finding a church was more difficult. The Valley had almost as many churches as it had bars, and we visited several. The Cordwells were Lutheran, and that was okay, but just not us, somehow. We attended a Baptist church in Pinehurst, six miles west, for a while. The church elders were cautious about this from the first. Finally, after some hemming and hawing, it developed that they didn't want to accept a family with "communist ties," by which they meant my father's recent presidency of the National Council of Churches.

Okay-y … we thought that kind of odd, but we looked further.

While I was away for a week promoting missions, Lois found a small American Baptist church in Osburn, seven miles east. We joined them, and they became our church family.

33

Pacifism Revisited

As ex-patriates overseas, Lois and I had exercised our absentee ballots in USA, but we had not had enough language skills to follow local Burmese politics closely. I remember the dismay I felt that so few of my hospital staff had voted in the 1960 Burmese national election. I never knew if local politicians had harrassed them, or whether they just assumed that U Nu would stay in power, so why vote?

Closer to home, in the late 1960s with the Vietnam war in full swing, I reconsidered my political stand. I found I was less of a pacifist than I had been a decade earlier.

The turning point, I think, had been the Shan insurgent activity in Kengtung in 1961 and 62. Intellectually, I sympathized with the Shan desire for state autonomy within Burma. As a pacifist, I didn't like the idea of the Burmese soldiers beating up civilians, as I had occasionally witnessed, nor the report of Shans tossing a grenade into a truck full of army wives and children. But I understood it as a part of war.

When the insurgents started mistreating their fellow Shans, that was different. They took away all the guns in the villages, then they fined anyone who owned a dog, and the villagers were finally defenseless. The Shans especially targeted teachers, as "collaborators with the Burma government." Men were summoned to their own execution in the night. Their only bargaining point was whether to go quietly, in which case the murderers would spare their wives and children.

Thieves or anyone with a grudge could act unopposed, I realized. And though I still believed that war was not a good answer, I saw that when the weapons are gone, people are physically defenseless.

As the Vietnam War heated up, I saw the same process again. Vietnam partitioned North and South into communist and non-communist areas respectively. A million citizens allegedly migrated from north to south (and some in reverse direction.) But the Communist Viet Cong preached that all should be "liberated," and they behaved much as the Shan insurgents had toward their own people. It's true that the South Vietnamese government and American troops sometimes behaved like the Burmese military, but they appeared to me to usually support at least some degree of freedom of choice.

And so, after I came back from Asia and lived in Idaho, I often sided against the Vietnam War protesters. At the Baptist Convention in Seattle in 1969, some delegates organized a public demonstration for peace in Vietnam. I asked if everybody could carry a sign. Sure, the leader said, everyone has the right to free speech. So I made a sign that said,

> "Peace will come to Southeast Asia when North Vietnam
> gets out of South Vietnam and Cambodia and Laos"

and I got into the line of marchers circulating around the Seattle Center grounds. Nobody read the signs, they just saw the marchers. Two soldiers walking by criticized me for marching. I asked them, "Hey, have you even read my sign?" They looked at it a moment and said, "Oh. Okay," and walked off. A fellow peace marcher then amiably peered over to see what I had written, recoiled with a shocked expletive, and moved away from me as far as he could get.

And that's kind of where I stood, for the next couple of decades, gaining a prickly reputation during twelve years of serving on the General Board of the American Baptist Churches/USA. I and another Board member, an Air Force colonel, were the Board's token hawks in those years. It took me a long while to see that there was a third alternative to being a hawk or a dove.

34

Medicine in a Mining Town

Small town medical practice is largely the same across the nation, yet each town has its special health features. In Kellogg, the first day of deer and elk hunting season usually brings in a couple of gunshot casualties. Some eager novices seem unable to tell an antlered four-legged beast from an orange-clad hunter or a child waiting at a school bus stop.

A chain saw injures an occasional logger when it hits a knot, bucks, and leaves a series of parallel gashes in his thigh.

But hard rock miners have the most danger. My partners arranged for mine safety supervisors to take me underground to orient me to my patients' work environment. I found it a totally new and fascinating experience. John Parker, our neighbor down the street, took me to the "dry house" one morning, fitted me with safety boots, hard hat, and battery-powered head lamp. We climbed aboard the train of steel-roofed man-cars with the rest of the day-shift men and rode two miles into the mountain through the dark, damp, echoing Kellogg Tunnel. The miners were friendly; some of them had already been my patients, and were glad to have me learn about their work. We arrived at the hoist room, where the ten-feet diameter electric-powered drum and its mile-long cable lowered the "skip" (elevator) down the slanting shaft. The bottom level of the mine was nearly a mile below us, and about 1,500 feet below sea level. We got off at one of the intermediate stops that are two hundred vertical feet apart. The air was warm and humid, the floor muddy. We walked to the end of a horizontal tunnel where a pair of miners were drilling a pattern of holes eight feet into the rock with a compressed air jack-leg drill. The noise level was about the same as up close to a jack hammer. Near the end of their shift, they would fill the holes with blasting powder, wire them to detonators, and after they left, the blast would be fired, extending the tunnel eight more feet. The next shift would "muck out" the broken rock, shore up the tunnel roof, and drill another eight feet. The same process in the mineral veins would produce silver-lead-zinc-bearing ore (galena and sphalerite.) Mechanically powered scoops dumped the rock down an auxiliary shaft to mine cars waiting on the next level below. It was dangerous work. Several times a year, falling rock would engulf or trap miners, sending them to the hospital or the mortuary. There is little leeway for error or inattention.

Above-ground again, I toured the concentrator, following the ore-bearing rock through the crushing and separating stages and onward to the smelter, a mile away. The smelter workers had a different set of hazards—burns from the large crucibles of molten lead or silver, and toxic absorption of lead dust. The latter danger could even extend to the miner's family unless he was always careful to shower and change clothes before driving the family car home. Lead-poisoning could cause stomach cramps, muscle pains and weakness, anemia, and various nerve defects including seizures and coma. It rarely got that bad because the safety program required periodic blood tests for every smelter worker. We doctors would treat anyone whose blood lead level reached 60 micrograms per 100 ml. Treatment in those days used "EDTA" (calcium versenate), which usually cleared it out of the system. Smoking or eating on the job was forbidden outside the cafeteria, to minimize oral lead intake.

The thousand employees at the zinc plant had their own illnesses. Here the zinc ore powder was smelted and cast into slabs and refined electrolytically into 99.99 % pure zinc. Entry-level workers had the endless job of stripping sixty-pound plates of zinc off the electrodes, in a vast room with row upon row of vats of sulfuric acid. Back injuries from the constant lifting, and nosebleeds from the fumes were common. Some men worked at the zinc plant all their lives and rose to positions of responsibility. Others quit after a few days, or even on their first day, which was why Doctors' Clinic had so many new employment physicals each day.

Mining was a tradition in many Silver Valley families, some with three or four generations of miners. The men underground were the elite. The pay was good; a "gypo" (contract) miner could earn $60,000 a year in the 1970's. Although Kellogg High School produced many graduates who went on to college and higher, many others saw no point in studying hard. Play football in school and then walk into a well-paying job on graduation. Marry your high school sweetheart and soon have your own honkin' big pickup truck with a gun rack in the back window.

It worked fine, if your back didn't give out under the hundred-pound loads a miner has to lift. Once your back went, the only way to survive was education. The state rehab program provided courses in auto repair and welding. Workman's compensation laws provided pensions to the truly disabled, if they could prove the injury was job-related. The doctor rated the disability according to a precise table of range-of-motion measurements published by the State Industrial Board. Naturally, there was pressure on the doctor from injured workers with a family to support. Such exams required the mind-set of a major-league baseball umpire, to separate truly injured from malingerer. There is no way to precisely measure back pain, although a number of tests gave us a pretty good idea.

All this was in addition to the chest colds, earaches, stomach ulcers, cancer, heart attacks and diagnostic problems. And accidents.

I found auto accidents to be as frequent in the USA as they were on the roads around Mae Sariang, in that era before seatbelt laws. I could usually expect three waves of Emergency Room patients on a Friday night. The first was at about 11:30 PM, when Dad got home from working swing shift and Mom decided that little Johnny's croup or stomach ache really shouldn't wait until morning. The second wave arrived after 2 AM, when the bars closed.

The third wave arrived by ambulance at three or four in the morning, when the high school crowd came back from their keg parties up the river. The Coeur d'Alene River's North Fork wound sixty miles through the hills of Shoshone County. The river road was icy in winter, and life's end in summer, for some of the kids speeding around its curves with a few beers under their belts. At least in the emergency room, those who were dead-at-the-scene had already been screened out, and there was equipment ready at hand to repair the torn faces and broken bones of the survivors.

The worst were the accidents I came upon while driving, where first aid really wasn't enough during the long wait for the ambulance. A mother yelled, "*Do* something!" while her eighteen-year-old quickly bled to death on the pavement, his arm torn off at the shoulder. Or there was the motorcyclist with his knee twisted 270 degrees, and the kneecap lying on the other side of the road. Or the flaming wreck on I-90 where the father was fatally burned while rescuing his three children. His wife never got out and was only an outline of gray ash in the car when the fire truck arrived. Reckless driving is not a funny topic. Ever.

But by far the greatest disaster was to begin on May 2, 1972, in my fifth year of practice in Kellogg.

35

United By Tragedy

Tuesday, May 2, 1972, started out calmly for the Sunshine Mining Co. at Big Creek, three miles east of Kellogg. The stockholders were in their annual meeting in Coeur d'Alene, forty miles away. At the time, Sunshine produced the most primary (new) silver of any mine in America, eight million ounces a year. A thousand-ounce pure silver ingot is about the size of a loaf of bread.

I had toured the Sunshine a year or two earlier, going along with a shift boss to the lowest level of the mine while he inspected a malfunctioning air conditioner. That required descent in the Jewell Shaft from the mine portal to the 3,700 foot level, followed by travel a mile over to Number Ten Shaft, and then further descent 2,200 feet to where a crew was developing a new level at the shaft's bottom. The natural temperature there at the 6,000-foot level exceeded 110 degrees Fahrenheit, and sweat dripped off my elbows in a steady stream. I had felt a long way from the earth's surface.

On May 2, I was working as usual in the Clinic. Around noon, we began to get rumors of a fire in the Sunshine Mine. No one knew the extent, but the general feeling was, a hard-rock mine had little to catch fire. We doctors conferred about emergency measures for burns and possible other trauma, and continued our regular work while we waited for the first casualties.

Only two had arrived at the hospital by the time I made rounds that evening. One of them I knew personally—Byron Schultz, a cage (elevator) operator at the Number Ten Shaft—who came in with smoke inhalation and probable carbon monoxide poisoning. Later newspaper accounts said that, after the initial evacuation of miners, the first rescue crew to descend that afternoon had found Byron attempting to make his way out through thick smoke on the 3100 level. He was near collapse, and a member of the rescue team gave him his own oxygen apparatus to breathe, but soon collapsed himself. When Byron had revived enough to talk, he told the rescue team, "They're all dead back there!" The team's monoxide detector showed dangerously high levels. Beginning to suffer toxic symptoms themselves, they returned to the surface. Byron recovered, and got credit for saving several miners that day by staying at his post until the smoke drove him out. About sixty of the day shift escaped, warned by a pungent skunk-like odor dumped into the underground ventilation system to signal urgently *Get out NOW!* More than ninety others, including some who had re-entered the mine on rescue missions, were still underground.

A patient of mine arrived at the hospital just at the end of evening rounds. Hysterically she wept, "I just know my husband's dead!" There was little to offer her, beyond a listening ear and a sedative. I privately thought she might be right.

The following day was my day off, and with some hesitation I phoned the mine office, asking if a doctor could be of any help. The switchboard operator gave me an emphatic yes.

I drove over, parked outside the gate, and identified myself to the police officer keeping the crowd at bay outside. He allowed me in; I passed through a gathering of family members anxiously awaiting news of husbands, sons, and fathers, and I climbed the stairs to the mine operations office. Miners, company officials and rescue crew members crowded around a large table covered with ventilation diagrams, cold coffee cups, and half-eaten sandwiches. They had been working for hours to get some safe ventilation scheme to clear the mine's air without feeding the fire, which appeared to be centered on the 3,400 level.

I had worked in Kellogg five years now; my patients included some of the state police, telephone operators, miners and mine officials. I could go freely about the mine premises, but not into the mine entrance where the air was still poisonous. My first job was to attend a mine security man who had breathed some monoxide, but who recovered without trouble. Otherwise there was nothing to do but stay available if needed.

I wandered among the crowd outside, who were being attended by Red Cross and local volunteers serving free soup, sandwiches, and coffee. Someone set up rows of cots in a warehouse where people could rest during their vigil.

About noon that day, an electric donkey engine towing a string of flat-bed mine cars brought out six more bodies wrapped in blankets. I examined them briefly, identified them, officially pronounced them dead, and sent them to a temporary morgue in Kellogg. One was the husband of my anxious patient of the night before.

My mind focused on incidental features, to keep me from the enormity of the tragedy unfoldng around me. First aid texts often describe monoxide victims as having a cherry-red color. Actually, their color resembled sunburn, quite unexpected in men who work underground, away from the sun. None had any burns or significant wounds. Because the rescue crews could carry only a two-hour supply of oxygen with them, and most of that was used in getting to and from the work area, the recovery of these six bodies had required the full efforts of two rescue crews. Thereafter, all attention was directed toward finding possible survivors. Bodies encountered underground were left there till later, which led to other problems in the very moist, warm, underground air.

The six bodies went by car into Kellogg. Members of the miners' families in the waiting crowd made it plain that they would break the head of any news reporter outside the gate who tried to take pictures.

A chance question about medical help underground got me an invitation to join the next mine rescue class. Curious about the training, I joined about thirty-five miners for an eight-hour condensed course in fire control, gas monitoring, and oxygen apparatus. We learned to dismantle, check, and reassemble each valve and tube in our McCaa oxygen packs, working as carefully as a sky-diver packing his own parachute. We donned the apparatus and climbed in tandem up a steep slope to get used to the forty-two pound weight on our backs and the sweat fogging the inside of our masks.

As it turned out, they needed little medical aid underground, but my classmates spent many hours searching for survivors, and later recovering bodies and fighting fire. I still have my Bureau of Mines certificate qualifying me for underground rescue (long obsolete, 35 years later) but I never had any work to do underground.

I stayed part of the night. Nothing on paper can reproduce the feeling of standing in the crowd, that chilly night, watching the air-exhaust stack on the hill above us propelling a constant billowing stream of smoke into the air, or speculating what the sudden turning of the big wheel atop the mine shaft structure might mean.

Help now poured in from everywhere. Experienced mine rescue teams from British Columbia, Montana, and Utah joined the local crews. Improved oxygen equipment, lighter in weight, arrived by air from England. It allowed three hours underground, and used liquid oxygen that cooled the wearer. All sorts of ingenious devices arrived: body cooling equipment for survivors, closed-circuit TV adapted to underground use, even a special two-man capsule that could be lowered down an air shaft which became the prototype of capsules used in later mine disasters.

High school students volunteered for the Red Cross, or for church-operated baby sitting services. Food poured in. A soft drink company set up a free fountain. All the stores and bars collected funds for the families. The Bean Association of America, whatever that was, donated six tons of beans. One offers what one has.

KWAL, the local radio station, stayed on the air all night with news bulletins and music. The disk-jockey told Burley Herrin, a local minister volunteering at the mine, "No matter what kind of music I play, people call up and complain. What should I do?"

"Play two westerns and a hymn," the minister advised.

The eleven-man county medical society set up a schedule to put a doctor at the mine around the clock, and the nurses did the same. We did mine rescue physical exams, assembled supplies for when survivors might need them, treated headaches and sunburn in the crowd. We stood by while family members told grandpa, "who has a bad heart," that his son was among the dead.

Two morticians volunteered for mine rescue training in order to go underground and stabilize the bodies until there was time to bring them out. Unfortunately, both men had been working without sleep for so long that they could not pass the necessary physical exam.

The only group apparently pursuing its own agenda was the national news media. The reporters had a tendency to draw a conclusion first, then seek evidence to support it. Perhaps their editors back home had told them to look for tear-jerker pictures, or statements against mine management. Anyway, it wasn't long before the crowd excluded them from the premises. They then took station across the road from the mine entrance and interviewed people coming out and going in. Occasionally the police allowed a pool photographer in to picture some special event like the governor's tour.

Day after day went by, with no apparent progress. Number Ten Hoist had heavy smoke damage to be cleaned from its switches and motor before rescuers could even travel down to the working areas of the mine. Mine timbers and the plastic material of the ventilation pipes themselves continued to feed the fire. The rescue teams sealed off bulkheads, only to have smoke appear from another of the many connecting tunnels. Underground power lines broke; underground power substations overheated. Smoke and moisture fouled electric contacts in the hoist machinery and had to be cleaned and dried. Many of the trapped men worked in the newest part of the mine, served only by Number Ten hoist.

There were other escape routes, but I tried to imagine climbing twenty stories up a ladder even in good air. If I had done so, I would only have reached the next level above, and would have to repeat that ten more times to reach the 3700-foot level that connected to the Jewel Shaft a mile away. The mine rescue leaders were correct in refusing to risk rescuers' lives until they had dependable hoist machinery and communications.

The one surge of joy and hope came after a week of vigil, when rescuers found two miners alive on 4800 level. Word came that they were in good shape and had refused stretchers. They came up one at a time through a ventilation shaft, riding the new rescue capsule to the 3700 level. Everyone gathered around the tunnel entrance, jostling for a better view, the two miners' families in front. Even the less emotional among us joined the cheering as Ron Flory and Tom Wilkerson, both bearded, smiling, and hanging on to their lunch pails, walked out under their own power, though supported by rescuers. Their wives joined them in the ambulances as they drove off to the hospital for an overnight checkup. They owed their survival to the air ventilation shaft and a door protecting them from the monoxide.

Every wife still missing a husband then believed her man would come out alive. But when Number Ten Hoist finally came back in operation, on the tenth day, rescue crews found only dead men, finally accounting for all the missing. The coroner determined that all had died that first day, some still sitting around their coffee cups at lunch break, perhaps not even aware of their danger. Carbon monoxide is colorless and odorless, and often precedes the smell of smoke.

I saved a chart from the mine rescue class, showing the effects of carbon monoxide at various concentrations and time exposures. One tenth of one percent concentration causes unconsciousness if breathed for an hour. Three days after the fire's outbreak, the 3700 foot level still measured 4.5% monoxide, enough to cause almost instant death without a respirator.

That fire changed mine safety rules nation-wide. The Safety Department no longer locks up self-rescue masks to prevent pilfering. (Miners had found that they made great inhalators while spray-painting rooms at home.) Everyone going underground now carries a canteen-sized rescue breather on his belt, allowing him an hour of breathing in an emergency. Oxygen equipment at the hoistrooms allows operators to stay at their posts until all miners are out.

Most miners won't work anywhere but underground. Many of the fire-fighters we examined in the weeks following the disaster had the same surnames as those who had died. Next to the Big Creek exit of Interstate 90, a larger-than-life statue of a hard rock miner and his drill, by sculptor Ken Lonn, memorializes those 91 men lost that day.

Sunshine Mine remained closed for several years. It meant the loss of more than 300 jobs, and nearly one hundred families without a bread-winner. The Sunshine Fire contributed to an era of economic decline affecting the Silver Valley for years afterward.

36

Going Solo

The six of us partners in Doctors' Clinic—Dr. Staley had died in 1968—mostly saw eye to eye in medical matters. We each took fifty hours per year of accredited medical education courses. We opened a Coronary Intensive Care unit at the hospital and most of us took ACLS (advanced cardiac life support) training, updating as new standards developed over the years. We held mock disaster drills. We often consulted each other, or specialists in Coeur d'Alene, Spokane, or Seattle about problems in diagnosis or treatment. I trusted my partners' professional judgment.

But we disagreed constantly on how to conduct the business side of the practice.

All my adult life, I had lived on a low income budget: *Use it up, wear it out; make it do, or do without.* On the mission field, all missionaries were paid the same basic salary plus a cost of living adjustment for location and number of children. My first-year monthly salary in Kellogg was a magnificent increase, and starting the second year, as a full partner, it averaged considerably higher than that, although cost of buying into the partnership reduced it.

My partners, however, had higher financial goals and, since we shared equally in the net proceeds, every time I charged a low-income patient less than they did, it decreased every partner's income. The office manager explained to me that each Christmas, the partners chose one family of deserving poor and canceled their bill. Others were expected to pay in full. Some were taken to small claims court.

I objected to charging a doctor's office visit when the patient only saw the nurse, for a repeat shot of "pen-and-strep". They countered that, since they "took responsibility," the charge should be for a doctor's visit even when he wasn't in the building. Two or three of them objected to my not always charging a full fee for brief follow-up visits. I objected when they charged a full "new patient exam" after merely glancing at a new patient's red throat.

There were other differences. Most of them had the office staff fill up every appointment slot in advance, and then tried to "work in" the emergencies that inevitably arrive each day. Sometimes they even scheduled extra patients every hour, saying that probably some wouldn't show up. All this meant that patients sat in the waiting room for as much as three hours after their appointment time. The patients complained, but my partners accepted this as the way things were. I thought that was not only insensitive but ridiculous. Since there would be walk-ins every day, leave some time open for them. It was better public relations, would probably eventually increase our practice, and would reduce the pressure on us. They said it would be less efficient. I thought that reducing the time spent at morning coffee break would boost efficiency better.

During my visit with Dr. Seagrave, ten years earlier, he had given me some good advice. "Your patients come first," he said, "your workers come second; then you."

At the Clinic one day, an office worker told me that this day was one clerk's twenty-fifth anniversary of working for the Clinic. I congratulated the lady, and later learned I was the only doctor who had even mentioned it to her.

We partners had a business meeting once a month where financial report, performance, and other matters were discussed. Every decision was voted on, but the vote usually found me in the minority. I realized that I was letting frustration and anger get control of me, and for two months after they voted to have the front office decide all charges, I went along with it.

But finally I thought, *I can manage a medical practice better than this.* I considered it for several months, talked with my wife about it, and with my father while on walks when he came for a visit (Mother had died in 1968.) I went for long walks alone and prayed about it. *Can I do this by myself? Have I the business sense to manage my office all alone? Am I just being self-centered and petulant?*

At the end of May, 1974, after seven years at Doctors Clinic, I gave my two months notice in writing. This surprised them, I think, but I pointed out the advantages. Separating our financial accounts helped give them the higher income they expected. And if we agreed to still take turns covering night call for each other, we would all still have the same amount of time off.

I would work out of Wallace, fulfilling the contract requirement to not compete within ten miles of the Clinic. All of us already had staff privileges in both the Kellogg hospital and the one near Wallace. Their buy-out of my share of the practice (which I had paid into for the first several years) and my share of receipts for patients seen up to the date of my departure would fund my start-up costs, until my own patient fees started coming in.

In late July, my family and I took a two-week vacation, driving to the Canadian Rockies. That was about the time Richard Nixon resigned from the Presidency. When we came back, I moved into office space owned by Harry Magnuson in Wallace, a remodeled grocery store with 4,000 square feet of floor space at a busy corner downtown. A few of my Kellogg patients followed me, but most of my practice came from the east end of the county. Lois couldn't work for me and still be at home when the kids got out of school, so she kept her job as school nurse. I thought assembling a staff would be my biggest problem, but it turned out that I had developed a reputation.

I was reading a medical journal in my new office, waiting for patients, when one of the Clinic employees paid me a visit. "I want to work for you," she said. Karen Hoskins was in her early twenties, very personable and intelligent. She had worked in the Clinic business office and as an X-ray tech. She took over the front desk after giving her notice at the Clinic.

Others soon came. Ann Wilson had experience in both laboratory and X-ray. Sharon Connors had worked as my office nurse at the Clinic a couple of years earlier. My first year in Kellogg, I had given the graduation address at her LPN class. "You called us ladies, and no one during nursing school ever had," she said as the reason she came. Mary Ann Hull had been a nursing instructor of that LPN class, and she also applied. Pam Sagdal, another RN, and Judy Haug, a lab technician, worked later on, to fill in when others were absent. I had a full staff at any one time: secretary, technician, and nurse. Later, when office collections were sometimes a problem, Alice Wolfinger and Martha Herrin came to work part time on the phone, reminding patients who had delinquent accounts, but I never took a patient to court. A part time cleaning crew did the floors each night and shoveled the sidewalks in winter.

The office staff got along well together, and the Wallace doctors accepted my presence, though we remained only acquaintances. I met the rent and the payroll and other expenses each month (with the help of residual income from my time as a Clinic partner), and I put the Wallace fees back into the expenses until my accounts were in the black. At the end of 1974, after 5 months in solo practice, I had recovered nearly all my expenses, both capital and operating. In January, 1975, I took home a small paycheck from net profits, and for the whole of 1975, only a little less than that of my partnership years.

I didn't worry about occasional gaps in the appointment schedule. I used those times to catch up on new developments from my medical journals. I continued night call schedule at the Kellogg Hospital, and delivered babies at both hospitals until one occasion when labor patients appeared at both places at the same time. That gave me an anxious night, and a quick trip between hospitals. After that, I accepted baby deliveries only in Kellogg, a one-mile trip from my home instead of ten.

After two years, Karen asked for a conference. "It's time for me to move on. I'll have to give you notice; I'm moving to Missoula, Montana," she said. "But I'll send my Mom to work in my place; she'll take care of the office."

"Wait a minute," I said, "what does Mom know about a medical office?" Not much, Karen admitted, but she had worked as postmaster in Page (population about 200). "And I'll coach her," she assured me.

I was sorry to see her leave. The patients all thought she was great. Ann Hoskins, Karen's mother, was as nervous as I about the front-office switch. She and Karen and I laugh about it now, but Ann could never stand the sight of blood, and one of our patients that first day had an injured hand he wanted to show her. "No, no, let's wait for the doctor

Keith Dahlberg

to unwrap it!" she said. But her daughter was right; Ann was every bit as good a secretary-receptionist as Karen had been.

I am proud of my Wallace office staff. One moved on to become the CEO of Missoula General Hospital. Another became chairman of the Idaho Democratic Party. One went on to work for more than twenty-five more years as county social worker, helping low income families get access to medical care. Still another managed her own visiting nurse company. Another now works as a lab and x-ray technician. And one became one of the first woman hard rock miners, at the Lucky Friday Mine in Mullan, repairing diesel engines underground.

37

Serving on the Mission Board

After I had worked four or five years as a family doctor in northern Idaho, the American Baptist Churches Committee on World Hunger invited me to join them, because of my experience with malnutrition in Southeast Asia. Many committee members, political types or social activists, felt the committee's job was to "raise consciousness" about the starving. Others thought that was certainly important in well-fed America, but the churches should be doing more than that. I did too, after one politically correct lady savaged a male committee member for bringing an apple to an evening session. "I can't *believe*," she hissed, "that anyone would be so insensitive as to bring *snacks* into a committee meeting on *world hunger!*"

The man kept on chewing. "This apple is all the dinner I had tonight," he said.

Although the Hunger Committee didn't get much done, my experience there and overseas got me nominated to the ABC/USA General Board in 1972. This two-hundred-member congress decides policy for the 1½ million-member American Baptist Churches (a.k.a. Northern Baptists.) The membership committee assigned one-fourth of us to International Ministries, to oversee missions in about fifteen foreign countries.

American Baptists on average hold more liberal views than the much larger Southern Baptist group, and have more diversity; many of their 6,000 churches in America are Afro-American, Hispanic, Asian, or mixed. The Board meets for three days twice a year, usually near Philadelphia, or in whatever city the biennial convention is held.

The Board recognized new missionary appointments and new retirees, received on-going reports of mission work overseas, and supervised the work of headquarters staff at Valley Forge. Congo, Haiti, Nicaragua, Burma, India, and Thailand were among our largest fields, with smaller endeavors in other countries in Europe, Asia and Latin America. The present number of Baptists resulting from efforts in all these foreign lands, during 150 years, is now double the number of American Baptists in the USA.

I found that many Board members considered me a backwoods Idaho redneck, while many of the Idaho and Washington churches I represented thought me overly liberal for showing interest in any concerns outside the local church. I myself was skeptical of deciding theological or social issues by majority vote. Making resolutions was a big thing to many of the Board members, on subjects ranging from boycotting African chromium ore to deciding the will of God.

I remember the Board members in heated debate one afternoon about assigning blame to victims of AIDS. Some conservative members saw no problem. Others were shocked that the pejorative word "blame" even arose, especially for children or for recepients of blood transfusions. I stood up and addressed the chair:

"You can can call it whatever you like," I said, "but there are consequences to what people do."

The room erupted in hostile argument, exactly what I had wished to halt or bypass in order to redirect our discussion to useful remedies.

I kept track of the mission in Thailand from my position on the Board. Bina Sawyer was still the only doctor in Mae Sariang Hospital. The work was expanding, both in hospital census and in outreach to the hill villages. At about this time, the Australian Baptists and Swedish Baptists began working with us in Thailand, and had new plans for the work. The Swedes wanted to increase the hospital to twenty-five or more beds, but this would need at least two doctors. The surgeon they had planned to send had decided not to come, although several Swedish families, including two nurses, did arrive.

Bina and I knew each other; she had been a pediatrics resident at Syracuse when I was a senior medical student. We had both been members of the same church in Syracuse, and we both had worked as doctors in Burma. But she had no surgical experience, and the operating room was barely used. Besides that, the hospital at Mae Sariang had reached a size where two doctors really were needed.

I felt fulfilled practicing medicine in America, but I missed the exotic diseases and scenery of Southeast Asia. Restlessness probably played a part too, and guilt at having an easy life in the USA when there was still so much need in the Third World. Lois was less enthusiastic about returning to Thailand, but agreeable. Our older three children were in colleges away from home; Nancy was in junior high school. I began talks with the Mission Board's candidate secretary about going back to Thailand.

Yes, they did accept previous missionaries within ten years of leaving the field, and I still met that criterion, barely. They required professional psychologic testing to screen out those with mid-life crises or other problems. I could certainly agree with that, after seeing several missionaries with nervous breakdowns overseas. We agreed to pursue matters further.

My fourteen-year-old daughter was shocked. "You're going to see a *shrink?*"

"Yes," I said, "both your Mom and me."

"I'm involved in this too. How come nobody asks *me* to see the Mission Shrink?"

"I'll find out," I said.

"Well, we've only done that in one other case," was the answer, "but yes. If she's interested, we'll include her."

So the three of us flew to Berkeley, California, to a counseling office that did occasional work for the mission. All three of us had filled out psychological tests and personality inventories at home, and took more tests at their office. Much of it questioned our reasons for wanting to leave Kellogg. I couldn't honestly think of any, except distaste for winter weather.

We discovered that I had a personality half-way between a leader and a follower, good for understanding other people's points of view. Dr. De Graf had a comment for Lois. "Mrs. Dahlberg, I notice that every time I ask you a question, you turn to look at your husband." I almost made a comment, and then thought, Oops! Wait for her to answer. I needed some consciousness-raising, myself.

189

The doctor learned that we planned to take three months of Thai language review in Chiangmai, and that Nancy would go to school there first before starting high school in Bangkok. He had a suggestion: study language in Bangkok, and enter Nancy in International School there from the first, so she would make friends before moving into the missionary kids' hostel. She would have enough insecurity to cope with in any case, he said. We agreed that sounded wise; Lois resolved to express her own opinions more readily, and I agreed to listen more, instead of firing off suggestions first. Other than such comments, the team gave us a good rating of mental health, and the mission accepted us again, to leave for Thailand in August of that year, 1977.

I gave my patients and office staff notice. An accountant would oversee bill collections, tax payments, and medical record transfers.

Our oldest daughter, Susan, had graduated from Whitman College in Walla Walla, and had found that her bachelor's degree in sociology/anthropology would get her no jobs without taking graduate work. She had become friends with the Kellogg hospital's respiratory therapist, Barbara Boye; had worked for her for the past year, and found she liked it. Now Sue decided to become a nurse, and enrolled at North Idaho College in Coeur d'Alene. She would live in our house and commute.

Pat was entering her senior year of nursing school at Pacific Lutheran in Tacoma. John would be a sophomore at Texas Christian. They were both used to living away from home. Nancy would go to Thailand with us.

Being an employee of the mission meant resigning from their board of directors. After four years of debating "resolutions," this requirement didn't upset me too much. I was re-commissioned as a missionary at the convention in San Diego.

We traveled to Tacoma, pulling a U-Haul trailer carrying Patsy's furniture, got her settled at Pacific Lutheran, and departed via Sea-Tac for Bangkok, with rest stops at Honolulu and Guam.

Realizing that age fourteen is a difficult time to uproot one's life, Lois and I had planned the trip overseas in easy stages, with interesting things to do at the stopovers. Our Honolulu hotel room on the seventh floor overlooked Waikiki Beach a block or two away. "How do you like this view, Nancy?" I asked, as we stood on the balcony.

In a low voice she said, "I feel like jumping over the railing."

38

Thailand in 1977

I was aghast, not to mention alarmed. *How big a mistake have I made?* I thought, as we moved back into the hotel room. I did not have a restful night.

It wasn't until many years later that I understood Nancy's reaction. She was expressing grief at having had to say goodbye to all her friends, her home, and all the surroundings with which she had been familiar, and she was now facing the totally unknown. She had only her parents to take with her, and they were responsible for all this. She had been only four when we had left Thailand previously; now she was fourteen.

Next morning, Nancy seemed her usual self, eager to see the sights of Oahu. We rented a car for the day, saw pineapple plantations and a visitors' center show introducing tourists to Hawaiian culture. She seemed to have regained her good spirits as we reboarded our plane that evening. Guam was not as interesting; an environmental spill had made the beach unswimmable, we felt jet-lagged, and the scenery was much like Thailand.

Our friend, Cecil Carder, met us at Bangkok's airport with his family, including his daughter Jeanette, about Nancy's age. Bangkok appeared even more crowded and traffic-jammed than when we had left ten years before. The mission had rented an apartment for us on the corner of Sathorn and Saladaeng. We did our own cooking and

191

cleaning, scrubbing the dust and soot off the hardwood floors every Saturday.

Language school was at the other end of Saladaeng Road, a few minutes walk each morning. Lois studied reading and writing Thai; I studied mostly medical Thai and elementary sociology. Rosa, the new Puerto Rican nurse-midwife assigned to Mae Sariang, had an apartment in the same building with us. She was just beginning language study, and would stay in Bangkok for a year. Fluent in both Spanish and English from childhood—her mother was from North Dakota—beginning Thai in her twenties sometimes put a strain on her temper, but she later proved to be a great help at the hospital.

Nancy quickly adapted to International School, joining the drama group in the production *Harvey* and taking weekly ballet lessons in Thai. She relearned enough Thai language to navigate Bangkok's bus system on her own, no small feat.

I discovered that, besides running the hospital at Mae Sariang, Bina Sawyer and I were responsible for keeping the other mission hospital alive at Sangklaburi. Kwai River Christian Hospital had no doctor at that time, and the staff had shrunk to three nurses: two Australian and one Karen. Until they could find a permanent doctor, one of us had to spend a few days there every three months, fulfilling the minimum requirements to keep the hospital's license valid. Reaching Sangklaburi in those days took a half-day bus trip to Kanchanaburi, the provincial capital, and then another day by boat up the Kwai River. I think each of us made the trip two or three times, until Dr. Phil McDaniel became full-time doctor there. He changed it from a small clinic to a center for Burma refugee work and study of tropical fevers over the next two decades.

I realized that Thailand's border country was still unsettled, that first trip, when no transportation had met us at the boat, and three of us carried our bags two kilometers to the hospital. As we crossed a small bridge over a ravine, someone said, "The Governor's coming." Here came an official with four stars on each shoulder, walking in a hollow square of about ten soldiers holding their automatic weapons at the ready. He eyed us foreigners loaded with baggage, stopped and inquired in English, "Where are you going?"

I looked at all the weapons and replied gravely, "We are going to the hospital."

He said, "Ah, yes," and moved on. He had helicoptered into this outpost of his province on a show-the-flag tour for the day.

Kwai River Hospital didn't really demand much attention in those days. A few patients came to the sleepy one-building facility; the nurses visited a few more by boat or motorbike. Five years later, it would change dramatically, but that's a later story.

After three months review of Thai language, Lois, Nancy and I took the train north to Chiangmai. It was almost Christmas, and we bought a four-foot-tall potted Australian pine to take out to Mae Sariang as our Christmas tree.

Our house of fourteen years ago had burned to the ground one morning, several years earlier. We would stay in the Coats's old house next door—they were no longer stationed in Mae Sariang. Bina had a house down the hill, across the street from the hospital.

The old hospital disappointed us at first sight. Instead of the light brown oil originally used on its walls, cheaper ordinary earth-oil had attracted all the wind-blown dirt and soot of a decade. The window screens and floors needed scrubbing. It gave us something to occupy our minds those first weeks.

After Christmas vacation, we planned to put Nancy on the bus to Chiangmai, where other missionaries would pick her up and accompany all the kids down to Bangkok. She developed intractable vomiting that morning; we canceled the bus, and our day's work, and drove her to Chiangmai. I should add that Nancy did well at the student hostel thereafter and developed close friendships that have lasted life-long. In her junior year at International High School in Bangkok she was elected school president ("I gave the shortest campaign speech," she modestly explained) and became producer of the drama group's road tour of Thailand during her last year. She came home for vacations; Lois (and sometimes I) visited her at least twice a year in Bangkok.

Another good feature of working for the American Baptists was that they paid for one field visit for each child in the USA, at some time during their college years. Patsy came out at the end of her senior year to get a taste of Third World nursing. She and Lois spent part of November and December of 1978 at Nancy's hostel in Bangkok, to give the house parents a work-break. We had two of our children in

Mae Sariang for Christmas that year, and Sue and John each came out to Thailand for a visit later.

I quickly became accustomed to rural Asian medicine again. One day a woman arrived bleeding, reportedly three months pregnant. There was something in her uterus all right, but it didn't feel like a baby. I couldn't get hold of it, though it appeared unattached to anything. When it finally came out, it was a baby's head—nothing more—and appeared to be about five months size. Under further questioning, she revised her story. The baby had miscarried at home, feet first, and then stuck. She pulled as hard as she could, with obvious results. She had kept calm, told her husband she was having bloody diarrhea and was going to ride the bus to the hospital (an hour's journey.) I was able to assure her that the baby would not have survived in any case.

The hospital staff still conducted "medical box conferences" for villagers who lived far from the hospital, and this time they held one for village midwives, conducted in Karen language by our head nurse, Christabelle. It lasted a week, and covered hygiene, nutrition, and elementary modern obstetrics. Lois was honorary diploma-passer and one of the speech makers at graduation. The other speaker was a dignified Karen woman from the hills, who spoke about her experiences delivering babies when she was young. Some of the women at the conference were totally without formal education, to the point where an experienced older woman would team with a younger girl, who could read the medicine labels and take notes. They watched several deliveries in the hospital, including one baby needing resuscitation for cord around the neck. Even female anatomy was new to them; they were accustomed to working with their hands under the patient's skirt without seeing the birth canal.

One midwife confided to the teacher that she thought the new birth control pills were really great. She never used to get any sleep; someone was always calling her to go deliver a baby. Now she often slept a whole night through.

Two months after returning to Mae Sariang, Lois and I celebrated our silver wedding anniversary. We felt far from home, thinking about how to celebrate. The occasion called for more than going downtown for a bowl of noodles. We resolved to hold open house for the whole neighborhood. We borrowed dishes from the church, bought out the town market supply of the cakes and sweets with which Thais celebrate.

We brewed Kool-Aid for the kids, and a cauldron of strong tea with four cans of sweetened condensed milk in it for the grown-ups. Almost a hundred people came, crowding our living room and spreading over onto the kitchen floor. The Karen pastor led a brief prayer meeting, the hostel students sang, and the food vanished as if into a vacuum cleaner. But we mainly remember the winged ants. One night a year they come out to fly in great clouds around any light source, and this turned out to be their night. Guests sitting directly under lights were busy recovering large wiggling ants from down their necks, but otherwise the evening was a success. The guests thought twenty-five years of marriage was a rather odd number to celebrate; Asians celebrate anniversaries in cycles of twelve years. But one of the nurses explained the concept of silver anniversary to some, and the rest probably thought we had to celebrate 25 because we weren't in Mae Sariang on the 24th year.

1978 and 79 saw the replacement of the old out-patient clinic building with a new structure behind it, with examining rooms, nurses' station, additional toilets, and a new laboratory and X-ray space (with walls of concrete instead of X-ray-transparent wood.) This was the first phase of the Swedish Baptist expansion. My reaction to supervising the construction for a year was "never again!" At the ribbon-cutting ceremony, the chairman of the hospital board, with tongue in cheek, acknowledged, "Dr. Dahlberg's continual arguing got the job done right."

The Thailand Baptist Missionary Fellowship now had grown to a coalition of the American, Australian, and Swedish Baptist missionaries, with a few co-workers from Great Britain and Germany. Mae Sariang was the focus of most of the Swedish work, and we had two Swedish nurses, plus a couple of families who worked with translation and evangelism among the Pwo Karens, a different dialect and culture from the predominant Sgaw Karen group. The Swedes were subsidized by their government, which had become heavily involved in social progress in the Third World. A Swedish Baptist mission executive had big plans for Mae Sariang Hospital.

He saw no reason why we should not aim to provide Western medical treatment to the whole Mae Sariang district, which by now had a population around 80,000. Twenty-five beds, forty beds, whatever it took; Sweden could pay for it. I was for keeping the mission hospital as a pilot project to stimulate growth of the Thai government program, foreseeing the phase-out of the mission medical work when the government system became more effective in rural areas.

Having just finished one new building construction, I didn't look forward to still more, with ever-expanding patient loads. But within a year, the whole thrust of Christian medical mission work in Thailand changed direction.

39

The Darkest Side of War

In 1979, Communist Viet Nam invaded Communist Cambodia, where Pol Pot had set up his Khmer Rouge government. The Khmer Rouge are said to have executed between one and two million of their own citizens during Pol Pot's doctrinaire rule. During rainy season, the mud kept the two armies apart. But in late October, the Vietnamese tanks could move across the land again, pinning the Khmer Rouge army against the Thai border. Many Thais feared that the Vietnamese tank columns would continue into Thailand.

Each army tried to deny food to the other, and so each side destroyed crops wherever they found them. Hundreds of thousands of Cambodian refugees, mixed with fleeing Khmer Rouge soldiers, were caught in the hill forests of southwestern Cambodia. They had no food except leaves on the trees, and no protection from malaria and other forest diseases. As the Vietnamese army drew closer, a half-million or more sick and starving human beings fled across the border into Thailand.

There was nowhere to put them. The daily newspapers carried pictures of dying children and mass burials. Thirty-thousand refugees flooded across the border in one day, near the border town of Aranya Prathet, and were vulnerable to the mortar shells of the pursuing Vietnamese. The Thai army assembled dozens of buses to move the refugees away from the border, and set up the first of many camps by clearing a field near the town of Sa Kaew.

Up in Mae Sariang 500 miles to the northwest, I wrote to our former neighbors Bob and Pat Coats who now worked at mission headquarters in Bangkok:

We understand that some 91,000 have come across the border from Cambodia this month, that a great many need medical help, and medical workers are swamped. We try to look at this realistically and not let our emotions run away with us. But the thought persists that here we are, in our slack season, seeing patients for only 3 to 5 hours a day, when there is this shortage of medical help down on the border. We could spare doctor for a month or so if you can use us. We don't know if this is God's will or not, but thought we would make the offer and see what he does with it.

A telegram asked us to come as soon as possible. Lois and I were in the first group to go, along with Rosa Crespo-Harris, Mala (a Karen nurse) and Weena, a Karen nurse-aide. We drove to Chiangmai next day and took the overnight train to Bangkok, where Bob and Pat Coats met us, fed us breakfast (and had thoughtfully invited our daughter Nancy from the school hostel.) They explained that we would be on loan to CAMA Services, the relief arm of the Christian and Missionary Alliance Church. We would work at the Sa Kaew camp, three hours drive east of Bangkok, where the Red Cross was setting up a tent hospital. CAMA had a permanent medical team coming from Holland, but they wouldn't arrive for two weeks. Rescue workers said thousands more refugees were scattered about the border area, many of them too weak to walk. The camp had existed for four days when we arrived, and of the 30,000 refugees, 1,200 of them were in the make-shift camp hospital. Some ill Communist soldiers were among them, but those strong enough to fight were still across the border in Cambodia. Sa Kaew was far enough back from the border to make hot pursuit by the Vietnamese unlikely.

Our driver turned off the highway and stopped at a Thai Army checkpoint, where a Red Cross worker gave us ID cards. My first impressions were of a sea of mud, surrounded by barbed wire. Thousands of make-shift lean-tos—blue plastic sheets supported by a few sticks—crowded the fields. The refugees all wore clothing a uniform charcoal shade of black, with purple-checkered head cloths. Our first problem was to navigate the deep mud. We picked our way from rock to tree root; at one point, Lois had to reach elbow-deep into the mud to retrieve a shoe. The hospital area was on slightly higher, more solid ground.

The refugees were deathly afraid of the Khmer Rouge among them, and we had no way of telling who was who. We just treated them all as the severely ill humans they were. We didn't even have a translator for the first two or three days.

That first day was chaos. We were put to work immediately on arrival, I with another new doctor, Lois over in a large tent full of orphan children, and we lost track of the other team members. None of us knew where things were, or even what was available. Each of us scrounged through the supply tents to find whatever might be useful. At dusk, another truck convoy arrived, bearing yet more starved, feverish, even unconscious people with meager bundles of cook pots or other small possessions. Some made no move to get down from the truck, and workers clambered up to pass them down to those of us waiting on the ground. Another worker and I struggled to carry a comatose man on a piece of box-cardboard over to the perimeter fence and pass him through the barbwire to others inside.

Severe starvation resembles being isolated in a blizzard. First you burn the firewood to keep warm. When the firewood is gone, you break up the furniture, and finally the walls of the house itself, to ward off death. Many of these people had lived off nothing but their own body tissues for weeks, and had arms and legs scarcely bigger around than their skin-covered bones. They had lost all fat and most of their muscle, to fuel the remaining small spark of life. Even the proteins to make digestive juices were gone.

We had to be very careful not to overload their digestive tracts those first few days. We started with clear broth, with a little rice and vegetables added. Some couldn't even handle that, and quietly died after reaching the camp. After a day or two, we added protein gruel, "Kaset food" made by Kasetsart University in Bangkok. Weena carried a pail of it back and forth, ladling out a cup twice a day to each of our ward's hundred and fifty patients. Later still, rice and curry came from a central kitchen for all 30,000 in the camp. Different volunteer groups managed each of the dozen or so tent-wards; we cooperated with each other, but we were too fatigued to socialize much.

We treated malaria, diarrhea, pneumonia, parasitic worms, anemia, and nutritional deficiencies. That first day, we had nothing to clean patients with, nor any change of clothing for those who had soiled themselves. Each morning when we came to work, those who had died in the night were left outside the tent, rolled up in their bamboo mats. We took the dead to the penetrating stench of the morgue tent at the far edge of the hospital area, to await burial in mass graves by Buddhist monks who had volunteered their service.

Those first few days, silence reigned in the hospital tents except for coughing. Not even a baby crying. Everyone lay there on mats, too weak to move. I remember how, during the first week, they gradually began to talk and even smile and walk around as they grew stronger. In particular I remember two men, an amputee and a blind man, who often walked together, the cripple on his crutches, holding a guide-stick for his blind friend to grasp and follow.

Daily bus-loads of volunteers swarmed out from Bangkok to respond to the need. Leaders of Bangkok society mingled with students, digging ditches, feeding patients, acting as go-fers. My daughter Nancy and some of her schoolmates used a holiday to come help. One elderly European man, with whom I could only converse in Thai, adopted an old Cambodian who was too weak to lift a spoon by himself, and stayed with him night and day till the old man died.

Bob Jono, a CAMA supervisor about half my age, saw to the medical team's needs. He found us a Khmer man who spoke Thai, and a Khmer girl who had returned from her home in New Zealand to help her fellow Cambodians, despite her terror that the Khmer Rouge would murder her. Jono and his crew also made sure that a hot meal awaited us back at our house in town each night. The camp had a security curfew, not even medics were allowed to stay after dark, except for a single team to keep watch over the whole thousand-bed hospital from six p,m. until eight a.m. Jono and I had to stay after the rest of the team left, for staff meeting at the Red Cross tent, where the day's problems were worked out. I got back to town each night about 7:30 p.m. after a thirteen-hour day, ate supper, and fell into bed.

The second week was a little better. Fewer died, and many were obviously recovering. A lab technician appeared from somewhere, and set up a blood transfusion service. He split every pint in two; even a half pint is enough to help someone with a hematocrit of only six. By mutual consent, the medical teams refused interviews unless the reporter could show his receipt for donating blood.

Lois and I had even taken our turn on the all-night hospital crew. There isn't much you can do for a thousand patients, most of whom you've never seen before. The four of us (another nurse, Ruth Jones, and Tan, the translator) tried to visit every ward at least every three hours and be sure the IVs were running properly. We removed two patients who had died; checked one teenager with diarrhea, and a couple of women in labor.

About three o'clock in the morning, I took a few minutes to take a break and gossip with the Israeli doctor in the triage tent, the one other medic who was allowed to stay all night. We watched a team of workers adjust the new lighting on a scaffold outside, where a drilling crew was sinking a well. As we looked up at the scaffold, I said meditatively, "Haman built a gallows, fifty cubits high …"

Startled, the Israeli demanded, "How did you know what I was thinking! Where did you hear that story?"

"Hey, the book of Esther is in our scriptures too, just like yours."

News media were everywhere, every day. A man squatted beside me with a hand microphone as I treated a pneumonia case, and I am told I was on Voice of America Radio the next night. A few days later, a television crew from NBC taped the hospital. Letters from back home later told me I had appeared in all the bars in Kellogg, to shouts of "Hey! There's Doc Dahlberg on TV!" The broadcast was repeated several times all over USA and Europe, probably the only time in my life I will ever speak to over a hundred million people. At the time, I was more concerned with tucking my feet under me so the camera wouldn't show how swollen my legs had become from long hours without rest.

Rosalynn Carter talked with Lois when the First Lady toured our tent. (I missed that because I was at a meeting back in town that day, orienting a group of newly arrived doctors.) Mrs. Carter asked her several questions, but Lois says her own finest moment was in response to all the newsmen, who nearly trampled our patients as they shouted at her, "Get down! Get down!" so they could get a clear photo of the

President's wife. Lois said, "If the reporters would move back a few feet, they wouldn't be standing in the patients' latrine ditch." A lady in the group said, "Oh dear! I wish I'd known that a little sooner." And one of Mrs. Carter's Secret Service men grinned to Lois, "Say it louder. We're being recorded."

We were more tired every day than I can ever remember being. And I felt a dull anger as I watched some of my patients die, anonymous and alone, an anger at those who start wars and let others pay the consequences. But you suppress your emotions after the first day or two, because you have to choose between emoting about the tragedy, or doing something to fix it. I found I don't have enough personal resources to do both.

But the feeling I remember most, and am most grateful for, came to me one evening after the nightly staff meeting, as I drove back to town alone in the warm night air. Through the open car window I inhaled the pungent, vinegar smell of the tapioca crop drying in the farmyards I passed. I felt at peace, tired but no longer drooping with fatigue.

We had taken everything that Sa Kaew camp had thrown at us, and most of our patients were getting well. And I thought, I can do this! I can practice medicine under the worst conditions, and still look anyone in the eye and know without any doubting, *I am a doctor!* No one will ever take that away from me.

40

Back at Mae Sariang

After two weeks, our team left Tent Number 8 in the hands of Eva Hartog, a Dutch TV personality, who arrived with eight nurses from Holland to work with the American doctors who would cover our ward. The nurses had spent most of the last two years in Bible school, and were a little uncertain how to give an injection at first, but we heard later that they learned and were doing well. I couldn't have cared less who took our places, I was so glad to have respite. In Chiangmai, on the way back to Mae Sariang, the Mission co-opted me to brief a visiting tour group. Someone taped it and sent me a copy, which I still have. I spoke in a monotone through a fog of fatigue, with long pauses. I guess the tape helped raise funds for refugee relief.

Dr. Sawyer took her turn, along with some of the other hospital nurses, at another camp a month later. The new waves of refugees had war wounds in addition to hunger and disease.

One unexpected result of the camp tour was a severe asthmatic cough I developed a month later. By the end of December, my blood had a white cell count of 16,000 with 79% eosinophils (normally less that 5%.) The doctor at McCormick Hospital in Chiengmai diagnosed tropical eosinophilia, and put me on diethylcarbamazine. It was a logical choice, but it did nothing for my blood count, cough, or general malaise. I finally self-diagnosed strongyloidiasis, a type of tropical parasite that penetrates the skin of bare feet and migrates through the bloodstream to the lungs. I recalled that during the first few days at the camp, with patients crowded together on mats, I had often left my rubber sandals by the edge of the mat to reach patients more conveniently. The medicine, thiabendazole, made me smell like dead mice for a few days, but it worked—the cough and my blood count both cleared. Meanwhile, back at Mae Sariang Hospital, work continued to be full of surprises.

In January, 1980, on Thailand's annual Children's Day, the Thai army sponsored demonstrations, exhibits, and baby contests at a field just outside Mae Sariang. One exhibit was an array of weapons, well guarded. Some young fool from high school snatched a phosphorus flare from the exhibit and pulled the pin, possibly to impress his girl friend. One of the guards shouted "No!" and grabbed for it to toss it beyond the crowd, but it went off too soon.

Phosphorus-burned patients flooded both hospitals. We received twenty-two, the government about the same, and the army helicoptered some of the worst cases to Chiangmai. A phosphorus burn smokes. Applying water makes both the pain and the smoking worse. Copper sulfate solution will neutralize the phosphorus, but no one at the hospital knew the Thai word for it. I found a text which suggested using potassium permanganate (*yaa daeng htaptim* in Thai—"ruby-red medicine".) We did have that in stock, quickly made up a dilute solution, and it neutralized the phosphorus residue.

Six people died in the incident, the student, his girlfriend, and the soldier among them. No one ever explained to me why the army used live ammo in its exhibit. And nothing about the incident ever appeared in the news, as far as I know.

On a happier note, we received a visit from a group of Thai ear-nose-throat specialists. They came with their own surgical crew, preceded by public radio announcements inviting anyone with ENT problems to appear at our hospital on a certain day. The response was overwhelming. Besides the 90 ordinary patients the hospital staff saw that day, the eighteen-member ENT team saw 168 more, with ten surgeries. We fed and housed the team overnight, and they taught me the needed post-op care for the surgical cases, most of which were minor. The really rewarding result was a fifteen-year-old, born with a double hare lip, who had been too ashamed of her appearance to ever venture out of her village. The surgeon's repair turned her into a pretty girl, once she learned to hold her head up and to no longer cover her mouth with her hand.

Sometimes a case was so easily solved, it made me weep for the years the patient had suffered. A man carried his teen-age daughter to us, bed-ridden for five years. Every time she had tried to sit up, she became so dizzy she had to lie down again. Her step-mother thought her worthless and ignored her, but the father hoped we could help. We put her in a bed, tried to help her sit up; she couldn't tolerate it. Lab work showed hookworm and anemia. The father left her with us while he went to get something to eat. The nurse and I tried a different approach: we cranked up the head of the bed about ten degrees and waited a few minutes. Then another ten degrees and waited. Okay so far, try it again. One of my best memories is the look of wonder on her father's face when he returned a half-hour later and saw his daughter sitting erect, dangling her feet over the edge of the bed. We kept her a week or so, treated the anemia, dosed her for hookworm, and slowly exercised her. I have a photo of her climbing the stairway up the hillside. One of our aides, Mului, is steadying her, and she holds a Karen Bible Mului had given her.

Some cases are best left alone. Karens from back in the hills brought in a boy about twelve years old. Someone had shot him in the head as he walked along a trail. No one knew who, although I sensed that the full story might be different. On examination, he had weakness in one arm and couldn't speak, but otherwise was calm and cooperative. The entrance wound was in the back of his skull. X-rays showed the bullet lodged in the front of his brain close to the midline. I am not a brain surgeon, and chose to do nothing, except to protect him against tetanus and infection. He stayed a few days, and gradually regained part of his speech. Probably still has that bullet in his head.

Other times, whatever is done is not enough. Dai Wan, another teen-ager, of the Pwo Karen tribe was the first patient ever from her village. Big spleen, fever, anemic—my first thought was malaria. But I had learned to think second and third thoughts too; the sound of hoof beats doesn't always mean horses; sometimes they are zebras instead.

In Dai Wan's case, her blood count showed acute leukemia. We hadn't much to use for that, didn't diagnose it often. But I tried mercaptopurine, and she got better. She would come in every few weeks to be sure her blood count was staying down and her spleen still shrinking. She and her family took notice of the way the nurses treated her, and after a few months she became a Christian, one of the first Pwo Karens from her area to do so.

Dai Wan became worse again two months after her baptism, with increasing white blood cell count and enlarging spleen in spite of her medicine. The Karen church elders met with her one night, placed their hands on her head and prayed for her recovery. At her next weekly checkup, her white count had dropped from 76,000 to a normal 7,000 with no additional medicine, and her spleen had shrunk to half its size.

It would be nice to stop there, but Dai Wan became worse again, and died in Chiangmai University Hospital a few months later. At her funeral, her non-Christian kinfolk were angry. "It's because you neglected your offerings to the spirits," they told her parents. "Why do you think these Christians have a hospital next to their church, if it isn't because those who give up the old ways get sick and die!"

The thought crossed my mind that God, in his kindness, may have had her improve to show that he loved her and respected what the Karen Christians tried to do, but that he had other plans for Dai Wan.

Two years later, her sister appeared at the home of one of the missionaries, asking about the Christian faith. Her village now has its own church, which many of the villagers have joined.

Sometimes Baptists argue about whether it's proper to cooperate with other groups—Methodists, for example, or Catholics. We got along just fine with the Catholic leprosy workers in Kengtung, the Israeli doctors in the next tent at Sa Kaew, and the Buddhist ENT doctors and nurses who helped us at Mae Sariang. God never expressed any objection that I am aware of. The farther we were from headquarters, the easier it seemed to be to cooperate.

41

Armies in the Hills

When the British gave back independence to Burma in 1947, peace did not last long. Assassins invaded Parliament with machine guns blazing, killing the nation's leader, General Aung San. Within the year, Burma erupted in warfare among political and racial groups. Fighting has continued for at least fifty-five years. Neither civil government nor dictatorship by the army generals has been able to bring peace.

One of the strongest insurgent forces in the hills surrounding Burma's central plain has been the Karen National Union. The KNU originally fought in response to documented Burma army attacks on their villages and churches in the 1940s. There were many Karen officers and soldiers trained by the British, and the Karens were able to defend their territory, about 30 to 50 miles wide and 300 miles long, along the border with Thailand opposite Mae Sariang. They declared themselves the independent nation of Kawthulay, but have never gained diplomatic recognition from other nations.

Karens live on both sides of the Burma-Thai border; many came to the hospital, and some of our staff were themselves Karen political refugees from Burma. Mae Sariang is on one of the smuggling routes for black market goods in and out of Burma; timber, high grade tin or tungsten ore, perhaps jade, traded for western products not widely available in Burma.

When Lois's elderly language teacher, Pi Ler Say, passed along an invitation for us to visit a Karen border village, we accepted. Her son, the village headman there, was going to celebrate his daughter's second birthday, the invitation said. That's nice, I thought, now let's go see what the real reason is.

Leaving the hospital in the hands of a visiting doctor, we set out in a Land-rover, with a nurse, Christabelle, her young son, and a Karen lady evangelist. The 2½-hour car trip forded a small stream fifty-eight times by actual count, before coming out into the Salween River valley.

The Salween is a big river, 1,300 miles long and about the size of the Columbia back in the U.S. The road ends at the bustling village of Mae Sam Laep, where we left the car at the house of one of Christabelle's relatives. The river was at its lowest dry-season level, and people moved back and forth across the white sand carrying crates of goods to boats and bringing small heavy burlap sacks back to waiting trucks. Tungsten ore, someone told me. Burma (or Kawthulay) lay on the opposite bank. Much of Kawthulay's revenue comes from taxing goods in transit. Unlike other insurgents farther north, they did not permit opium trade and are anti-Communist. Many have been Christian for several generations past. They are, however, some of the most hard-bitten, tough-looking characters I have ever met, having survived by their guns for, at that time, thirty-three years.

The river boats are long and narrow, motor-powered and traveling better than twenty miles per hour through wilderness territory. About fifteen miles down the Salween and up a branch, we landed on the Thai side in a deserted-looking spot, climbed through sand and a screen of jungle, and discovered a 100-house village hidden in a small valley. We parked our baggage at the headman's house, had lunch and a siesta, and went on a village tour. This village had only been there two months. The townspeople had recently fled from Burma when the Burmese army began drafting villagers to carry supplies, or to go ahead of the troops as human minesweepers. Thanks to several aid groups, there were chickens, goats and pigs everywhere. Crops would be planted when the rains started.

Pi Ler Say's son and his family were up most of the night preparing the next day's feast. We were told that the Kawthulay supreme commander, General Bo Mya, would attend the service. He strolled in a half-hour later, accompanied by armed guards and a team of Thai doctors who would hold a medical clinic later. He left his rifle at the door, and sat down next to the evangelist leading the birthday prayer meeting. At the meal that followed, Lois found herself seated next to the general, who never said a word the whole meal. (Most Kawthulay leaders speak excellent English, but not the general.)

His adjutant introduced himself and invited us on a tour of the headquarters village to see their hospital. We took another boat ride up a branch river, past an armed guard post, to the family encampment (not military HQ.) This village had more comfortable wooden houses, with electricity and piped-in water. We had tea at the adjutant's house, met the medical officer, and toured his hospital, a little bigger than ours, but lacking much equipment. A lab and X-ray building was under construction.

The Kawthulay Nation maintained its own educational system, with a high school located at this village. The headmistress, Pi Emma, had been a patient of mine, so we paid her a visit. She was over seventy, vivacious, with excellent grammar and a lilting speech that was almost musical. She was preparing lessons, not only in modern Karen and English (a required subject from kindergarten on up, in Kawthulay) but in the ancient "chicken-track" script to maintain her students' sense of heritage. The village church had a single pastor who held a Baptist service on Sunday and a Seventh Day Adventist service on Saturday.

When patients came to Mae Sariang Hospital, we didn't ask a lot of questions about where they came from. Thus, when I overheard a woman behind me say, "There's Dr. Dahlberg," I asked the adjutant if I should know her.

"Colonel Gladstone's wife," he said. "I believe you took care of her last year." She had a hysterectomy, Christabelle said. Evidently she came disguised as a farmer's wife.

On our way back to Mae Sariang, Christabelle told of her own refugee journey from Burma seventeen years earlier, when Burmese planes bombed her school at Papun.

I know very little of the Karens' armed forces except by news reports, but they have continued to maintain independence in their territory for twenty more years. Only in 2003, when the Burma army no longer insisted that the Karens lay down their arms before any conference, have the two sides begun cease-fire talks. But by 2006, the talks had gone nowhere, and the Burma Army was again closing in on the shrinking Karen territory.

Years later, refugees from Burma would be a greater part of my life than those from Cambodia had recently been.

42

Planning Ahead

Our term of service at Mae Sariang would be up in July of 1981. Bina had had her year's furlough back home in Maine, and a Philippine doctor, Eli Cong, would arrive soon with a three-year commitment after finishing his surgical training.

Changing jobs again made me wonder if I knew what I was doing. Mae Sariang was a pleasant place, and Lois and I were able to make good use of our talents, at least in the medical work. But I found hospital administration as tension-producing as I had ten years earlier, and did not look forward to being the Swedish Baptist Union's on-site architect and contractor for the rest of their planned hospital expansion.

There were a number of reasons favoring moving back to America. Being a parent at a distance half-way around the world is possible, but it lacks contact. Susan, commuting daily between nursing school and home forty miles apart, had fallen asleep at the wheel and totaled her car. Pat's romance with Dave, whom we'd never met, was warming up. John was still looking for a permanent job after graduating from TCU. Nancy and some of her classmates in Bangkok had just taken a trip to Rangoon, and she was now producer and properties manager in the school drama group's road tour, but was still 500 miles away most of the year. We could communicate love and interest with all of them by mail, but we missed being there to talk together.

I could handle most medical crises, but dealing with a patient's anxiety or family problems in a foreign language was another matter altogether. Moreover, I had noticed that my medical missionary colleagues in their isolated posts tended to fall behind in medical progress while becoming more set in their ways and opinions. Perhaps it is the price to pay for the life goals they choose.

I pressed the mission board to state their future plans for medical mission work. There were no local people in the medical pipeline. Mae Sariang High School's science department was almost non-existent, and the kids were never able to pass med-school entrance exams. Almost all Christian Thai doctors were ethnic Chinese, and their culture did not steer them toward low-income rural practice. American doctor candidates—how should I put this—the mission board sometimes rejected them for seemingly trivial reasons. One excellent doctor had visited Mae Sariang for a month and expressed interest in a missionary career, but the mission board refused his application because his wife had been a divorcee. (Another mission quickly hired the couple for work in Africa.) I thought new doctors were more important than new buildings. I wasn't willing to commit to managing a hospital instead of practicing medicine, and a lone doctor could not do both jobs well.

I had no clear picture of God's will for my future. I thought perhaps I was just seeing greener pastures across the fence. But I resolved that if no path was pointed out in these last months in Mae Sariang, I would restart medical practice near Kellogg.

Alderson-Broaddus, a Baptist college in West Virginia, invited me to their commencement ceremony in May to receive an honorary degree, and they "believed I would be interested to see what we have going here in health service." They appeared to be offering me a job in their physician's assistant training program. Full-time teaching did not appeal to me as much as office medical practice. I appreciated the offer, but one doctor degree is really enough. And if I was to live in the mountains, I wanted the real mountains of the west. I thanked them, but pointed out that my daughter would not have finished high school that soon, nor would Dr. Sawyer return to relieve me until June.

Lois, Nancy, and I flew home on British Airways, with a stop in England, where we spent a week in Devonshire exploring King Arthur country, and another week driving through Denmark, Germany, and

Belgium. With my sister Margaret's help, we bought a low-priced car in Massachusetts and went on westward to Idaho.

We had expected to find our yard at home knee-deep in hay—Susan had moved to Seattle to work, leaving the house empty for a year. But we drove up McKinley Avenue to find a neatly mowed lawn, flowers outside and inside our house, and a kitchen stocked with food. We had more thoughtful neighbors than we had realized.

Our daughter Pat and her fiancé Dave Cordier were two of our first visitors after returning home. They had first met when Pat was a lieutenant in the army nurse corps outside Seoul, Korea, and Dave was a sergeant at a missile battery near the Demilitarized Zone. We had heard much about Dave, but this was our first meeting with the tall, courteous, soft-spoken soldier. We were very favorably impressed. Evidently, the visit had settled any doubts he may have had about marrying into a missionary family. He and Pat told us that now we were back, they wanted to get married—how about Friday? And did we think that Grandpa would marry them?

Fine with us; we spent a day in Spokane getting some new clothes, the women drew up a list of about twenty friends and family for a home ceremony. My Dad and step-mother were off on one of their car trips at ages 88 and 71, respectively, and we had to send out an all-points bulletin to locate them in time. The Montana State Patrol spotted their Arizona license plate and pulled them over to tell them they had a wedding to perform.

A wedding on five-day notice is the best of both worlds—less fuss than when the women have time to make full plans, yet more sociable than elopement. One of Pat's high school friends was bridesmaid; Dave's brother came up from Missouri to be best man. Our home's narrow staircase made it awkward to escort the bride down the aisle, but everyone agreed that the ceremony and reception dinner went off very well.

We started looking for office space near Kellogg in late August. A week later, the Bunker Hill Mining and Smelting Company announced closure of more than two thousand jobs in Shoshone County.

43

The Office in Pinehurst

Opening a family practice when many of the area's families were moving away to find work elsewhere didn't sound like a good idea on the face of it. But the completion of Interstate 90 all the way to Spokane four years earlier had meant growth for the west end of Shoshone County. It was now much easier to reach, for those who worked in Spokane or Coeur d'Alene but wanted low-cost housing. There was no doctor in the forty miles between Kellogg and Coeur d'Alene. That gap had been in my mind for a long time.

Shoshone County's loss of more than two thousand jobs certainly gave me pause. But the other mines were still running, the timber was still there, and the highway itself supplied many with work, and gave skiers, elk-hunters, and other tourists easy access. Lois and I knew the people, and many of them already knew us.

Pinehurst was the obvious place for a doctor's office. Six miles west of Kellogg's hospital, close to the freeway and to several smaller towns, it already had a pharmacy and enough shops to draw people. The business community was eager to have a doctor in town. I began talking with building owners. There weren't many vacancies with enough space and the necessary plumbing and rooms, but I finally focused on a shop whose occupant wanted to move to smaller quarters in the shopping center a block away.

Tenants in the rest of the building warned me that the roof sometimes leaked. The heating system and small toilet were barely adequate, but the space could probably be partitioned, and cars could park by the side of the building. The landlord drew up a contract. I didn't know much about such things, but I knew enough to get a second opinion. I said I would run it by my attorney (I didn't have one yet, but I knew some in Kellogg) and we could close the deal in a few days.

Immediately, the landlord backed off. "If you're going to be that way, we're back to square one," he said. He rewrote the lease with higher rent. I said to give me a few days to consider it.

The hospital in Kellogg also had an interest in getting more doctors. An executive from their management company happened to be in town, and he was sympathetic to my dilemma. "Call this number down in Portland," he said, handing me a scribbled note. "They deal in pre-fabricated doctor's office buildings."

"Yes," they said when I called, "we have a double-wide on the lot now." Lois and I had a date to speak at a church in Walla Walla in a few days. I made an appointment with the pre-fab lot in Portland for the day following that. We arrived December 1.

"It was built three years ago," the salesman said. "We repossessed it earlier this year from a ski slope on Mount Hood." Lois and I inspected the two halves of a fifty-foot-long double-wide trailer, resting on cement blocks. Minor damage, needed a new paint job, but it was designed to be a doctor's office, with lab space and even a lead-lined X-ray room and dark room. Each half had an electric heater/air conditioner. I found the $37,000 price tag a little daunting.

"You can make monthly payments," the salesman assured me. "$715 a month, and if you decide to buy the building, one-half of each month's rent is credited to the purchase price." I thought we could handle seven hundred a month. We dickered a little, and the final price was 35,000. I told him it would take a week to arrange the financing. A security deposit of $6,035 borrowed from my life insurance policies sealed the deal.

We needed a place to put the building. The pharmacist in Pinehurst offered the empty lot next door to him, if we didn't mind his sign on a pole in the lot. It was at the end of the shopping center, with lots of parking space. The couple who owned the shopping center land proposed a land lease of $125 a month.

Bert McCauley, a friend in the real estate business at the time, passed the word to the landlord of the property I had been looking at the month before. "You should have quit while you were ahead."

"But aren't I the only game in town?" the man asked Bert.

"Not any more, looks like," Bert said.

I arranged for water, electricity, sewer and phone lines, and a foundation under the building. A hauling company delivered the two building halves the day after Christmas, and hook-ups were completed in a week. Even before we were in business, a few people climbed the temporary cement-block steps to ask for appointments. We opened January 4, 1982.

To save our shrinking capital funds, Lois was both nurse and receptionist; the only payroll the first month was for a night cleaning crew. We had hardly opened when Ann Hoskins, my former receptionist, paid us a call after hours. She had worked at the Doctors Clinic for the past four years, and was now in charge of their front office and patient scheduling. We visited a while and then she came to the point: "Can I come work for you again?"

Lois and I thought that was a great idea, but didn't know how we would pay her. Nor did I really want to irritate my former partners by stealing their office staff.

"Give us time to build up some income, Ann, and we'll talk again in a couple months."

But a week later, Lois and I were so mired down in accounts and insurance forms that I phoned Ann at her home. "It's okay to give them your two weeks notice, Ann. We need help!"

She was the one that kept that office running. She made the appointments, answered the phone, and kept the patients' accounts, sent the bills, seemingly without effort. She had time to visit with those sitting in our small waiting room, knew almost everybody in the Valley, told me which ones could pay and which were having trouble. I handled the office expense bills and payroll myself. Lois was nurse and lab tech. We sent patients who needed X-rays to the hospital, and they would bring the films back. After a few months, when Lois wanted some time off, we hired Gail Young, an RN who at the time was not working except to keep her husband's business accounts. Gail worked in Lois's place one week each month. And those three, Ann, Lois, and

Gail, were about all the office staff I ever needed. On rare occasions, a night duty nurse from the hospital filled in for a day.

I drew up an office policy notebook about handling patients, phone etiquette, and emergencies. It dealt with scheduling, sick leave, petty cash, overtime, patient privacy, and a lot of other matters.

I resolved that my patients would have no long waits unless I was detained by an emergency at the hospital. Ann would inform waiting patients of any delay, and offer to reschedule if they didn't want to wait. The hours 8 to 10 a.m. were saved for hospital rounds, or minor surgery in the office. During that time Lois also drew lab samples to send with the daily courier service, or did some of the simpler procedures herself (urinalysis, blood sugars, and the like.) The hours 10 to 12 and 1 to 4:30 were open for appointments. Our waiting room had only six chairs, and I wanted to keep them occupied only briefly. I tried to be on time and get done as close to 5 p.m. as possible, to let the staff go home on time. Most nights I could finish up my records and evening hospital rounds and still get home soon after six o'clock.

For ordinary patient visits I could see four per hour; new patients were allowed longer. I had Ann fill two of those four time slots each hour, ahead of the day. Another of the four was for those who phoned for an appointment on that day. The fourth spot each hour was kept open for emergencies and walk-ins. Most days, no one had to wait more than fifteen minutes. If some appointments were empty, I used the time to catch up on records or medical journals. I have never understood why all doctors don't use this simple, relaxing way of scheduling. Some still do.

The office was open Monday through Saturday noon. I saved Wednesday mornings for paying bills, catching up on letters, accounts, and other business matters. Wednesday afternoons we were closed. I have never swung a golf club in my life, but I did go fishing sometimes. Friday night was my turn to cover hospital emergency room calls for all the doctors. Each of us took care of his own hospital in-patients and baby deliveries each day.

I had learned that the very poor in the USA often stay away, rather than be embarrassed about being unable to pay, just as those in Thailand and Burma had done. I had to earn a living, so I tried a compromise. Ann enclosed a slip with each new patient's first bill:

"To my patients: (save this notice)
"My fees are comparable to those of other physicians in North Idaho. If, however, you are retired and living on a small fixed income, are temporarily out of work, or having other financial hardship, you may reduce my fee. The amount is up to you; I suggest a reduction of 25%, but you may choose a figure more or less than this.
"No explanation is necessary; simply mark the amount of reduction on your payment and send it in as promptly as possible. (Promptness, in turn, will help reduce my office overhead expenses.) Reduction is not offered on that portion of charges which are covered by insurance or other third party payments.Please do not advertise this offer. Keith Dahlberg, MD"

It seemed to work well, and drew favorable comments. Most doctors anticipate an average 90% collection ratio of total billing; mine ended in the high eighties. If a patient didn't respond with any payment at all after several monthly bills, Ann would mark the chart folder with a colored dot, prompting me to bring up the subject at the next visit. The only times I rejected patients for financial reasons was when the insurance company paid them directly, and they didn't pass my share on to me.

I financed my start-up expenses by borrowing $40,000 on life insurance policies. Patients and insurance companies pay about two months after the service is rendered. I sent out bills at the end of each month, and most companies paid the following month. Only a few patients paid at the time of the visit. By the end of January, we had collected $728. February brought in another $4,580. At the end of March, I was able to pay all current expenses and take home a paycheck for myself. We never got rich, but we always had enough and some to spare. With my small office staff, I was able to raise their pay-rate almost every year. About every three years, I had to raise the patient fees a little.

After three years, I took out another loan and paid off the rest of the price of the building. I continued to put $725 a month into loan repayment, and had the loan paid back by 1987. Money was hardly ever a cause for worry. Enough other problems would soon surface, however.

44

Working in the Community

Using the English language all day, with no need for interpreters, sped up my work. And with fewer night calls, I had more time for family and for community work.

Kellogg's hospital was going through difficult times. The shrinking population of Shoshone County wasn't enough to support both hospitals in the valley, but city rivalry stifled any talk of a merger. The two halves of the county each wanted separate school districts, separate fire districts, and separate hospital districts. At Kellogg in the early 1980s, moreover, medical staff and hospital management argued with each other continually, and many patients chose to go forty miles to Coeur d'Alene for care instead. The hospital was running in the red. Supplies were overpurchased and became outdated on the shelves. At one point many nurses were ready to resign because of the hospital board's micro-management of their work. The hospital had ended 1981 with a deficit of $90,000 for the year.

The hospital board hired a new administrator in1982. He trimmed the payroll, improved the purchasing system, boosted employee morale, and ended the year with a $100,000 surplus. I later served on the board to fill someone's unexpired term for a few months, enough to show interest, but not long enough to make everyone mad at me.

One area where doctors at both ends of the county cooperated was disaster preparedness. Interstate 90 carried more than a thousand big trucks per day, many with radioactive or toxic chemical loads. Commercial airlines flew over the county, homing on the radio beacon at Mullan Pass before turning to destinations farther east. Fire, ambulance, police, and medics all saw potential for disaster in this traffic corridor, and all cooperated in a disaster drill about twice a year, made as realistic as possible. High school students cheerfully played roles as victims, applying makeup to simulate realistic wounds.

In the early 1980s, the county disaster officer proposed adding another factor to the mix. Fairchild Air Force Base, eighty miles west, and upwind from us, was a prime target for nuclear attack if the Cold War with Russia ever grew hot. Washington, DC took notice of all the underground mines in Shoshone County—ideal shelter from atomic attack, some bureaucrat thought—and two hundred cots and some medical supplies arrived to be stored at the hospital. People fleeing from Spokane could take shelter here, was the idea.

Well, maybe. I had a minor interest in nuclear scenarios ever since my Burma days, when I had wondered if the USA would be radioactive when I returned home. I saw some holes in the present survival plan, and discussed it with some others in town. We finally formed a team— Jerry Cobb from Public Health, Dale Costa the Fire Chief, one of the Mine Rescue instructors, and occasionally a few others—and we explored mines, both active and abandoned, whenever we had time together.

We figured an atomic explosion eighty miles west would send radioactive fallout in our direction on prevailing winds, taking perhaps at least an hour to arrive. Miners had observed during the Mount St. Helens eruption in 1980, that volcanic ash drifted into the mine tunnels only a few hundred feet before sticking to the damp rock walls. Scientists at the time suggested that radioactivity of the dust would decline to one thousandth of its original level in about three weeks. Many mines had year-round warm temperature, natural air circulation, and water. With some planning, shelter might be feasible beyond 300 feet from the entrance.

Electric mine hoists probably wouldn't function after atomic attack, so we considered only areas where people could walk in. Intrigued by our mission, mine managers gave our team guided access to their properties—Bunker Hill, Galena, Atlas, Star, and many others; and to abandoned workings like the Sidney, Big It, and Nabob. Jerry arranged analysis of water samples at Public Health. Bacterial contamination was rarely a problem deep underground, but he found some water sources were too acid to drink, or contained too much zinc or other metals.

The mines were totally dark and damp, and radios would not work, but life was at least possible, with flashlights and food. We estimated the two-mile-long Kellogg Tunnel and main hoist room in the Bunker Hill had space for about 1,200 people to bed down, plus several hundred more in upper levels of the mine with separate outside access. Other mines' capacities varied from a few dozen people to a couple hundred.

Altogether, the mine tunnels might accommodate those of Shoshone County who were interested. (Some locals said that if atomic war ever happened, they personally planned to "sit on the front porch with a six-pack and watch the fireworks." You'd have to live here to appreciate that.) But we'd have to forget Spokane's population. There wouldn't be shelter for extra thousands, even for those who could keep ahead of the dust cloud.

We pursued our explorations for most of 1984. But when we noticed our mine safety expert casting worried glances at the rotting timbers in the old Nabob mine tunnel, we realized the risks we were taking. No one could reach us if one of these old tunnels collapsed, so we agreed to quit. By that time, we had disproved the theory of mass exodus and shelter for half of Spokane. And to be honest, we had been exploring the mines as much for the adventure as for serious purpose.

Other community projects engaged my attention, with more practical results.

Most people with jobs had health insurance in those days. A few employers tried to avoid paying benefits by hiring part-timers. People with no income usually qualified for Medicaid assistance. But the people with part time or minimum wage jobs were caught in between. They had income, but not enough to afford doctor visits and prescriptions. Hence, the origin of the "low income clinic."

It started as a one-night-a-week clinic at the Public Health office in Coeur d'Alene. I joined them one night a month at first, to help provide people an alternative to "toughing it out" with toothache or flu, at least if they had transportation. The clinic grew busier, and went to twice a week as more Kootenai County doctors volunteered, and then several people formed a board of directors for a clinic in Kellogg, meeting every Monday evening. Another doctor had charge of it, seeking volunteers and asking drug companies for free samples, but several of us each worked one night a month. Such clinics are not for serious acute injuries or illness, which we sent to the hospital emergency room, but they were well suited to the minor illnesses and prescription refill visits that eat up a minimum wage earner's pay.

Almost all the doctors volunteered a day per year to give free sports physicals to all the school athletic teams, or immunization shots at the schools.

Dr. Gnaedinger was county coroner, and he sometimes needed to be away. I volunteered to take some of his calls for a few months as assistant coroner, but I never was very good at it. I had read too many murder mysteries, and suspected foul play in every unexpected death. The police were very patient with me, but I could see they wished I would be quicker to sign the papers. About a year later, the local mortician became coroner; he did the exams during the course of his work, and didn't need a backup.

In an effort to stem the deaths from drunk drivers Idaho passed a law mandating that everyone convicted of drunken driving be examined by a physician, who would then advise the judge before the offender was sentenced. The doctor was to consider not only the present arrest, but advise the judge of any past episodes. It drove the defense lawyers crazy.

I usually gave the judge a favorable report on first offenders, but would recommend more severe penalty for repeaters, if that's what it took to change their ways. One attorney wrote me an irate letter asking what business I had digging up old records, and did I know that his client had had his driver's license taken away for a year this time? I replied that that was probably what the state legislature had in mind. Prudently, I asked pre-sentencing exam patients to pay in advance.

45

The L Word

Nothing chills a doctor's joy in his work like a letter with a lawyer's return address, asking for a patient's complete records. Asking for a single report usually means the lawyer is only trying to help his client get disability benefits. A demand for everything usually means the doctor is about to get a lawsuit notice. A doctor pays a lot for insurance against malpractice claims, no matter how carefully he practices medicine. In the 1980's, a family-practice doctor had to pay from five to ten thousand dollars insurance premium each year, if he practiced in a low risk area. An obstetrician or neurosurgeon practicing in, say, Florida, pays premiums ten times that, and in the last twenty years the rates have more than doubled yet again.

The doctor had best send the records promptly, keeping a copy of everything he sends. Holding back anything, or worse yet, trying to change the written record, will have disastrous results.

Several times in my professional life, lawyers have asked me for copies of my records. Idaho is one of the states that provides for a pre-trial hearing by a panel which usually includes an uninvolved doctor, an uninvolved lawyer, and one or two lay-people. This is to screen out cases which, after examining the evidence from both sides, appear to "have no merit." In some instances, a lawyer chooses to pursue the matter in court anyway, asking multimillion dollar damages. I am deeply thankful that I have never had to appear in a court trial as a defendant.

Several of my colleagues have, and I have testified as a witness a couple of times, but courtrooms are not one of my favorite scenes. One attorney asked me, under oath, what I thought of the jury system. With good conscience I was able to reply that I thought it the best we have, and he did not pursue that line of questioning further. But in my mind I recalled one doctor who asked his own attorney what he thought his own chances were in an upcoming malpractice trial. The attorney replied to the effect that he thought he would win the case; he [the attorney] didn't think that the doctor's actions caused the damages the plaintiff claimed, though no one could probably ever determine what had. But if the patient was brought into the courtroom in a wheelchair and exhibited before the court, a sympathetic jury might award full damages anyway.

Asking what were the chances of such an outcome, the doctor was told maybe fifty-fifty.

One of my acquaintances, convinced he had done nothing wrong, chose to fight such a case. He lost, and even after his malpractice insurer paid the amount it covered, he was left owing a million dollars.

After working in Asia, the chronic threat of lawsuit in America changed me. I felt vulnerable. I learned that if a doctor had not written it, then in the eyes of the court he had not done it. True or not, I spent more time writing my records. I did less surgery and OB, and what OB I still did, I spent all night if necessary, watching the labor patient personally.

Do I practice "defensive medicine"? You bet.

Over the past twenty years or more, doctors do all the tests that might possibly have *any* bearing on a diagnosis they are considering, not just a few tests to confirm or dismiss a possibility, expensive though all those tests may be. Frequent testing for high blood pressure in pregnancy is routine, to prevent a life-threatening complication called eclampsia, even though I have encountered only about three cases in the two thousand or so pregnancies I have seen in fifty years. Cancer screening, or measuring cholesterol or blood sugar—all might be called defensive medicine in a sense, and all add to the patient's costs. But to neglect such routine tests is to risk an avoidable death or disability in a few patients, and today's American medical standards are based on zero-risk, or at least minimal reasonable risk for the patient, and cost is a lesser priority. As cost of care continues to rise, that will someday change. But that's the way it is in the early twenty-first century.

46

Doctors Outside the Norm

Doctors are often pictured as golf-playing socialites, more concerned with their stock-brokers than their patients. I guess there are a few doctors like that. Doctors range across a whole spectrum of behavior, from the competent and caring to the careless loose cannon.

The six or eight full-time doctors at our local hospital took turns serving as chief of staff, that office being thought more an administrative burden than an honor. Sometimes the chief would have to counsel a fellow doctor whose patients had written complaints to the staff; sometimes for a lapse in standard of care, sometimes for behavior that had somehow offended the patient.

Some doctors' careers are both tragic and scary. A pair of my classmates in medical school, acclaimed for their superior grades and their medical research, became partners in an OB-GYN practice, high-income specialists in a big city. Twenty years later, the news media widely publicized their deaths from drug overdose, during what should have been the prime of life.

Even those of us who try to maintain and improve our skills can have lapses in ordinary sensitivity. A woman with complicated endocrine problems returned to her primary care doctor after referral to a specialist, to hear the results. She waited anxiously while the doctor studied the specialist's report and diagnosis. As he finished reading, she heard him murmur, "Hmm … My father died of that."

When an acquaintance of mine returned to her surgeon in a near-by city after her second back operation, still in severe pain, she said he did not see her, but sent his nurse out to the waiting room to say there was nothing further he could do.

A fifty-year-old man with cancer went to the emergency room after finishing a round of chemotherapy. He had a lump in his cheek and a sore mouth. With little or no examination, the ER doctor (according to the patient) told him this meant the cancer "had spread to his lymph nodes and he was going to die." Actually, the soreness and the enlarged lymph node cleared promptly after another doctor treated the mouth infection.

I recall an incident of my own insensitivity which, forty years later, still makes me wince with shame whenever I think of it. A teen-age boy had carried his father to the hospital in Kengtung. The man was having acute breathing difficulty and died within the first few minutes, before I could do anything useful. Fed up with families who tried every kind of quack treatment before finally coming to me, I raged aloud about how long the boy had waited before bringing his father. He had just lost his father, and I was scolding him! Only when I saw his tears did I pause and realize what I was doing.

Two highly respected North Idaho doctors mailed their colleagues letters many years ago seeking to fund a public relations campaign dealing with "government intrusion, malpractice crises, legislative and legal battles." One mentioned "brain-washed lay people" who thought medicine's reputation was deteriorating. As he saw medicine and surgery, the doctor went on, it is progressing at a tremendous rate with more and better hospitals and doctors, better medicines, better surgeries and diagnostic procedures ... This good news must get to the public, he said. The majority of us have kicked in to the war chest [of the IMA and the AMA] ... We can, then, be forgiven for having a wee bit of resentment towards those of our colleagues who share in our victories, but who have not so far paid for their share of the ammunition.

It was soon after my leaving the Doctors' Clinic partnership to go solo, and the letter nettled me enough that I thought it deserved a reply:

It's true that medicine is progressing at a tremendous rate [I wrote.] Organized medicine's efforts at public relations, on the other hand, seem to be going backward if they are going anywhere at all. It has reached the point where many Americans will seize almost any opportunity to express their hostility, and they don't need much brainwashing to do it ...

Our organization's attitude seems to be that if we just marshal enough money for a publicity campaign, we don't need to do anything about our patients waiting two hours past their appointment time. Nor about our business office charging a first-visit workup for a 30-second glance down a throat (or worse yet, charging a night call for phone instructions to an ER nurse without ever seeing the patient, 'for taking responsibility'.)

I have been speaking about these abuses for 5 years, but I am not aware that doctors listen much yet. I have worked hard to correct them where I am aware of them in my own practice. Contrary to predictions, it hasn't hurt my collection ratio.

Perhaps you will forgive me for feeling a little resentment too, I wrote. I feel like I am being asked to help repair a house that a lot of doctors are tearing down, even while they keep shelling out money on repair bills ... Since I am soon going overseas for a while, I don't object if the IMA and AMA take the unused portion of my dues to use for public relations. It about equals the amount being asked. But I don't really like to 'pay for ammunition' (as you put it) while so many of our colleagues keep supplying the 'enemy' with his.

In fairness to doctors, they are under a lot of pressure to perform. Patients rightfully don't want to wait three weeks for an appointment, but once they get into the examining room they want unlimited time to discuss their own problems while the next patient waits.

Special interest groups focus on their own single issue as the only thing needed to solve all medical care problems, and seem to have no difficulty in getting all the publicity they want. A religious group once invited me to attend a "Consultation on Health." Their advance literature complained that "medical professionals who are concerned with health spend all their time attending to the diagnosis and treatment of disease." The group claimed there is no solution to the problem of illness and asked, "Of what and how shall we die, once we cure cancer, heart disease, and stroke?"

Their purpose was to raise consciousness about "holistic medicine" to the exclusion of all else. In declining the invitation, I answered their question ["of what shall we die …"] half facetiously, "God will think of something. How about childhood leukemia, or rheumatic fever, or diabetes? Do you just tell the grieving parent, 'Aw, c'mon, Mom, everybody is going to die sooner or later'?"

One other bit of nonsense I could not let pass—their avowed "need for rigorous deprofessionalization of the health care system." Next time you are in an auto accident, I advised them, call a sociologist.

I don't worry a lot about where medicine is headed—there are still a few fast-buck artists, but many more doctors are competent, dedicated young people who nowadays know a lot more about medicine than I ever learned fifty years ago.

I do worry about the working poor who have no access to a system that demands seventy dollars or more up front before even entering the doctor's inner office. It does little good to offer them tax breaks or cheaper insurance, when they don't earn enough to be taxed, or to buy insurance. Many of them struggle just to pay the rent and the grocery bill. Now *there* is a problem to raise consciousness about!

47

Rent-a-Doc, International

As I approached age 65 the question arose, what to do with the rest of my life? I didn't want to stop work entirely; I still enjoyed it. But I dreamed of having no more call-outs to the hospital on freezing-cold winter nights. And I coveted vacation time that need no longer be pencilled in between maternity patients' due dates.

The Indian Health Service looked interesting. The Federal Prison system—well, maybe … And doctor on a cruise ship was a passing dream.

As retired missionaries, Lois and I were invited to attend a Ministers and Missionaries Benefit Board-sponsored conference on retirement for those of its clients approaching age 65. There we learned that we already had a good financial set-up, with diversified assets in a modest mission pension, social security, and IRA mutual funds. We had chosen one of our daughter Nancy's former college classmates several years earlier as our investment advisor, and he seemed to know his business.

The M&M Board also counseled its retirees about health, maintaining an active life, and planning for assisted living. We followed all their advice, except about assisted living. The facility where we were meeting featured shuffleboard and in-door gardening, and that didn't resonate with us at all. We visited several other senior citizen places in warmer climates, but living among old people had little appeal. We realized that one of us might someday have a stroke or dementia requiring assistance, but we also knew that about half of my elderly patients had lived at home until dying a natural death. We decided to keep our house and stay active. Our four children seemed to enjoy their work, and as far as we could tell, each made more income than we ever had. They needed no financial help from us.

The back pages of the *American Medical Association Journal* listed several firms supplying temporary replacements for doctors on vacation, those who were ill, or otherwise in need of short term-help. They sounded too good to be true—they paid travel costs, housing, insurance, licensing fees, and a take-home paycheck. No office expense or paper work beyond keeping patients' medical records up to date. The temporary doctor can choose how many weeks a year he wants to work, and where. The technical term is *locum tenens*, nick-named "rent-a-doc."

I considered hiring out, but about that same time, a letter came from Dr. Phil McDaniel in Sangklaburi, Thailand. Phil had been the doctor at Kwai River Christian Hospital for fifteen years. The hospital I used to visit to keep the place alive before his arrival was now a bustling center with three wards, full most of the time. He was due for a year's home leave starting in August, 1993. Would I come work during his absence? Lois and I talked it over; I wasn't 65 yet, but I would be by the time I finished at KRCH. My Thai medical license was still active. We hoped to attend our son's graduation in California (his employer had sent him to Stanford for a year's study) so we agreed to cover until May. Phil thought he could find someone else for the last few months.

I gave notice to my patients that I would close my office, after twelve years in Pinehurst, in June 1993 and arranged to transfer records to the new doctor of their choice. Ann would stay on for a few months part-time transferring records and depositing late payments. The hospital in Kellogg would put a new doctor in Pinehurst, but would give him new office space.

We had never been to Kwai River Hospital in its new location. The Thai government had built a dam halfway up the Kwai River, creating a lake reaching to its headwaters and submerging the old hospital and town. Paved road extended all the way to the new hospital now, an easy one-day journey from Bangkok by bus.

KRCH was still officially a ten-bed hospital (the maximum allowed for one doctor), but usually had fifteen or more in-patients. An almost completed addition provided for another twelve beds for long-term care of tuberculosis patients. The nursing staff was excellent, most departments well organized, and there was usually a visiting medical student or resident from America or Europe, getting a month's taste of tropical medicine.

Being on call day and night was daunting, but Phil had a well-run organization going, and the nurses allowed me every Wednesday afternoon off. I did surgery I wasn't really trained to do, with the textbook open on a stand Phil kept in the operating room. Most of the surgical scenes in my later novel, "Flame Tree" are based on KRCH, and there were many more. I amputated a woman's leg for a large cancer at the knee. A man whose stomach could not pass food onward (because of scar tissue from an old ulcer) could be saved from starvation by a bypass connection from stomach to intestine (gastroduodenostomy) I removed a three-pound cyst from one woman's abdomen, and did several C-sections for women hemorrhaging in late pregnancy.

KRCH offered only three choices of anesthesia—spinal, ketamine, or local lidocaine. I would give the anesthetic, and then do the surgery while a nurse monitored the patient's IV and vital signs. Sometimes one or more of us had to donate a pint of blood before surgery, if no family members were available or willing.

Usually, we had no practical way to refer patients to big city hospitals, even if the patient could tolerate the five-hour ride. Many patients were undocumented aliens from Burma, and wouldn't get past the police checkpoints. If we didn't overdo it, the government hospital in Sangklaburi, ten miles away, would accept emergency referrals and send them to the city in their ambulance, which had less trouble with the police. Depending on the government doctor on duty, some had even less surgical experience than I, and sometimes even referred surgery to me.

Refugee camp clinics along the border sent cases to us. A young unconscious woman in labor came in after two convulsions at the camp. Her blood pressure was very high, she was swollen with retained fluid, the classic picture of eclampsia—a condition rare in America anymore. The baby's heart was very slow, but we could hear it. She went directly to the delivery room. Luckily the baby's head was almost ready to come out; I applied forceps, and (while the mother was having another convulsion) the baby came out alive. Both mother and child recovered.

Sometimes, of course, a patient was entirely beyond our help. A Danish tourist had been trampled by an elephant—the side of his crushed head had a clearly outlined footprint—and I could do nothing except lead the simple funeral service his companion requested, and later try to explain to the family, by long-distance phone, what had happened. Some patients arrived too deep in shock, or with fever that failed to respond to anything we tried, or who needed surgery I didn't even dare attempt. A team of eye surgeons visited every three months, to take care of cataracts and to fit glasses.

But our little mission looked like a big-city hospital in contrast with the make-shift facilities out on the Burma border. Once a week, the Immigration Department in Bangkok deported two or three hundred illegal Burmese workers, one hundred per truck, using the road that went by KRCH. They might drop off a patient too weak to walk across the border; we would treat him, and then keep him in a safe-house until he was stronger. Thailand used this road to deport aliens because the road ended at an area of Burma under Mon tribal control, where Burmese police could not arrest them. Medicine-Without-Borders had a clinic there, just across the border, and would refer cases to us.

Some of us drove out there one afternoon, about ten miles west. Holakani, in Mon insurgent territory, is a town entirely of thatch huts stretching two or three kilometers along a narrow valley—about 5,000 population. No electricity, no running water, no farmable land. We visited the Medicine-Without-Borders people in their large thatch hut. They had a microscope to detect malaria, using sunlight and a mirror for illumination. Several patients lay on the floor getting intravenous fluids. Perhaps twenty patients in all. I never again complained when they sent us a patient.

In 1995, Lois and I worked five weeks with the Bible translators at Ukarumpa, in the highlands of Papua New Guinea. The resident doctor there was recovering from a chronic illness, and needed some temporary help. Ukarumpa is the central town for about 200 linguists who spend half of each year in back-country villages, putting the local languages into writing. Papua New Guinea has about eight hundred separate languages, the most of any nation in the world. Officially, foreign doctors can only treat other foreigners, of whom there are many at the translation center. In practice, we assisted local PNG nurse-practitioners with some of their more serious cases too. We also attended monthly clinics in villages, and we gave emergency counsel over a two-way radio network spanning all their outposts across the nation.

Practice in PNG was more limited than in SE Asia. The public health department limits treatment to a bare minimum, attainable by their own medical and nursing people. On the other hand, the translation experts seem to have abundant resources for their work, with a large linguistic library, computerized translation, a small fleet of airplanes, and a centralized school from first to twelfth grade for all the ex-patriate children.

Our month in Ukarumpa let us experience a different type of Third World Nation, newly independent from Australia's supervision. It also let us see the degree of cooperation possible among diverse Christian groups when they focus more on a uniting common task and less on divisive doctrine.

The following year brought opportunity to revisit Burma after an absence of thirty-four years.

48

A New Look at Burma

By the 1990's Burma's economy had deteriorated so far that the army generals began to seek new sources of income. They permitted tourism in a few supervised spots like the city of Mandalay and the ancient pagodas at Pagan. The government also accepted outside consultants in a few projects to benefit the nation.

A Seattle group had a contract for improving rural health in the Kachin State, the northernmost region of Burma. The local director had been a missionary kid himself, about the same age as our children, and knew about our village health work in Thailand. He wrote and invited Lois and me to spend some time in Burma with his project in 1996.

We had missed life in Burma since we left Kengtung in 1962, and eagerly accepted his offer. The Burma Government (which had renamed the country Myanmar) had approved the health project, following the cease-fire with the Kachin insurgents in 1994. Government officials gave us no trouble about entry or about working in areas still closed to tourists.

It was like going back in time thirty-five years. We could speak no Kachin, but between our Burmese and the team's English, we got along all right. The team leader and we two were the only foreigners. The rest were nurses, a doctor, and sanitation workers, all Burmese, eight or ten of us in all. A police intelligence officer accompanied us, a standard requirement for all foreigners. He sat in on some of our teaching sessions and left after three days, satisfied that we were indeed teaching public health and not anti-government propaganda. We stayed in Myitkyina between trips to villages, and were free to visit local shops and restaurants and talk with people on the street. (The city itself was open to tourists.) While on tour we stayed mostly in local homes.

Our first trip took us fifty miles down the Irrawaddy River to a farm town of about 6,000 people, where we helped teach examination and treatment of common diseases to village women chosen by their village headmen. Other team members taught disease prevention, clean water supply, nutrition, and immunization. Part of Lois's and my job was to sit in the back of the room while we ouselves were not teaching and observe the students to see how much of the program they appeared to be absorbing. In that first village, we stayed in a vacant wood-and-bamboo house, with the outhouse in a neighbor's back yard. Meals were shared with other team members, who slept in the village school. For anyone under age thirty-five in that village, we may have been the first Caucasians they had ever seen.

Many scenes from this trip are paraphrased in my novel *Flame Tree*. There are too many tales to summarize in a single chapter, but one adventure stands out. We would have missed it if we had surrendered to early morning rain and turned our pickup truck back toward Myitkyina. The team had been surveying villages down the Ledo Road to the south, accompanied by our policeman and his army corporal assistant again. We had been turned back near Kandawyang by an army unit attached to Bhamo command, that knew nothing of our project or our travel permits.

We spent that night in a cheap Chinese hotel in Waimaw, then headed through a light rain toward Sadon, high in the hills along the Chinese border, up over a mountain pass and down into the valley beyond. The local commander there, a Burmese major, knew about us and directed us to a picturesque yellow-and-red Chinese inn. A small sign near the gate identified it as the guest house of the National Democratic Army, a rival of the Kachin Independence Army. Each small sparsely furnished room offered two wooden bed frames, a table, and a candle. Facilities were up a hillside path out back, and the proprietor offered hot water for an outside bathing area   each morning.

That afternoon we drove up higher in the mountains to the local hospital, built on the remains of an old British border fort. The whole hospital staff was lined up in the driveway to greet us, a young Burmese doctor, and four nurses in their caps, white blouses, long red skirts, and radiant smiles. They had a conference room set up where we went over the statistics of nearby villages, accessibility, and the potential for training health workers on a later visit. The doctor proudly led us on a tour of his operating room, with its three hemostats (one broken) and two needle holders.

The team ate dinner at the inn where we were to spend the night. It had no electricity; only candle light. As we enjoyed the excellent Chinese curry and rice the proprietor and his wife had served us, a man of perhaps forty sat down with us uninvited, placed a large automatic pistol on the table, covered it with his hat, and kept both hands near it. He introduced himself as the information officer of the National Democratic Army.

He apparently thought that we represented American officialdom, and wanted to offer us a deal to clear the area of opium fields (for a price, presumably.) He pulled several poppy pods from his jacket pocket to show us. I noticed the parallel scratch marks on each pod, evidence the opium had already been harvested. I had the impression he was more interested in money than in crusading against narcotics. Our team leader apparently reached the same conclusion. He explained that we were a health-teaching team, not goverhment agents, and the man soon left.

Lois came to me as we finished dinner and said the youngest team nurse was afraid and had asked Lois to sleep in her room with her.

"She should feel safe this close to an army camp," I said.

"That's who she's afraid of," Lois pointed out. So I shared the team leader's room.

The next day, after holding a clinic in a valley town, we experienced probably the most frightening ride of our lives, a view shared by most of the Burmese team. We were headed for a Kachin village three miles from the inn along a one-lane rock-strewn road going up a steep grade on the mountainside, with a sheer drop of over a thousand feet. The driver had to gun the motor around every blind curve to keep his momentum, not knowing if we would meet fallen rock in the road or an on-coming vehicle. The wheels were inches from the edge of the drop-off. I kept my terror at bay by continually assuring God that I was aware of our being in his hands. After about twenty minutes of this, we finally reached a parking spot and continued on foot down one slope and up another to a mountain-top village.

The whole population was waiting to welcome us in style. The elders were in their best clothes and turbans, ceremonial swords at their sides. Two Kachin young women, in brilliant red-and-black clothing heavily decorated with silver, handed each of us a flower as we arrived at the top. Everyone shook our hands, and seated the team under an awning. Two nurses from the hospital (located over on the next mountain) served refreshments to the crowd of some two hundred people. As the speech-making went on, I surveyed the crowd of villagers—many with large goiters, two mentally retarded, one boy on crutches, one young man with horn-rimmed glasses, taking notes. As the speeches continued, the hospital doctor quietly invited me to consult with him about an ill village girl. She appeared to have active rheumatic fever, and we agreed on a regimen of penicillin and aspirin, both of which he had among his supplies.

On the walk back to the truck, I descended the hill and climbed the opposite slope to where the truck stood, stopped to catch my breath, then turned around to find the oldest village elder following me. His sword was in a silver scabbard at his side, three rows of medals on his chest. Although he was bent over his walking stick, he did not appear winded in the least after the climb. "He's ninety-six!" someone nearby proudly told me. He smiled and shook my hand once more before turning back.

The trip down the mountain wasn't as frightening as the trip up, except when one wheel dropped over the edge for an instant on a tight curve. We returned to the inn, loaded our baggage, and were in Waimaw three hours later to catch the river-ferry to Myitkyina. The police officer and his army corporal insisted on carrying our luggage down to the shore, and waved us farewell as the ferry pulled out.

We returned to Myitkyina in 1998 to see how the project fared. It now had three teams and ranged over parts of the Shan and Karen States as well. We joined a team already at Putao, the farthest-north outpost town in Burma. The weather was chill and rainy, but on the two or three sunny days during our ten-day stay, the Himalaya Mountains gleamed white with snow on the northwest horizon. We had no police officer with us this time, but the local authorities assigned us to a guest house in the middle of the police compound, to keep track of us at night. We were so cold each evening that we had no desire to wander the town, but were in our sleeping bags by nine.

The team was teaching 105 students this time, divided into two groups; one taught in Burmese and the other in local Kachin dialect. The team not only taught their previous syllabus, but had a generator-powered TV with video tapes about dysentery, malaria, pneumonia, and AIDS. Two senior medical students were along this time, volunteering while waiting for medical school to re-open so they could finish their degrees. (The government has since allowed universities to re-open after a two-year closure.) A retired RN proved herself a masterful teacher by clearly demonstrating an entire labor and delivery with only a cardboard box and an improvised rag-doll baby for props.

Later, we returned to the original village where we had taught in 1996, to see how much our students had retained. We went with them to clinic sessions in several of their villages with one of the medical students to translate. As it turned out, many of the women understood and taught sanitation, clean water, and disease prevention rather well. But when it came to diagnosing and treating, most went from the patient's main symptom directly to a guess (usually wrong) about what medicine to use. Burmese education is geared to rote memory, and most students ranged from barely acceptable to clueless when making reasoned decisions. They did remember what they had been taught, but didn't know how to apply it.

Most of the villagers came over to the med student and me or the Kachin doctor. We told them, no, your neighbor is your care-giver. The med student and I (and the Kachin doctor and a nurse across the room) then worked with each village worker, going through several cases step by step. In one example, with some coaching, the village worker correctly noted that the child had fever, jaundice, and a big spleen; cautiously told me she thought it was malaria, and chose the right medicine from her limited supply.

In summarizing to the teams later, I suggested that this mentoring process be a regular feature of return visits, unless a backlog of waiting patients required faster processing. The village workers seemed to gain little from merely watching the visiting doctor at work, and felt themselves sidelined.

Altogether, at that time, the project had trained 500 village health workers. Their training was inadequate to their task, but was better than the untrained medicine-men, midwives, and injectors in the rural villages beyond the road's end.

Back in Myitkyina, we were privileged to hear the personal journey of Saboi Jum and several other Kachin leaders who had struggled with the cease-fire process and government relations over the past decade. The Kachins also invited us to a meeting with assistants of Senators Joseph Biden and Jesse Helms that evening, together with people from the U.S. State Department, about aid to education.

There has not been much change during the years in Burma since then. The military government is still in firm control; Burma's opposition leader, Daw Aung San Suu Kyi, is again under house arrest, and many of the generals see no need for anything other than a military solution to the nation's political and economic woes. There is little meeting of the minds, while the clock keeps ticking away.

49

Rent-a-Doc, USA

After returning from our nine months in Thailand in 1994, I wrote my former receptionist, Karen Hoskins Foster. She and her husband had visited Mae Sariang a few years before, and now wanted to hear about our latest trip. She wrote back, asking if I was now free, would I consider working a month for her? A clinic in Kalispell, Montana, wanted a temporary family practitioner.

Kalispell Regional Medical Center proved to be a beautiful campus of medical offices and a hospital, just north of the city. Karen was in charge of doctor recruitment there. She assigned me to a group of six family practitioners. Lois and I had the loan of a small house in town, and Lois found volunteer work at a local nursing home. It was December; the arts center in nearby Big Fork and the local school system provided spectacular Christmas music and drama, and Lois and I were quickly hooked on the *locum tenens* lifestyle.

Vista Staffing Solutions in Salt Lake City then signed me on, after thoroughly reviewing my credentials. I told them I wanted work only in towns of less than 10,000 people. They sent me first to Oneonta, NY, in January, 1995 to work a month in a three-doctor group. Lois again worked, as a school library volunteer, and part-time in an art store (where she had no experience, but learned a lot about paintings.)

Later that year I worked for Kearny County Hospital in Lakin, Kansas, a unique hospital sitting on one of the biggest natural gas fields

240

in America. It had a friendly staff and a budget that could afford almost anything. I worked in Lakin four times in the next two years. One child with chronic disabilities remained an in-patient the whole two years, his county welfare bills covered by gas-tax revenue.

During a month in Michigan, I divided my time between Hillman and a branch clinic in Atlanta twelve miles to the west, and the hospital in Alpena, thirty miles east. Not all advanced-neglect cases are in the Third World. A man living alone in Michigan had behaved strangely for weeks according to a neighbor. When he undressed for his hospital examination, his socks spilled live, wriggling maggots onto the table. He remained cheerfully nonchalant. My first thought, brain tumor in his frontal lobes, was not far wrong. A CAT scan showed a massive frontal lobe stroke, destroying the area governing the sense of social norms, but with little damage to motor skills or speech.

Over a five-year period with Vista, I worked in New York, Nebraska, Michigan, Colorado, Kansas, West Virginia, Idaho, Montana, and a South Dakota Indian reservation. Locum tenens is a wonderful way to wind down into retirement (or, for young doctors, to explore a variety of places to work), and the pay checks financed my medical volunteer trips overseas.

In the same period, I worked occasional twelve-hour shifts in Kellogg Hospital's emergency room. I kept my certificates up to date in advanced cardiac, trauma, and pediatric life support. Emergency work has changed a good deal over thirty-five years. Now that seat belts are mandated by law, the driver doesn't hit the steering wheel and bruise his heart so often. Passengers rarely eject from the car, and are their bodies are less likely to bounce around inside the car while the driver is struggling to regain control. And without heads smashing the windshield, the ER doctor has fewer torn faces to repair.

We treat heart attacks much more aggressively now. I remember when I was an intern in Denver, helplessly watching a 43-year-old father-of-three die of a heart attack. Nowadays we routinely hook such a patient up to a heart monitor, intravenous lines, and oxygen on arrival, and confirm his heart attack by immediate EKG and lab work. Then we inject a $1,200 vial of a medicine called tPA to dissolve the blockage in his coronary artery. Finally, after his condition is stable, most such patients go by helicopter to an advanced-care hospital for further management—coronary bypass surgery, perhaps, or placement of a stent. Now he usually lives to see his grandchildren graduate, because within minutes of the time someone dials 911, he is attended by ambulance people, nurses, doctors, and medevac teams who know what to do to keep him alive.

But the most fulfilling memories are not of the methods, hospital wards, and buildings, but of people. Lois and I were having dinner at a local restaurant not long ago, when a man stopped by our table. "Doc, I saw you here, and just wanted to say thank you for what you did for me when I was in that explosion at the smelter years ago." I had forgotten the event, but his words helped make worthwhile all those Friday nights on call.

A woman behind me, as I was standing in line to collect my car at a local tire shop one day, introduced me to her twenty-one-year-old son. "This is the man who delivered you," she told him.

"He came six weeks early," she reminded me, "and you C-sectioned me because I was bleeding so much. The placenta was too big and covered the mouth of my uterus." I didn't recognize her six-foot-tall son, of course—newborns change a lot in twenty-one years. Almost all the babies I delivered have now graduated from high school. They and their families have meant a lot to me, and I hope my presence was a help to them, too.

Different doctors work until different ages; some hang it up at sixty-five; some work part-time until eighty or more. As I entered my seventies, I began to sense that my memory has a slower response time, and I have less stamina. My hands have a slight tremor, and I've had to start wearing glasses again. I decided it was better to quit before I made some major error, and so I worked my last ER shift in August 2002 at age 73. I continued taking my once-a-month turn at the local low-income clinic for another year. Now I devote my working hours to writing books.

On request, I made one last trip to Thailand in 2004 to fill in for a month at Kwai River Christian Hospital again when the missionary doctor was called back to America, temporarily leaving only one doctor on the staff. I worried that I would have to do major surgery, after three years away from the operating room, but God apparently saw no problem. A visiting general surgeon came to spend a weekend doing thirteen cases, catching up the backlog of hernias, fixing a non-united tibia fracture, and removing an acute appendix. I performed one forceps delivery during the month, and referred a gangrenous hand (cobra-bitten four days before the patient reached us) to the government hospital. Otherwise all my practice was medical.

Kwai River Christian had became a major player in tropical fever research at the turn of the century, when AFRIMS (the Armed Forces Research Institute for Medical Sciences, a joint US/Thai army group) set up a ward to identify causes of jungle fevers. Their doctors and nurses visit the hospital to consult, and do serology and other tests on all patients with fever. At one point during my stay they held a seminar in the nearby town of Sanklaburi to report on their first 900 fever cases. Aside from readily diagnosable diseases (malaria, pneumonia, dysentery, etc.) their antibody studies showed that we were seeing rat bite fever, mellioidosis, scrub typhus, and many other conditions, all masquerading as "fever of unknown origin" but often treatable with antibiotics.

Perhaps their most important contribution was a rapid bedside test for malaria. In thirty seconds it detects the presence of malaria and identifies the type. No microscope needed. Cost: less than a dollar. During my last few days there, I used their test strips to identify malaria in three cases (all confirmed by microscope.) In one, a mother who had brought her baby as a patient collapsed into coma herself. The test identified falciparum malaria and we had artesunate flowing in her IV within less than thirty minutes of her collapse.

Two months after my visit, Dr. Sakda, the first Thai Karen medical graduate, completed his three-year surgical residency in Bangkok and joined the KRCH staff. Perhaps outside doctors will no longer be needed.

50

Conflict Mediation

Political and religious beliefs often raise such heated debate in America that some social groups frown on even their discussion. Such debate has its good and bad points. It has ensured our basic freedoms in the Constitution; it has also caused acrimony among otherwise friendly groups.

Nowhere is this more obvious than among the Baptists. From the splitting off of the Rhode Island Colony from Massachusetts, and later splitting into the Northern and Southern Baptists in the 1840s over the issues of slavery and power sharing, more than forty different Baptist groups now exist in America, usually differing over literal word-for-word interpretation of the Bible versus seeking the spirit of the message.

In the geographic region to which my own local church belongs (Washington, Idaho, Montana, and Utah) matters again came to a head in 1999. Two prominent American Baptist churches had affiliated with the Association of Welcoming and Affirming Baptists (AWAB welcomes both gay and straight Christians.) Several other churches in the region strongly opposed AWAB. The opposers threatened to call a vote at the next region meeting to "disfellowship" (expel) the two churches. Others in the region did not want to cause yet another split by redefining faith around a single issue.

In March of 2000, the Region called a mediation conference representing the whole spectrum of conservative, moderate, and liberal viewpoints. Two professional mediators from the Mennonites chaired the meeting of about forty invited clergy and lay people, including myself. We spent two full days, working until midnight.

I had visited both of the AWAB-affiliated churches several times over the years. While I might describe their preaching on matters of social justice as a little shrill at times, I had been impressed with the resources they contributed to sheltering refugees, and feeding and clothing the poor. I also have friends from among the churches strongly opposing them, and knew them to be sincere in their attempts to define family values. I admit to some difficulty understanding their vehemence on the homosexual issue, almost to the exclusion of, say, marital abuse, infidelity, or uninhibited pursuit of wealth or war.

In the two-day conference, none of us tried to interrupt or convince those with whom we disagreed; we listened to each other instead. The purpose was not to debate homosexuality or any other issue on which beliefs or priorities differ, but to discover whether all of us could continue in one fellowship of faith.

We learned, somewhat to my surprise, that the Afro-American and Oriental church leaders said that homosexuality was a non-issue among their people, low on their agendas. We also discovered that our fellow conferees, of whatever stripe, were people with whom we really wanted to maintain fellowship as one region, if at all possible. But we failed to reach consensus. Some said their members back home would never agree to abandon their interpretation of Bible passages that labelled homosexuality a sin. They did think, however, that a split could be avoided, at least for the present, if the two AWAB churches would withdraw from formal membership in the Association of Welcoming and Affirming Baptists.

The AWAB churches responded that they could not, in conscience, turn their backs on Christians who had been rejected by almost every other aspect of society. But to avoid prolonged argument in the approaching region meeting, they volunteered to withdraw from Northwest Region. They would form a new association with any other Baptist churches who, whatever their personal positions on homosexuality, still upheld the traditional Baptist responsibility to interpret the Bible's message "according to the leading of the Holy Spirit in one's own heart."

Some issues of personal belief are not resolved by majority vote. As a group, we failed to see a higher level on which the goals of both sides truly coincide. Three months later, at the Biennial Region Convention, and after much further debate, the majority of about three hundred delegates voted to accept the withdrawal of the two churches. Thirty-four other churches have since joined the new group.

Interestingly, the American Baptist Women's group refused to divide, and continue to meet as a single group at their annual conference and other events.

As I gathered my belongings to make the forty-mile trip home that midnight in March at the end of the failed mediation, I found one conferee quietly weeping in an otherwise empty room. Another friend was leaning slumped against a post outside as I left the building. Medical instinct alerted, I stopped beside him. "Are you okay?" I asked.

He shook his bowed head. "No," he replied slowly, "and I'm not sure I ever will be again."

51

Writing

When a doctor writes the patient's history, examination, and ongoing treatment, the record usually stays confidential. Only a few nurses and doctors and perhaps the patient ever read it.

An author, on the other hand, intentionally writes to a large audience. Success is measured by how the reader perceives truths behind the facts, and how well that audience of strangers identifies with the author's view. The only common ground between doctor and author is that both must write clearly, concisely, and honestly. In the transition from doctor to author, everything else must be learned.

When I closed my office practice in 1993, I bought a computer and printer and began learning about word-processing, e-mail, and the Internet. I have never learned proper typing, but have reached moderate speed with two fingers. Stories, ideas, essays, letters and computer printouts fill several file drawers in my home.

My first published book was a biography of my father, started as a family project from the letters he wrote us every week. For years he traveled the globe, first for the World Council of Churches, and later as president of the National Council of Churches USA, during the height of the McCarthy years and the Vietnam war. He often spoke on topics of peace and justice, and sometimes met with President Eisenhower, Martin Luther King Jr., or leaders of Congress and industry. I soon changed the focus of the story from purely his own life to his contribution to the history of the mid-twentieth century.

When I began writing, he had already died at age ninety-three, but had left behind audiotapes about his life in the early 1900s. The American Baptist Historical Society in Rochester, NY, had fifteen feet of shelf filled with files of his documents and pictures. I interviewed some of his surviving colleagues and opponents, sifted materials to extract what I considered his essence, and finally put together a story with which to remember him and what he stood for.

That's when I learned that writing the book is only half the job. An author also has to verify every quote, with written permit to reproduce it. He has to rewrite and rewrite again to smooth out the prose, and then try to sell it to a publisher. I sent queries to every place listed in *Writer's Market* that I thought might be even remotely interested, and I learned a lot about rejection letters. Finally, a year later, an editor at Judson Press phoned to express interest. She thought it wouldn't sell many copies, but American Baptist National Ministries sought some way to pay tribute to Dad's sixty years of service with the American Baptist Churches. The book came out in 1998 in hardcover under the title *Edwin T. Dahlberg: Pastor, Peacemaker, Prophet*. (As with many books, the publisher chose the title.)

While marketing Dad's story, I also tried my hand at writing fiction. During my time in Burma, teaching village health in 1996, the Burma government's treatment of its citizens made me recall an episode in the comic strip *Peanuts* some years before. In it, Linus asks his big sister, Lucy, the meaning of the expression "Butterflies are free." Lucy is watching TV, and doesn't want to be bothered. She dismisses him with, "It means you can have all the butterflies you want."

Adapting that kind of dismissal to Burma's treatment of its "free" but conscripted workers (an incident that finally settled into place midway in the story), I wondered what might happen if the ethnic insurgents and the Burmese Government finally started to listen to each other. Would they ever reach common ground? The result was the book *Flame Tree, a Novel of Modern Burma*. A renegade colonel with his own agenda wants to keep the fighting going. An American doctor and his wife discover the origin of the resulting battle, and their information proves critical in reaching a cease-fire.

By this time, I had more writing experience, after attending several summer seminars at North Idaho College, and a critique by a professor at Lewis and Clark College. I rewrote parts, proof-read endlessly, and began the rounds of publishers and literary agents again.

Mainstream publishers who bothered to comment said Burma was too obscure a place to interest enough readers. Several university presses said they liked it, but they never accepted fiction. But a group called *PeaceHope* sponsors an annual international peacewriting competition, and my story won a finalist award for novels submitted in 2001.

A friend had just self-published a memoir of her two years in pre-war Afghanistan, through 1stBooks (now AuthorHouse), a print-on-demand publisher. POD was a new concept then, printing only the number of copies required each week, from a permanent electronic template. They have no need to warehouse thousands of copies. I asked her how she liked it. She said the company did a fair job of printing, and posted a brief promotion on their website, but did no editing or marketing. I ordered a copy of her book, *Guests in the Land of Buzkashi,* and a couple of others from 1stBooks, and after checking the quality, decided to try them.

The first copy came about five months after original contact, faster than traditional publishing. With some marketing costs and revisions added, I paid around one thousand dollars total costs. It could have been done for half of that, I learned later.

Over the next two years, I promoted it on personal trips, and with picture cards in a Christmas letter mailing. Bookstores had only lukewarm interest; an occasional one took some copies on consignment, but only North Idaho stores sold many. Public libraries were more receptive, especially those close enough to consider me a local author. The University of Arkansas English Department hosted a successful book signing in 2003, but after that interest began to wane. Financially, I barely broke even.

The Irrawaddy, a Burmese ex-patriate magazine in Thailand, published several of my articles on Burma. I submitted a query to a Thai publisher who had advertised on their back cover. In due course, Orchid Press of Bangkok wrote me that yes, they wanted to see Flame Tree. We signed a contract for a 2004 edition of 1,000 copies, in English but with a different cover. Such traditional publishers have the advantage of better marketing and distribution ability.

Like many first-novel writers, I put too much of my personal experiences into the plot, disguised as happening to a fictitious doctor. This may be a fault of doctor-authors in general—when there are so many real-life anecdotes to draw on, why imagine others? Most of the medical events in the story happened, but the villain and his exploits drift into the imaginary after the real-life insurgent officer lays his gun on the restaurant table.

In 1997 I joined a local group of writers in Shoshone County, ID, *Pen and Quill,* meeting every second Saturday morning. Most members have novels, memoirs, or poetry in progress. In earlier meetings, a few members seemed reluctant to read—even books from the public library—lest their minds be cluttered with ideas other than their own. Others show real talent but may lack the time, finances or health to make progress. Perhaps the group's greatest value lies in keeping each of us accountable and at work.

I enjoy writing, but unless it serves a purpose, unless it contributes to some change for the betterment of the world, it is unfulfilling. Hence, I still pursue answers to the elusive themes of peace, justice, and integrity. Writing lets me discover where I have been, and why; and where the journey might take me in the time ahead.

Where to go next? I have a second novel in its final stages, based in Papua New Guinea, but have to polish it more before seeking an agent or publisher. Or maybe the next project will be essays on the present problems of American medicine.

I sometimes feel like the fictitious grandfather whose doctor told him to exercise by walking five miles every day. He took that advice, and nobody knows where the heck he is now.

52

Confronting Mortality

Trouble can start simply enough, as it did for me on a May morning in 2006. I was mowing the lawn and suddenly felt unable to push the power mower up the gentle slope even one more time. I was overwhelmed, flooded with fatigue, my pulse racing. I sat down on the steps, while my wife finished the few remaining strips of grass. Minutes later, I was okay again, and the following week I could do the whole lawn without pause. Even so, I mentioned it to our family doctor, Fred Haller, at my next visit.

I try to maintain my own health, although I do consult Fred for the big stuff. But I had never been much concerned about my heart. Blood pressure, cholesterol, and weight had almost always been near normal; I exercise on the bike trail five days a week, and don't smoke.

"My heart sounds louder, doesn't it?" I commented, as he finished listening to my chest. "Especially when I lean forward a little. Do you think it's my aortic valve?" Retired doctors who are now patients are always ready to offer guidance. Doctors like Fred who *have* doctors as patients tend to use a low-key, diplomatic approach.

"Mm ... well, I still think the mitral valve is the problem. Let's schedule an ultrasound and look."

Fred referred me to Dr. Canaday, the heart specialist who comes over to Kellogg every three weeks. The latter studied my ultrasound pictures. "I see the size of the aorta, just above the valve, has gone from

48 millimeters last year to 54 now. No chest pain or dizziness, you say?"

"Never. Just fatigue. So, how many years till I'll need surgery?" I joked. This isn't really happening, I assured myself.

"Let's make sure you don't have other heart problems, before we discuss that. I'll have my office send you instructions and an appointment for a CT angiogram."

But if anything, the angiogram on June 13th showed the aortic bulge a little bigger. Fred came to my house after work one evening to discuss the report. "I know you've already been through a lot of testing, but the surgeon wants a cardiac cath before he operates." He was half apologetic.

Surgeon? "You're saying I need surgery *now*?"

"Well, that aneurysm's not going to get any smaller." Fred was gentle but persistent. "Fifty-four millimeter size is starting to push the safety limit. It's a lot easier to operate before it tears apart."

I remembered the night my daughter Susan was born, when I was an intern. I had worked hours that night, trying to save a man with chest pain, only to have his autopsy show that he had ruptured his aorta, untreatable even from the time he had entered the hospital. I didn't really want to play out that scenario with me as the patient.

"Let me talk with my family and think about it, Fred."

I'm seventy-seven, I thought during the next few days. I've already ended my medical career, and the writing I do nowadays doesn't seem to be going anywhere much.

What reason do I have to prolong my life? Should I accept this risk of sudden death, when the alternative might be dying from cancer or stroke later on? Could I ethically continue to drive a car if I didn't have the surgery? I recalled my Uncle Albert, Mother's brother, who had died suddenly at the wheel of his car, its front wheels on the edge of a cliff when it finally came to a stop. Mother had been a passenger in his car at the time.

But replacing a section of the aorta, the main artery, is big surgery. During the time it takes to replace it with a graft, my heart will be stopped, and my life will depend on a pump outside my body, to supply blood and oxygen to my brain and other vital organs. A lot of things can go wrong. The surgeon has to be quick and competent. Would I end up an invalid, watching in paralyzed frustration while our family's life savings drain away into a nursing home?

But what about my wife, family, and friends? Do I want to abdicate all relationships, all responsibilities, give up all chance to know each of them better, choose to stop learning and loving and growing, all just for fear of complications that may never happen? Finally I agreed to surgery, and it was scheduled for July 14th.

When I finally met Dr. Icenogle, the Spokane chest surgeon, on the day before surgery was scheduled, he had further news. I had three branches of my left coronary artery (the blood supply to the heart muscle itself) each narrowed 70 to 90 per cent. He also saw a structural defect of the heart's aortic valve, which he would study further when he opened my chest. The good news was that all of these repairs could be done in a single operation, and that the overall function of my heart was still good (expressed as an "ejection fraction" of 70% of the heart's blood load with each heartbeat.) I knew that Dr. Icenogle had been doing heart transplants and other major heart surgeries in Spokane for ten years or more, and I had complete trust in him. My trust was further bolstered by his matter-of-fact recital of the precise chances of complications in his own series of cases like mine, including stroke, bleeding, infection, death, etc.

But he postponed my surgery a week, because he had been up all the previous night doing an emergency heart transplant. Even though he had gone thirty-six hours without sleep at the time of our first meeting, he still spent most of an hour explaining just what my operation would involve, and took time to answer my family's questions. The postponement was okay with us; we preferred the doctor awake and alert when my turn on the operating table came.

Sacred Heart Medical Center provides a night's free accommodation at a nearby motel for out-of-town patients who have to report for surgery at 5 a.m. The 23rd Psalm's mention of the Valley of the Shadow of Death will henceforth always remind me of that two-block walk Lois and I took over to the hospital's door, the street silent and empty in the quiet early dawn of July 20, 2006.

We met our daughter Sue by the hospital admissions desk. The paperwork, shaving, prepping, and insertion of IV lines went smoothly, and by the time the nurses took me to anesthesia all three daughters and our church pastor, Paul Hegg, were there. From that point until several hours after surgery ended, my memory is blank.

The family waited in a surgical area to which a nurse phones progress reports from the operating room every hour or two. Lois saw our daughters getting restless when my time "on the pump" began to exceed two hours. They had all worked in operating rooms and intensive care units, and knew that complication rates rise steeply after the first two hours. By the time the OR phoned to say I was now off the pump, I had been on it three hours and eight minutes, and Lois says all three daughters were quietly frantic. Altogether the surgical team worked seven hours to replace my ascending aorta with an artificial graft, do three by-pass grafts, and replace the aortic valve with a tissue graft. The doctor told me later that I had been born with an aortic valve having only two leaflets instead of the usual three; the resulting fish-mouth shape of the opening had directed the heart's outflow as a smaller, more forceful stream, perhaps causing the aortic aneurysm.

All the family could visit me in the intensive care unit. Usually enough nurses work there to give one-on-one care. That first night, things were busy, and care was one-on-two, or even one nurse for every three patients. Because I was one of the less serious cases that day, the ICU nurses allowed my daughters to help in my nursing care, with frequent checks by the ICU nurse herself. According to Pat, I was very restless and paranoid that first night. I didn't know who all these people were. Certainly not nurses. I needed to get out of here.

"Let's blow this place and go out for ice cream," she says I told her, soon after my tracheal tube was removed.

"Dad, I'll *bring* you some ice cream, but you have to stay in bed; you still have all kinds of tubes and drains in you."

"No, I'll go with you." I struggled to get up.

She or Nancy was at my bedside most of that first night, keeping me quiet. The second night, I was improved enough to turn over and go to sleep when they told me to.

But even a couple days later, in the "step-down care unit," I had spells of confusion. When Dr. Canaday and his assistant came in to make rounds, I thought they were janitors and asked them to help boost me up in bed. And I still had doubts about the nurses actually being nurses, although in fact they were very competent and helpful.

I went home six days after surgery with instructions to not raise my arms or spread them, or pull or push anything for eight weeks (lest the two halves of my breastbone come apart.) I attended physical therapy class with a dozen other post-ops three times a week for a month and a half, wearing a heart monitor, all of us parading in line around the hall, alternately raising one arm and then the other, or riding stationary bikes. Dr. Canaday thinks my spell of fatigue, that day in May, was "silent angina", just as valid a warning of future heart attack as chest pain is.

As I write this first draft, four months later, I feel fine and am almost back to full excercise. After three units of blood transfused during surgery and three months on iron supplement, my blood is up to full strength again, and a pill to keep blood pressure low is the only added medicine. My brain function is almost back to normal, and Lois and I have gone on brief trips of two or three hundred miles to points of interest. Maybe farther, next year.

Following the ongoing lives of my wife, children, grandchildren, and the world in general were the main factors in deciding to have the surgery. And a good Medicare supplement plan helps, too.

But when God tells me, "It's time, now," I'll be willing to go.

53

Peace—A Third Plan

Pacifism is a concept whose time has not yet come. In a world with terrorists, genocide, and other means of mass brutality, armed force may still be a necessary last resort. But the pacifist has a valid role in the modern world as a reminder that war is not the answer to most of humanity's problems. It may in fact be the cause of some of them.

I was a firm pacifist all the time I was growing up, until the Shan insurgency in 1961. There the behavior of both sides made me rethink my position. The pattern is all too familiar now, in the twenty-first century. The Burma Army, attempting to root out insurgents, burned villages and arrested or drove off or killed the villagers. The opposing Shans killed informers, exploded bombs, took away from their own people whatever guns the Burmese hadn't already seized. The average citizen just wanted to be left alone, to grow his rice and be able to keep it, eat it, or sell it, without fear.

During the Viet Nam war, the Communist definition of "peace" appeared to mean complete obedience to their own philosophy and rule. The South Vietnamese government and the Communist Viet Cong behaved much as I had seen the Burmese and Shans do a decade earlier. I began to perceive that people sometimes must defend themselves in order to survive.

That being said, I had to think yet again in the 1990s. By that time, we had seen the first Gulf War, Bosnia, the Rwandan genocide, and

Somalia. The Irish civil war had been going on a long time, and so had the Israeli-Palestinian conflict, with little net progress toward peace in either case.

The fighting in Burma, which had begun in 1947, still continues sixty years later, with neither side really winning. The nation has been on a long downward slide into economic and political chaos. And I began to wonder: not only "Is peace worth the price?" but "Is *war* worth the price?" Might there be some third alternative, besides battle or surrender?

A possible answer appeared during our visits to Burma after a thirty year absence, when Lois and I worked in the Kachin State in the 1990s.

The Kachins used to be an American Baptist mission field from around 1890 to 1965. Even after General Ne Win expelled all foreigners from Burma, the Kachin church kept on growing rapidly, and maintained a cordial relationship with American Baptists. For thirty-five years, the Kachin Independence Army had been fighting the Burmese government. They are good fighters, these Kachin Christians, but in all that time neither side could gain victory. Travel and trade were almost impossible, and men abandoned their farms to escape the soldiers. Many people did not have enough to eat.

In the early 1990s some of the Kachin leaders declared, "This is not the way God wanted it to be." After working with other Christian groups in Asia and Europe, and contacting the Carter Peace Center in Atlanta, they had reached an armed cease-fire with the Burma government in 1994. According to the terms, neither army could enter the other's territory, but postal workers, medics, and other unarmed people may go back and forth. Both sides in fact approved the medical training teams that Lois and I were invited to work with. When we arrived in early 1996, snipers were no longer firing upon trains and river boats. Farmers had begun working their fields again and bringing their crops to market. We did not observe the wide-spread malnutrition we had been led to expect. The government could possibly have contrived this in the city, and perhaps in a few towns, but we drove through many villages and made impromptu stops in several. The cease-fire's temporary success was not all staged just for outsiders' benefit.

Present-day Burma certainly has not solved all its problems. At the time I write, the government still dictates the law. The legally elected parliament still cannot meet, and dissenters still go to jail. Around 1999, the Burma army started moving hill tribe people out of their villages and setting up free-fire zones. If anyone returned home to harvest his crops or to retrieve something he forgot, the soldiers reportedly shot to kill without further warning.

But the Kachins have decided they are going to get on with their lives again, as far as is possible under present government. Many still privately disagree with the way the country is being run, but they have decided that killing is not the solution.

They still have problems: Chinese entrepreneurs are taking over much of the jade and timber trade, and drugs and AIDS are overwhelming the state. The Myanmar government spends its time and resources fortifying a new national capital near Pyinmana, rather than dealing with poverty and education. The government apparently sees no problem with the status quo—often the case with the side that holds all the power.

Now the world struggles to restore peace in Iraq, North Korea, Israel/Palestine, Burma, Haiti, Sudan, and many more regions. I can only repeat the Kachins' observation, "This is not the way God wanted it to be," and prayerfully continue to seek a remedy.

There is a popular saying, "Don't get mad, get even." But the error in this is that getting even is only another term for vengeance, and vengeance escalates. An alternative could be a maxim my father sometimes quoted: "Get rid of the enmity, not the enemy."

Gradually, beginning about 2003, I saw new ideas surfacing where there had once been only repetitive rhetoric. Some writers among Burma's refugees, some ex-patriate leaders, and some inside Burma are exploring ways of living with military dictatorship. More than fifty years of fighting, and fifteen years of economic sanctions, have only made the common citizens poorer. Economic sanctions increase the poverty of the ordinary people, without much affecting those in power. Too many Asian nations—China, India, Singapore, and Thailand among them—willingly trade with or supply arms to Burma as they jockey for strategic trade positions in the twenty-first century.

So far, the Government has shuffled leadership and talked, without doing much else. Senior General Than Shwe has purged the army of some of the more moderate leaders who had at least considered dialog with the opposing groups. Many of the older field commanders who remain see no difficulty with solving the ethnic problem by military means alone. Those in power will have to change this, if they want a stable nation.

Peace and integrity are built, not from the top down but from the inside, person by person. In Burma, both sides have a long road ahead, learning to work together.

54

Medicine and Faith

Every now and then, the newspapers report a child with some dire disease—leukemia or diabetes perhaps—whose parents refuse medical treatment, saying they will depend on God alone to heal the child.

If these same parents were caught with their child in the middle of a raging flood, or some other natural disaster, I think that in most cases they would not hesitate to accept rescue by boat or helicopter, acknowledging that God sometimes sends help by way of such things in this world. It puzzles me why they might think that medicine is less a part of God's created world than a helicopter is. Maybe it's the way they perceive the offer, perhaps with a requirement for cash in advance, or offered with arrogance; or because someone they heard of died anyway. Be that as it may, there is a need for both faith and medicine in medical crises.

To take diabetes as an example, one feature of this disease is a lack of insulin, a natural body product, which the body needs to regulate the way it uses food for energy. Damage to the insulin-producing cells in the body results in diabetes, and if not treated can cause death. Giving daily doses of insulin allows the person to continue to live. It's not wise to treat a child's diabetes with prayer alone, when she urgently needs insulin to survive.

Many cases of diabetes in adults, however, are caused by an unhealthy life style which "wears out" the insulin-producing cells.

In early cases, simply modifying one's food intake and life style can restore health. But the person may find it very difficult to change life-long habits. Even though he understands what he must do, he finds he hasn't enough willpower to maintain the change. I have seen prayer and faith make that change possible in some cases.

Faith in what or whom? Some advise self-reliance—"I am the master of my fate; I am the captain of my soul." Others depend upon another person, a spouse perhaps, or a work partner, or a doctor or counselor. Some trust in following the rules set down by their particular religious group. Some others hope to be lucky.

This is a touchy subject. In matters of faith, those who claim to have all the answers often feel threatened and insecure if anyone argues against their particular interpretation. Many other people, more secure in their own faith, may suspect the person with "all the answers" has not yet addressed all the questions.

As Benjamin Franklin put it: "[Most suppose themselves] in possession of all truth, and those who differ are so far in the wrong. Like a man traveling in foggy weather, those at some distance before him on the road he sees wrapped up in the fog, as well as those behind him, and the people in the fields on each side. But near him all appears clear, tho' in truth he is as much in the fog as any of them."

I freely admit being a follower of Jesus, even though an imperfect one. I believe in a Creator God who takes benevolent interest in each of us and who has a plan for our lives if we, in our freedom of choice, choose to trust God. That's my basic life view.

Some people reject this, blaming God for making the world the way it is and causing so much suffering. But before we cast blame, it makes sense to do everything possible to correct the wrongs we ourselves (or others) have caused or could have prevented. Among these causes that might be remedied I see infection, injury, ignorance, greed, demand for vengeance, and misguided desires or life-styles, to name a few.

There are some events, such as volcanic eruption, or earthquakes, over which we have little control. Perhaps God allows such misfortunes as a test of our faith, or to teach us how to help each other, or to teach nations how to get their priorities straight. That's only a perhaps. I don't claim to know the answer.

Whether dealing with disease or disaster, it makes sense to use the facts of science as far as they can be applied. But there is a point beyond which intellect alone is not enough to fight mass murder and indifference, once we cease to acknowledge God.

If God exists and created the world, as Christians suppose, God is not a genie in a bottle. We do not bargain with God, or order God around. If this world is God's creation, we can choose to accept it and seek to learn how best to live in it, or we can choose to be angry about it and raise our blood pressure to unhealthy levels. Rather than complain or panic when confronted with crisis, I often find it useful to ask for God's help.

Some quite intelligent people believe that what I call answers to prayer are no more than coincidence. Perhaps so. My father used to remark that when people pray, coincidences happen more often. I tend to agree with him. I have seen many separate instances where something was accomplished by several people happening to be in "the right place at the right time." To always ascribe such results to blind chance appears unlikely, considering the odds. There is a lot we don't comprehend about God and the universe. But to state that the world depends on random chance is merely another way of saying that we don't yet completely understand how order comes out of chaos.

How then is faith relevant? To me, it's the infrastructure of life. It is the fiber, the substance of what we call integrity, dependability, honesty, character. Without it, life and direction begin to wobble, become indecisive, or even collapse.

It is not faith's function to abolish all trouble, but to deal with it effectively, whether by prayer or the scientific methods God provides through his servants.

"There is no narrowing so deadly as the narrowing of a man's hunger for spiritual things. No worse evil could befall him in his course on earth than to lose sight of Heaven. And it is not civilization that can prevent this; it is not civilization that can compensate for it. No widening of science, no possession of abstract truths can indemnify for an enfeebled hold on the highest and central truths of humanity. "What shall a man give in exchange for his soul?"

Inscribed at Stanford University Chapel, Palo Alto, California

55

Children

I can't end my story without mentioning my children more fully. Parents sometimes seek a doctor's sympathy or advice about their out-of-control teenagers. I usually tell them, "Don't burn your bridges. If you can get them up to age eighteen and beyond, they often turn out to be quite entertaining adults." Not only can you watch them get payback time when their own children act bratty, but they may become very capable humans. Lois and I were blessed with all four of ours.

Each of them became a "Third Culture Kid" (TCK), belonging fully neither to American nor foreign culture, but having some attributes of both. TCKs come from military, diplomatic, missionary, or overseas business families, and experience uprooting and transplanting several times during childhood and adolescence. Most have difficulty discovering their personal identity and where they fit in. They truly identify only with other TCKs because none of their other friends, either at home or abroad, have the same interests and viewpoints. This can be disastrous to a few, but most eventually adapt and become very able citizens with a wide world-view.

Susan is the gregarious one. At age four, in Burma, she always had a following of neighborhood kids trooping through our house, and soon spoke four languages fluently: English, Burmese, Shan, and Lahu.

(That talent lapsed on return to America, where such knowledge wasn't "cool.")

Friends were supremely important in her teen years. On our family's first trip through Yellowstone Park, Sue stayed in the car at each sightseeing stop, buried her nose in a magazine, and asked how soon we would be back in Kellogg.

She majored in sociology and anthropology at Whitman College, but discovered there were no jobs for a BA degree with that combination, so she drifted into a job in respiratory therapy and found she liked it. She returned to school at North Idaho College at her own expense, studied nursing and eventually got a job in coronary care at Seattle's Harborview Hospital. She later worked in the U. of Washington's electrophysiology lab, and became the ultimate Seattle-ite with morning workouts in a fitness center, followed by a bagel and latte.

She married Cleve Ashcraft, a mathematician at Boeing, and they are raising three daughters. Dissatisfied with city life after twenty years in Seattle, they moved to North Idaho. Cleve now works from his computer at home for a California company, studying metal stress in cars. He has also moonlighted for an oil company, mapping out petroleum reserves, coaches local school kids in math, coaches the soccer team, and manages his forty-acre wood lot. Sue works part time in several jobs, usually related to cardiology, and is a soccer mom, and on the local hospital board.

I recall a Christmas during her Seattle years when she wrote us that she stopped to pick up some bagels, and saw three street-people warming themselves on a grating outside the shop. She got three extra bagels and coffees, went outside and told them, "Okay, guys, here's breakfast," and was on her way.

I have already mentioned our daughter Pat and her husband, Dave Cordier. Pat has always wanted the world to be fair. She was the three-year-old who, unable to climb the tree in our front yard one day, angrily bit its trunk. She was the teenager who declared "It's not *fair!*" as she campaigned for a student smoking area to match the one in the teachers' lounge.

She's the young army nurse who signed up for three years, and found herself retiring from the army twenty-six years later. She has plaques on her wall at home from subordinates, thanking her for support in conflicts with the brass higher up. Her eyes sparkle with delight as she shows me:

> LTC Patricia Cordier
> Madigan Army Medical Center
> Aug 97–Jun 00
> "The Surgeons Met Their Match"

Another plaque refers to her protests to higher command when ordered to do more work with fewer nurses (alluding to Exodus 5: 10–18):

> "More Bricks, No Straw"

She received perhaps her highest compliment when the chief surgeon at Fort Lewis's Madigan Hospital introduced her to the new surgical staff when she returned there to be head operating room nurse. He said, "To those of you who haven't met Colonel Cordier before, I can only say, 'Thank God she's back.'"

Pat has now reached army retirement, has two teen-age children and an older step-daughter. Her husband has worked as a substitute teacher, and a volunteer with a group called CASA, helping young kids avoid a career in jail. At the time of this writing, Dave is working in building construction and is considering returning to college to get his Washington State teacher's papers. Pat works as a civilian consultant for purchasing surgical supplies for the armed services.

John was the kid who could never resist the temptation to press every button and throw every switch he passed. He was the one who came bucketing down a hillside on his bicycle, disdaining the brakes, and crashed into a fence head-on. He was the high school football player who pretended to dumb down so his teammates wouldn't know he got A's in class.

Low self esteem has never been John's problem. After graduating from Texas Christian University, he told us he would accept employment in any corporation that offered entry at a senior executive level. Failing to get such an offer, he started as a waiter in an upscale Fort Worth restaurant, then signed on with a succession of computer companies that led him to California, and then overseas to Hong Kong and Singapore.

While troubleshooting computers in Singapore's Central Provident Fund (similar to USA's Social Security system), he met and married a young computer supervisor who "was more interesting than her computer problems." Duan Meng is a slim, attractive Singaporean with a master's degree from Illinois Institute of Technology. She became vice-president for application systems in Star Hub, a Singapore telecom firm, later scaled back her working hours to spend more time at home. She is a good match for John, his equal in intellect and arguing skills, bringing him down to earth when he occasionally gets carried away by his imagination. They have two sons and a daughter.

After a series of computer jobs, Citibank sent John to Stanford's Graduate School of Business for a year as a Sloan Fellow; and he later moved to Development Bank of Singapore, and then headed Group Operations and Technology at Oversea Chinese Banking Corporation. I don't comprehend exactly what he does, any more than I do my son-in-law Cleve's mathematics. A couple of jobs ago John explained, using the analogy of the optimist's half-full glass and the pessimist's half-empty one, "My job is to tell each of them, 'It looks like you have twice as much glass as you need.'"

More importantly, I have known him to take the side of his employees in disputes with upper management, when the rule book goes against common sense.

He recently embarked on a new project to empower the "under-banked," those hundreds of millions of people in East Asia who must, until now, depend on loan sharks who charge high rates of interest.

John recently brought me a black T-shirt from a business trip to the former Nyassaland, whose postage stamp had expressed my childhood dream of travel. The shirt front pictures two elephants emerging from the forest, with the inscription "Malawi—The Warm Heart of Africa".

If you never reach one of your goals, someday perhaps your son or daughter will.

Nancy, our youngest, was the one who at age three, inspecting her first butterfly in our garden, asked timidly, "Does it bite?" She is the one who felt insecure about our return to Thailand, yet became president of the high-school student body at Bangkok's International School.

She favored the underdog in her high school friendships, and once predicted that 50% of her Kellogg friends in sixth grade would end up in the state penitentiary. (Actually only about 5 % did.)

She got her BSN at Pacific Lutheran University, and later told us, "I want to experience a different culture."

"You could go back to Thailand and work," I suggested.

"No, I've already been there. Something different."

She chose King Faisal Hospital in Saudi Arabia, and stayed five years during the first Gulf War era when so many other nurses left. "Don't worry about me," she assured us, "we have gas masks and a bomb shelter," and she sent us a picture of her studying while using both. What she didn't show us until later was a picture of a Patriot missile hitting an enemy Scud, photographed from the hospital roof. She helped develop the first Saudi pain clinic, and used her earnings from overseas to finance her studies for a master's degree in nursing.

At the time of this writing, Lois and I have just returned from a weekend with our three daughters and our two grandcats at Nancy's house in Kennewick, WA. (Their brother enjoys such meetings too, but prefers to bring his family home in December to ski.) The three girls get together each year at grape harvest time to tour some of Central Washington's many wineries. They use a parent as designated driver, but have never yet required one, getting bored after a sip at each of about six stops and then heading back to Nancy's house. On one such visit, after dinner at a Thai restaurant, Lois asked Nancy, "Show us the new building where you work."

Nancy took us to Kadlec Medical Center, where she manages the Critical Care Unit, and showed us an unoccupied room. During fifty years of medical practice, I had never seen anything like it. Each large single-bed room holds two floor-to-ceiling columns with multiple monitors, suction ports, and oxygen outlets, plus banks of light switches for every conceivable need. The elevators and doorways are big enough for an entire resuscitation team to hurry a patient and his bed to surgery without interrupting either monitoring or care.

As we were leaving, Lois said, "We haven't seen your office." Nancy's sisters had seen nursing offices before, and went ahead to the car. She took Lois and me to a room containing her computer, bookcases, diplomas from Pacific Lutheran and the University of Texas, and a dish of chocolate mini-bars by the visitor's chair. "No memento from Riyadh?" I asked.

"That's a map of Saudi Arabia on my mouse pad." As she led us back to the elevator, we passed near the critical-care nurses' station. The nurses taking report at shift-change swiveled their heads at this unexpected appearance of the manager. "It's Saturday night," called one, "go home!"

Nancy gestured toward us. "Just showing my parents where I work." There was an affectionate chorus of "Aw-w-w." behind us as the elevator doors closed.

I am proud of each of our four children and the three spouses, each of the seven with multi-talent technical competence, but each also with a human side which is both caring and practical. When they are all home, their conversations around the kitchen table often last until after midnight, remembering their childhood, and their parents' peculiarities.

My own grandfather, Elof Dahlberg, expressed it well in his diary: "Considering our ups and downs, we regard our children's educations, all developing a good honest character to render service to mankind, to be our most valuable assets."

Most of my nine grandchildren—Ryder, Marah, and Bekka Ashcraft; Melisa, Rachel, and Michael Cordier; Matthew, Joshua, and Sarah Dahlberg—are still in a young formative stage. They show promise of being, each of them, every bit as entertaining, surprising, and praiseworthy as their parents. But they'll have to write their own stories at a later day.

I have often regretted not taking enough time to understand people and illness more deeply. I also regret not having been able to give undivided attention to my family and friends, while filling the needs of my patients and my profession. There is a fine line doctors must walk between conflicting demands. I have sometimes felt like I schedule family events in pencil but professional appointments in ink, but I am very grateful to my wife, children, and grandchildren, who have kept me in their love and life in spite of this.

56

Summing it up

My friend Roger Fredrikson sat with me outside the guest house in Bangkok, one warm quiet evening when we were both in our sixties. The guest house is on a back street, away from the noisy traffic and crowds, a relaxing place to talk. Roger and I go a long way back; we were in the National Baptist Youth Fellowship together in the 1940's, and he later became a leading American Baptist minister.

"Keith, whatever happened to our plans to change the world, back in our younger days?" He was reminiscing, but he really wanted to know, too.

I thought about it. "We did make some changes, Roger. We just didn't realize how big the world really is."

What does happen to the goals of younger days? I still enjoy the fascinations of my childhood—travel and science—but I see them now as vehicles that carried me to further goals I had not yet thought of. When I was twenty years old, medical school admissions committees dismissed me as an immature idealist for "wanting to help people." But I have realized, over the years, that the rebuff was not for idealism but for expressing it too shallowly. I finally found my niche as a doctor among those who had little access to modern medicine.

My medical career reached its high point at the Sa Kaew refugee camp, where "helping people" took on a more intense life-and-death meaning, and where the latest brand-name medicines and techniques

269

were mostly irrelevant. I will never dispute the need to expand medicine's borders by further research. But more than ever, after that experience, I am aware that our first priority is applying skills and knowledge that we already have, but are neglecting.

I realize now that the basic needs of medical practice include the doctor getting the sick patient into his office without a three-week wait for an appointment, and without demanding a large payment up front. I found that I could follow that policy and still have a successful practice.

The basics include starting appropriate treatment today, not "after the test results are back." We can modify the treatment any time those test reports suggest a change is needed, but beginning the relief of pain and anxiety is needed at the first visit.

The basics include the doctor talking with the patient and family about the results of treatment so far and the options ahead, listening to the patient's goals and adapting the treatment sensibly. Not abruptly lecturing about what the doctor thinks the patient should want.

The basics include caring for the patient even when we can do little or nothing about the disease. Although I was already aware of this, an event in 1995 etched it on my brain:

On a weekend off, during the month I worked in Oneonta, NY, I flew to Dayton, Ohio, to visit my long-time friend Ambrose Smith. Soon after retirement, Amby had developed cancer of the esophagus. He had had appropriate surgery and other measures, but now the cancer had spread to his brain, and he was on hospice care at home. His wife, Helen, had been a hospital volunteer for twenty years, but both she and I felt helpless in the face of this merciless disease that had turned her husband from a brilliant engineer into a dying man struggling to say a few words.

There was nothing I could do except sit there during the weekend, listen, converse when he felt like it, and be glad that at least I could be with him for a brief time. When I left again for the airport, I drove a few blocks and then pulled the car over to the curb and sobbed.

Helen said she never knew exactly what classified work Ambrose had done for the military. At Amby's retirement party, a colonel had told her the U. S. Air Force was losing one of its two most valuable civilian engineers. But I remember him best as a friend, and for the years of companionship we shared, hunting the rare rocks.

As I get older, physical factors begin to limit my activity. It takes me longer to recall names of people I know and medicines I prescribed. My curiosity is still active, and my zest for exploration is still alive. But with my hands less steady and my decision time a little slower, I was right to stop practicing medicine when I did. The ill and injured deserve better.

So in recent years, I have devoted my energy to writing about the work I used to do and the future that I dream about, where doctors not only understand the science of medicine better, but are more skilled at the art of applying it to improve the patient's life.

That's this book's premise. There are indeed bridges that appear in unexpected places, to help you achieve your goals. Choose your goals carefully, and then relax and enjoy your life journey. It may even be that your life will make a bridge for others to reach a worthwhile goal.

Bibliography

I add these notes only to help show where I am coming from in this memoir. These are a sampling of books that have influenced my life and thought on topics of peace, medicine, faith, biography, history, or simply enjoyment of a good story or writing style. There are, of course, other media—DVDs, music, poetry, magazines and other periodicals, etc., but I'll limit this to books. Those that are now out of print can often be found in the Amazon.com website or sources of old books.

Andrew, Brother. *God's Smuggler*. New York: Signet, 1967. biography.

Aung San Suu Kyi. *Freedom from Fear*. New York: Penguin, 1991.

Bankson, Russell A. *Beneath These Mountains*. New York: Vantage Press, 1966. A history of Idaho's Silver Valley.

Bible. available in many translations from many publishers.

Brands, H. W. *Andrew Jackson: His Life and Times*. New York: Anchor Books, 2006.

Bujold, Lois McMaster. *Komarr*. Riverdale, NY: Baen, 1999. science fiction, her Vorkosigan series.

Buttry, Daniel. *Christian Peacemaking*. Valley Forge, PA: Judson Press, 1994.

Carothers, Chaplain Merlin R. *Prison to Praise*. Watchung, NJ: Charisma Books, 1972.

Carter, Jimmy. *Palestine, Peace Not Apartheid*. New York: Simon &Schuster, 2006.

Churchill, Sir Winston. *The Second World War* (in six volumes). New York: Bantam, 1948.

Clarke, Arthur. *Rendezvous with Rama*. New York: Spectra, 1990. science fiction.

Crile, George. *Charlie Wilson's War*. New York: Atlantic Monthly Press, 2004. Where America dropped the ball in the Middle East.

Dahlberg, Edwin T. *I Pick Up Hitchhikers*. Valley Forge, PA: Judson Press, 1978.

Dodson, Kenneth. *Away All Boats*. New York: Little, Brown, 1954. World War II in the Pacific.

Doig, Ivan. *Ride With Me, Mariah Montana*. New York: Scribner, reprint 2005. part of Doig's Montana trilogy of the McCaskill family.

Fickett, Harold. *The Living Christ*. New York: Doubleday, 2002. vignettes of modern Christian lives in action.

Fischer, Louis. *Gandhi*. New York: Signet/Penguin, 1982. biography/history.

Francis, Dick. *The Edge*. New York: Fawcett Crest, 1988. Action adventure in Canadian horse-racing.

Heinlein, Robert. *Double Star*. New York: Signet, 1956. Classic science fiction, among his many.

Hersey, John. *The Call*. New York: Penguin, 1986. life of a missionary science teacher in China.

Hoover, Dorcas Sharp. *House Calls and Hitching Posts*. Intercourse, PA: Good Books Publishing, 1969. general medical practice among the Amish in Ohio.

Lawrence, Brother. *The Practice of the Presence of God*. Grand Rapids, MI: Spire Books, reprinted 2000. The classic writing of a lay brother in a 16th century monastery in France.

Lee, Harper. *To Kill a Mocking Bird*. New York: Perennial/Harper Collins, reprinted 2002.

Lee Kwan Yew. *The Singapore Story.* in two volumes. New York: Prentice Hall/Harper Collins, 1999/2002. autobiography and modern history.

Lewis, C. S. 2003 reprint. *Out of the Silent Planet.* New York: Scribner. Sci-fi; my favorite of C. S. Lewis's many Christianity-based books, which include the rest of his *Space Trilogy, The Chronicles of Narnia, The Screwtape Letters, The Great Divorce,* etc.

Lilje, Hans. *The Valley of the Shadow.* Philadelphia: Muhlenberg, circa 1950.

Lintner, Bertil. *Land of Jade.* Bangkok: White Orchid Press, 1990. A journalist's two-year trek among the Burmese ethnic insurgents.

Li Zhi-Sui. *The Private Life of Chairman Mao.* New York: Random House, 1996. A biography written by Mao's personal physician.

McCullough, David. *Truman.* New York: Simon & Schuster, 1993.

McFee, John. *Annals of the Former World.* New York: Farrar Straus and Giroux, 2000. a geologic narrative of America.

Monsarrat, Nicholas. 2000 reprint. *The Cruel Sea.* Springfield, NJ: Burford. classic British naval novel of World War II.

Newhall, Sue Mayes. *The Devil in God's Old Man.* New York: Norton, 1969

Niemoller, Martin. *From U-Boat to Pulpit.* New York: Willet Clark, circa 1937.

Paton, Alan. *Cry, the Beloved Country.* New York: Scribner, 1948. a novel of mid-20th century South Africa.

Seagrave, Gordon. *Burma Surgeon,* New York: Norton, 1943. His autobiography, in contrast to his later life by Sue Newhall, above.

Selth, Andrew. *Burma's Defence Expenditure and Arms Industries.* Canberra: Australian National University, 1997

Seuss, Dr. *The Sneetches and Other Stories.* New York: Random House, 1961. for a change of pace.

Severn, Bill. *John Marshall, the Man Who Made the Court Supreme.* New York, McKay, 1969.

Shute, Nevil. *A Town Like Alice*. London: Mandarin, 1990 reprint. my favorite of Shute's many novels.

Smith, Barbara. *The Circumstance of Death*. Charleston WV: Mountain State Press, 2001. A blistering novel of a family who falls between the cracks of the welfare system.

Solzhenitsyn, Alexander. *One Day in the Life of Ivan Denisovich*. New York: Farrar, Straus & Giroux, 2005 (new edition.) A classic from the labor camps of Soviet Russia.

Thompson, Morton. *Not as a Stranger*. New York: Scribners, 1954. A best-selling novel for every aspiring doctor.

Venter, J. Craig. *A Life Decoded*. New York: Viking, 2007. Deciphering the human genome.

Yeager, General Chuck Yeager and Leo Janos. *Yeager*. New York: Bantam, 1985. autobiography.

Printed in the United States
206086BV00001B/88-360/P